W9-AAU-651

THE BETTER
SEX GUIDE

THE BETTER
SEX GUIDE

HOW TO ENJOY AND MAINTAIN A HEALTHY
SEX LIFE IN A LOVING RELATIONSHIP –
THE BOOK FOR MODERN LOVERS EVERYWHERE

NITYA LACROIX

HERMES
HOUSE

To all lovers and partners and to those dedicated people who, through careful research, teaching and practice, have helped to shed a more open light on human sexuality.

The publishers and author would like to thank Richard Emerson for his contribution to this book; Catherine Hill and Mary Ling for their help in research; and Andy, Bernadette, Kay, Mark, Peter, Ralf, Sarah, Tina, Vijaya and Wendy for modelling.

This edition published by Hermes House
an imprint of
Anness Publishing Limited
Hermes House
88-89 Blackfriars Road
London SE1 8HA

All rights reserved. No part of this publication may be reproduced, stored in a retrieval system, or transmitted in any way or by any means, electronic, mechanical, photocopying, recording or otherwise, without the prior written permission of the copyright holder.

A CIP catalogue record for this book is available from the British Library

ISBN 1 84039 547 5

Publisher: Joanna Lorenz
Project editors: Casey Horton, Nicky Thompson
Editor: Richard Emerson
Design: Blackjacks
Special photography: Alistair Hughes
Additional photos: p206 Ron Sutherland/Science Photo Library;
p208 Jerry Wachter/Science Photo Library;
p209 Debbie Humphry © Photofusion
Hair and make-up: Bettina Graham

Also published as *Love, Sex and Intimacy*

Printed and bound in Singapore

©Anness Publishing Limited 1995
Updated © 2003
1 3 5 7 9 10 8 6 4 2

Contents

Introduction

Writing a book about love, sex and intimacy is akin to turning the key in a doorway, only to find that behind the entrance there are a thousand pathways – each signposted to indicate a different aspect of life. It is a labyrinth of hope and passion, joy and longing, full of tenderness and excitement and, yes, sometimes of fear, disappointment and emotional pain. One can explore the avenue along which lies the new romance; the first meeting of lovers, the anticipation and thrills, the tentative kiss, the courtship and the exploration of sensual play. In that scenario is the excitement of the unknown, the fear of uncertainty, the dissolving of egos and the delicious unravelling of the body's erotic responses. Yet another equally valid route is that of the long-term relationship, with its growing responsibilities and deepening bonds, its sexual compatibility and emotional companionship, the edge of complacency and the hint of boredom.

Write about sex techniques, on how to enhance arousal and orgasm, and one risks turning the book into a manual on physical mechanics, devoid of feeling and emotion, vulnerability, humour, and innocence – or any of the wonderful, poignant and tender gifts that each of us can bring to a sexual relationship. Yet, if we focus purely on love and intimacy, what happens to that glorious basic, instinctive energy of lust that stirs in our loins and lights up the body while intoxicating the mind? If we explore the possibility of attaining

That Special Feeling

▶ Love is an endless source of joy – yet this mysterious emotion can affect us profoundly in many other ways too.

ecstasy through love and sexuality, then we must also acknowledge the frustration and heartache that Cupid's arrow can leave in its path.

Our expectations and experiences of an intimate relationship are always subjective, for how we perceive it and what we seek within it is but a mirror to our own particular vision, fantasies and needs. A particular couple may have entirely different

agendas and views. Then there is the backdrop of religious, cultural and social factors – external voices that continue to influence us positively or negatively throughout our lives.

How can the definition of love, sex and intimacy mean the same to those who believe intercourse belongs solely within marriage, and that marriage is for life, as it does to those who have relished the sexual revolution and now see themselves as serial monogamists? Where is the meeting ground between those who believe oral-genital sex is a perversion, and those who testify that it is the best part of their sex lives? What about those who say sex is for procreation while others insist it is for recreation?

Love, sex and intimacy – the subject is so vast and complex it would be difficult to conceive of any one book that could do it justice. This book has attempted to embrace a wide spectrum of issues relevant to a loving relationship, while acknowledging that there will inevitably be areas of special interest that will not have been covered. However, it is our hope that couples will find helpful advice and information which can enrich their relationships and speed their pursuit of sexual happiness.

This book has taken an open approach to sexuality in the belief that any sexual practice which brings greater emotional and physical fulfilment, and adds variety, pleasure, love and joy to a sexual relationship has to be good. The message of this book is for partners to explore their erotic capacity, alone or together, and to embrace the fullness of sensual and sexual experience in their lives. It has no moral stand on sexual behaviour, other than that whatever transpires should be with the mutual consent of

both partners, is of psychological, emotional and sexual benefit to them both, and involves no risks to health.

In an era in which HIV/AIDS and other sexually transmitted diseases have made it imperative for sexually active people to re-evaluate and modify their sexual behaviour, the message of this book is that safer sex is an issue that all couples must consider. The programmes in this book are therefore based on the assumption that they will be followed by couples practising safer sex, or by those in committed relationships who are absolutely certain that neither partner's sexual history presents the slightest risk of contracting a sexually transmitted disease. Sex can be great fun, but it does have its risks – and so all sexually active people should take full responsibility for their own emotional and physical well-being.

Love, Sex and Intimacy has tried to find a balance between an individual's personal journey of growth and self-awareness, and the process of creating a harmonious relationship with another. Love and intimacy are longings to which most people aspire

and through which they hope to find not only sexual satisfaction, but also a friend and companion, and perhaps – even more – a soul-mate.

Love within a sexual partnership is a shared journey of heart and body, mind and spirit. Yet whether we are alone or with a partner, self-awareness is also an essential part of life's process. Feeling good about ourselves, in mind and body, and nurturing our own needs as well as another's, builds within us a solid foundation of self-esteem from which we can take responsibility for our own destiny and happiness.

Throughout this book, there are personal self-help tips and couple exercises to help the reader develop a sense of physical, emotional and sexual well-being. There are suggestions on how to signal your availability when you are seeking a partner, and how to create romance in your life. Sensuality, foreplay, basic and

Love in All its Forms
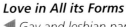 *Gay and lesbian partners have the same need for loving and nurturing relationships as heterosexual couples.*

adventurous lovemaking positions are discussed and illustrated, focusing on the importance of loving touching throughout intercourse; advice is also given on sexual positions which are most likely to bring emotional and orgasmic satisfaction to both partners. The book also acknowledges the problems which can arise through sexual dysfunction, and offers practical advice on self-help exercises for partners to overcome sexual problems. Communication techniques, massage techniques, physical game-playing – they are all there to help you enhance your relationship. So are suggestions on how to keep long-term and mature relationships alive and vital. Finally, the book looks at Tantric sexo-yogic practices, which allow the readers to explore a wholly different concept of lovemaking.

Relationships can take many forms. This book has focused specifically on heterosexuality, but issues of love, sex and intimacy are as relevant to gay and lesbian relationships as they are to opposite-sex partners. Whatever the individual's sexual orientation, and religious or moral background, what binds us together in our sexual diversity is the human need to love and be loved, to go deep with someone, to share and receive nourishment and pleasure, to have a playmate and an equal partner to travel with along the path of life.

Hearts and Minds in Union
 *The physical union of two bodies is the ultimate expression of a couple's emotional and spiritual bond.*

Chapter 1
Self-Awareness

Caring about your body and well-being is a major step in creating a strong sense of self-esteem. Developing a good relationship with yourself sets a solid foundation from which you can open yourself to a relationship with another person. The first place to begin is your body, because its health and vitality will give you the fitness and energy to enjoy your own life and to commit yourself with enthusiasm to another person. Simple steps can be taken which greatly enhance your life. A change to a healthy diet will give you the right balance of nutrition which will make you feel and look good. A regular programme of exercise, such as stretching, walking or aerobic work-outs will keep your muscles toned and your cardio-vascular system in good condition. Certain exercises, designed to deepen your breathing and unlock blocked emotional feelings, will bring you a greater sense of freedom and spontaneity. Then, taking good care of your skin and muscle tone by using self-massage techniques will help you to feel more relaxed and invigorated. Your self-awareness programme will make you feel positive about yourself and draw others to you.

Caring for Yourself

The gift of another person's love is a satisfying, fulfilling and nurturing force, but it is also important to gain that degree of caring and respect for yourself. We are not conditioned to love ourselves, but are encouraged to put our own well-being in second place in order to consider others. To create a secure sense of self-esteem involves a conscious drive towards self-awareness, and that is an ongoing process throughout our lives.

Building up your sense of self-worth will empower your life, and enable you to become less dependent on another person for your own feelings of personal value. This will sustain you in the times when you are on your own, and will also enrich any relationship you are involved in because you will have sufficient emotional resources to share.

You can start by planning a lifestyle that shows a real concern for the basics – a good diet, healthy exercise, and plenty of rest and relaxation. As well as enhancing your health and well-being, this will help you manage the tensions in your daily life so that stress becomes a power for good, for positive action and achievement, rather than a negative force that blocks and withholds your vital energy.

To have the confidence and enthusiasm you need to embark on a new relationship you have to feel good about yourself, and this means nurturing the essential you. This process of self-appreciation starts by ensuring you feel good internally and externally, so that your body is relaxed and full of energy and vitality, and your complexion is clear and glowing with life. Self-appreciation involves feeling good about your body so that you are content about yourself and life in general, as well as being very alive and spontaneous. It is also about preparing your physical self so that you are better able to fight disease and stay healthy, because ill health is a state of mind as well as body, and will dampen the enthusiasm and self-confidence you need to seek and sustain a loving relationship.

Ensuring you have adequate rest is an important part of this process. Never neglect your sleep routine because without sufficient rest and relaxation, your body is unable to replenish its resources, and you are unlikely to achieve the mental harmony you need to fulfil your potential.

Diet and Nutrition

Diet can often have the most direct and immediate effect on your well-being, and yet it is the one aspect of the average person's lifestyle that is most likely to be neglected. A healthy body must start with a healthy diet. That "you are what you eat" is an old adage – yet it is literally true, because the cells in your body are constantly being replaced by the molecules in your food. Food supplies the building blocks, in the form of amino acids and essential fatty acids, that repair and replenish your tissues, and ensure the normal functioning of the basic bodily processes. It also provides the vital energy you need to power you through the day and it will certainly add zest to your sexuality.

Mealtimes should be an important part of your daily activity. Instead of rushing your food, take time to sit down and relax as you eat. Turn your mealtimes into an occasion for mental relaxation as well as physical renewal. In this high-speed, high-pressure world it is tempting to forsake a good diet in favour of high-fat fast foods and sugar-rich snacks. This can only be a short-term solution and can have disastrous long-term consequences.

Vital Foods
◀ *A balanced diet that contains a wide range of foods, including plenty of fresh fruit and vegetables, will ensure you get all the vitamins and minerals you need for health and well-being.*

Eating too much of the wrong kinds of foods leads to a much higher risk of digestive disorders, heart disease, and certain types of cancer, as well as risking obesity and tooth decay. The body also needs adequate levels of essential nutrients, including vitamins and minerals, to stay healthy. Only by eating a balanced diet with a wide range of foods can you ensure that you are getting all the major nutritional components you need.

Highly processed foods invariably contain an excess of animal fats, and refined sugars, while much of the goodness, in the form of fibre and vitamins, is removed. These foods represent empty calories that add to your waistline but provide little else of benefit.

Physical well-being starts with a well-balanced diet. Normally, a person should aim to increase the percentage of complex carbohydrates, such as bread and potatoes, in the diet, and reduce the amount of refined sugars, such as cane sugar. Complex carbohydrates provide

Rest and Unwind

◀ *Sleep relaxes the mind as well as the body by helping to uncoil the cares and tensions that have been building up throughout the day. It also refreshes and revitalizes you for the day ahead.*

energy at a steady, sustainable rate, while simple sugars give a quick-acting energy surge that can make you edgy, hyperactive and irritable, and then leave you feeling drained and lethargic.

You should also try to cut down on saturated fat, obtained from meat and full-fat dairy products such as butter and cream, which clogs up the arteries and increases blood pressure levels. The ideal daily diet for a healthy adult should include:

❖ Up to eight glasses of pure water a day. This helps keep the kidneys functioning properly and flushes out the toxins and waste products that can build up in the body. You should also reduce your intake of stimulant drinks, such as tea, coffee and alcohol. These drinks can disrupt the body's fluid balance and over-stimulate the central nervous system, leading to insomnia, high blood pressure and raised heart rates, and aggravating stress disorders.

❖ Eat plenty of fresh fruit and vegetables, to provide the vitamins, minerals, and soluble and insoluble fibre you need.

❖ Have at least four servings a day of complex carbohydrates, such as bread (especially whole-wheat), pasta, rice, breakfast cereals, and potatoes.

❖ Include in your diet low-fat dairy foods, such as skimmed or semi-skimmed milk, yogurt, or

fromage frais. These provide the calcium and vitamins you need without significantly increasing your intake of saturated fats.

❖ Your daily intake of food should include two servings of protein foods such as chicken, fish, eggs, nuts, seeds, beans, peas and lentils. This gives the vital proteins needed to replace worn-out and damaged tissues. By including oily fish, such as herrings and mackerel, in your diet you will also be getting the essential fatty acids your body needs. A vegetarian diet can also be healthy and sustaining, but take care to ensure it contains the right balance of amino-acids.

Physical Fitness

It is important to take a well-balanced approach to your body. Without becoming neurotic about your size and weight, try to take an interest in your physical state because an enjoyable and invigorating fitness regime at a level you can sustain without undue stress can enhance your mental and physical well-being.

When you are unfit you tend to feel more lethargic and uninterested in the world and the people around you. If you are not in a current relationship, you may be less inclined to look for a partner. Low self-esteem about your own body may even transmit itself to others and be reflected in the way they regard you. Similarly, if you are in a partnership, your lack of vitality and enthusiasm could undermine your confidence and you may feel less inclined to put in the commitment required to sustain the relationship.

In addition, lovemaking is a physical activity and needs at least a minimum level of fitness. The fitter you are, the more likely it is that you will be in the mood for sex when your partner is feeling romantic, and the more enjoyment you will get out of lovemaking.

Regular exercise also provides major health benefits. It makes your heart, lungs and circulatory system work more efficiently, lowers cholesterol levels, and helps you to lose surplus fat and maintain your ideal weight once you have achieved it.

Releasing Vital Energy

In addition to the routines that help improve your general health and fitness, there are special exercises you can do to aid the release of muscular tensions within your body. Long-term tensions in the body, caused by emotional blocks and repressed feelings, can result in chronically tight muscles, and inhibit the free flow of vital energy – including sexual energy. This reduces your capacity to breathe deeply and prevents oxygen from reaching your inner core to replenish your vitality and nourish your cells and tissues.

Breath awareness, as described later in this book, and certain exercises can help relax and expand tense

Sideways Trunk Stretch

▲ *This stretch exercise will help improve flexibility in your neck and body. Stand with your feet apart and take a deep breath. Bend sideways and breathe out. Hold the stretch for ten seconds. Repeat with the other side.*

areas of the body, and allow for the release of pent-up emotional feelings. Chronic patterns of tension formed within the body are known as "muscular armour" and this needs to be released if the individual is to

gain greater emotional freedom and physical vitality.

The exercises shown here are based on Bioenergetic Therapy which is a system of bodywork devised by Alexander Lowen in the 1960s, and which has its roots in psychoanalysis. Lowen taught that a person's level of emotional stability is indicated by the degree of physical integration between one area of the body and another and the way he or she maintains contact with the earth through the feet and legs. This latter concept is termed "grounding". Grounded people "have their feet on the ground", literally as well as figuratively, and are rooted in the real world and in their physical reality, and so are better able to allow muscular-emotional release. Such individuals are better able to identify with the body and relate to their sexuality.

The following exercises – "the backward bow" and "the front drop" – may help you to increase your flexibility and sense of grounding by opening up areas of tension, and releasing stress, and so helping you gain access to your vital sexual energy. Try them to see if they are of benefit to you. Do

Limbering Up

Always start your exercise programme with a good limbering-up routine to stretch the stiffness out of the muscles and tendons. Be careful not to bounce or jerk as you do this or you may tear muscle fibres and damage joints.

Backward Bow
▶ *Stand with feet about 45cm/18in apart and toes turned in slightly. Make a fist with both hands and place them into your lower back. With knees well bent, and keeping your weight on the balls of your feet, arch your body backwards. Still keeping your weight forwards on your feet, breathe through the mouth and draw your breath deep down to your diaphragm. Hold this position for a minute to let the vibrations pass through your body.*

The Front Drop
◀ *Stand with your feet about 30cm/12in apart and your toes pointing in. Keeping your knees flexed, bend forward and touch the floor lightly with your fingers, without putting weight on your hands. Let your head hang down and keep your neck loose. Keep the weight of your body over the feet. Breathe easily through the mouth and take the breath a little deeper than usual. Slowly put the weight on the balls of the feet, without locking, or straightening the knees. Hold this position for a minute and then relax.*

both, one after the other, for about one minute each, and practise them every day, or three times a week, or whenever you feel the need to release tension. Always finish off with the front drop, even if you began with it, as this will release the tension from your lower back. (If you have a lower-back injury, these exercises should be used with caution or not undertaken until the condition has improved.)

Regarding the first exercise, the backward bow, Lowen points out in his book *The Betrayal of the Body* that the body arches like a bow to give itself impetus in various activities, such as when swinging an axe to cut wood, or serving a ball in a game of tennis. He states that this arc movement is basic to sexual functioning and that any tension or disturbance which prevents the body from achieving the bow position, thus inhibiting a forward thrust, can diminish a person's ability to achieve sexual satisfaction.

This exercise draws attention to areas of tension within your body, particularly the diaphragm and abdomen, but because that area is put under stress by the position, it can begin to release its tension. Breathing should be through the mouth and deep enough to expand your belly. The energy release is felt as a trembling and shaking and, if this happens, simply allow it to vibrate through your body.

The second exercise, the front drop, has a dual purpose. By leaning forward the person is releasing tension blocks in the diaphragm that enable the breathing to become deeper and more revitalizing. In addition, because of the position of the feet and legs and the flexing in the knees, an individual is more aware of the contact with the ground and of tensions in the calf muscles and hamstrings.

As tension releases, this may be experienced as a tremor or tingling in the legs and possibly up towards the pelvis as stress areas are released and energy is able to flow freely. However, do not worry if you fail to experience this vibration at once.

Press-Ups
▶ *This strength exercise improves muscle tone in the shoulders and abdomen. Lie face down on the floor with hands at shoulder level, palms facing downwards, and elbows bent. Raise your body by straightening your elbows, while keeping your back straight. Hold for ten seconds, and then lower. Repeat five times.*

If you practise this exercise, daily or several times a week, you should begin to notice an effect.

Skin Care

As well as bringing about internal physical changes to enhance your self-esteem, a health and self-awareness routine can also take into account your outward appearance. Good grooming and a concern for your appearance is just as important for men as it is for women.

Helping to keep your skin clean and youthful looking does not need to involve expensive bills at a beauty parlour, or costly cosmetic preparations, as a simple daily regime is usually sufficient. A nutritious and balanced diet, of course, is the best way to have a healthy skin.

Skin care is mainly aimed at counteracting the harmful effects of the sun and wind, and preventing the pores becoming blocked by removing dirt and excess grease along with the outer layer of dead skin cells. You should avoid wearing heavy make-up and use a cleanser to remove all cosmetics before you go to bed.

Looking Good
▲ *Good grooming is just as important for men as it is for women. By taking some care over your appearance you encourage others to take an interest in you.*

Self-Discovery

Using creams and lotions to moisturize and revitalize your skin can make you feel sensual and help you to get in touch with your body. The insidious effect of advertising and its constant encouragement to achieve unrealistic perfection can often lead people, particularly women, to develop a negative body image. By massaging your own body with a good quality moisturizing cream or lotion to help nourish your skin, you can take the opportunity to explore your body so you learn to appreciate yourself, lose your negative feelings, and feel more positive, as well as caring for your skin at the same time.

Starting with your face, spread upwards and outwards from your nose, working the cream into your forehead and then sweeping out to the temples. Slide your fingers along the sides of the nose and out over your cheekbones, then use your fingertips to stroke upwards and outwards from your chin over the jaw and up to the ears. Finish this area by rubbing the cream into your neck, using an upward motion to tone the muscles.

Now use light sensuous touches of your fingers and palms to spread the

Air and Exercise
◀ *Aerobic exercise, such as jogging, will boost the heart and lungs and draw oxygen into the tissues to improve your health, well-being and mental alertness.*

cream over your body. Working outwards from your heart, spread the cream across your chest, using an upward motion on your breasts, and then rub it over your shoulders and down your arms. Work from your lower breastbone over your belly and down your legs to your feet. Take time to rub the cream in well, particularly into the top and undersides of the feet, to squeeze out the muscular knots and tensions that can accumulate here.

Alternatively, using a similar technique, spread a rich massage oil over your body. A man should pay particular attention to the muscles around the shoulders and arms and in the legs, stroking and kneading the flesh with the fingertips to loosen and invigorate the muscle fibres.

To enhance the feeling of relaxation and contentment, blend one or more aromatherapy oils into your massage lotion. Lavender is a safe and attractive oil for relaxation and harmony which can also ease tired, stiff, or aching muscles, but there are many more you can choose.

By using these soothing caresses on your skin, you will begin to know and love your body, as well as nurturing your skin with the lotion to leave it soft and glowing. As you stroke over your skin, let your hands relax so they are able to slide smoothly and sculpt over your body's contours.

Self-Massage

A regular self-massage programme makes you look and feel more relaxed,

as well as stimulating the circulation and enlivening your skin so that you can become more sensually responsive. It can help you develop an awareness of your outer self, as well as dispelling negative thoughts, and improving your body image.

Start off by massaging the head, using tiny circular movements, as if shampooing your hair, and feel the scalp move under your fingers. Now massage the temples, using two fingers of each hand in a circular motion to relieve mental tension, and then work on the fleshy areas of your

Massage the Muscles

▼ *Spread a massage oil over your body, working it into the muscles of the shoulders, arms, and legs. Knead the flesh with the fingertips to loosen and relax the muscle fibres.*

Care and Attention

◄ *Apply a good quality moisturizing cream to nourish your skin, and explore your face and body at the same time, so you can learn to appreciate yourself as you care for your complexion.*

cheeks, using the flats of your fingers in large circular movements.

The next stage is to follow an invigorating sequence of massage strokes to refresh and revitalize your skin and muscles. Start with the face, and use the tips of your fingers to tap all over the facial muscles, jaw-line, forehead, temples and cheeks. Next, work on the shoulders and neck. Make a loose fist and use the flat surface of the fingers to pummel the muscles gently. Use the same technique to pummel the arms and down to the backs of the hands. Now do the same thing on the inside of the hands and arms, before using alter-

Pummel the Tissues

▼ *By making your hands into a loose fist you can gently pummel the body to release tension in the tissues and boost the blood circulation, leaving you feeling restored and invigorated.*

nate strokes to pound the ribcage vigorously. Finally, use a hacking motion with the side of the hands on the legs and feet to tone up the muscles and boost the circulation.

A very invigorating massage can be obtained by using a skin brush. This device, which is available from health shops, is used dry and stroked over the skin. It removes the outer layer of cells and allows the underlying cells to regenerate themselves. It revitalizes and tones the skin and enhances the body's ability to eliminate toxins, as well as leaving the skin soft and smooth to the touch.

Starting at your feet, work up your legs and then your arms, and over your body towards your heart, following the direction of your circulation. Follow it up with a shower to wash off any remaining dead skin cells. You can do this several times a week to leave your skin glowing with health and vigour, and silky soft to the touch.

Brush Your Skin

▼ *Use a skin brush to remove the dead outer layer of skin cells. It will revitalize and refresh the skin and also leave your body tingling and glowing with health and vitality.*

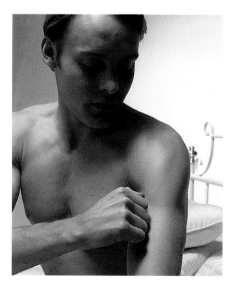

Chapter 2

The Sexual Body

Our sexual body is a miraculous part of our psychosomatic reality, yet generally we know little about how it develops and functions. In this chapter, we discuss how our sexual organs mature through adolescence to adulthood and begin to unravel the mysterious differences between the male and female reproductive systems. To understand our sexuality fully, we must first make the effort to get to know the geography of our sexual systems, and learn about their physical processes, strengths and weaknesses. Then we can go on a voyage of discovery in search of the body's secret pleasure zones – a journey which can bring us sexual happiness.

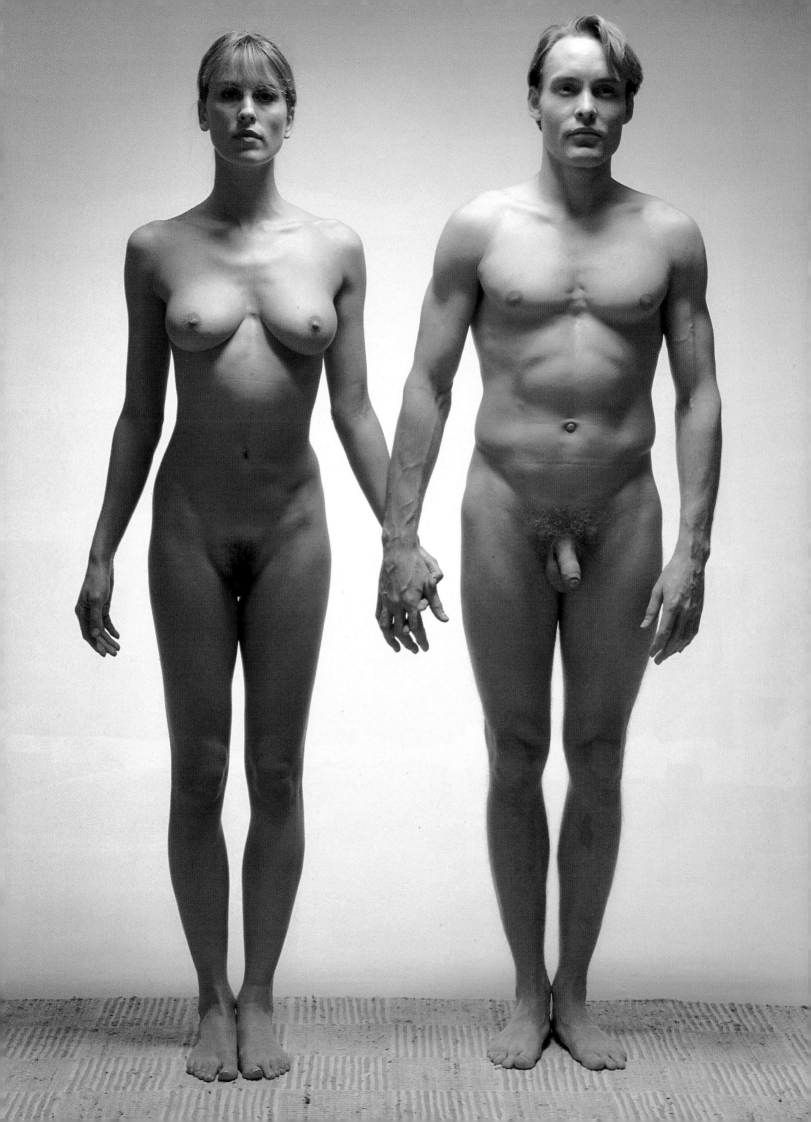

The Woman's Body

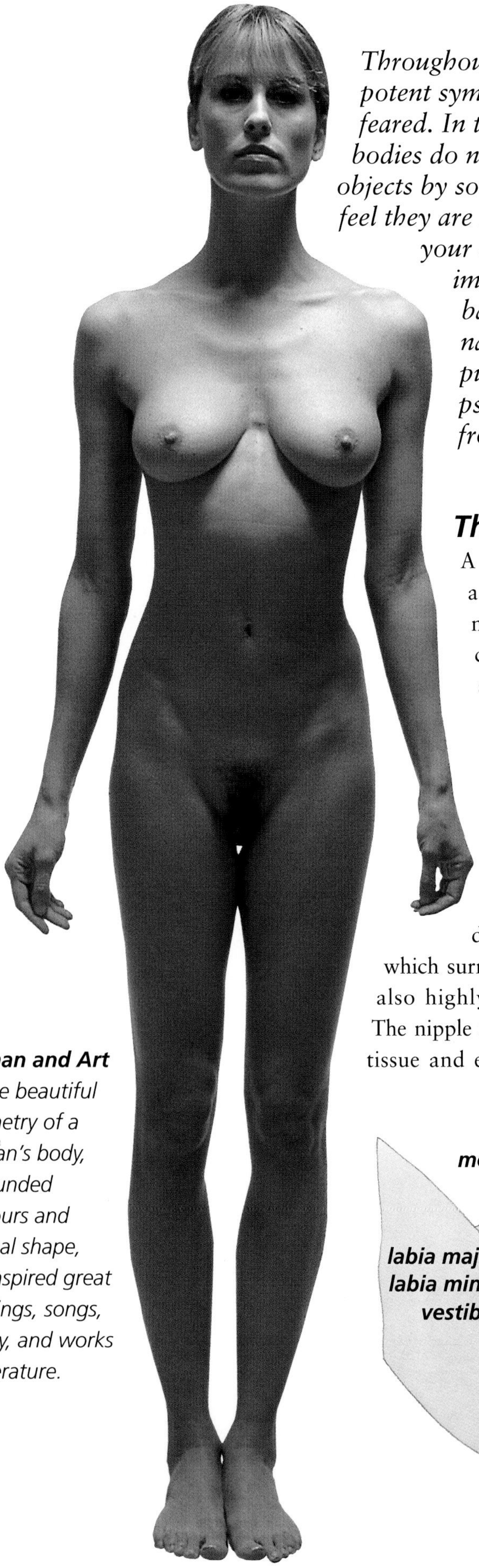

Throughout history, the female body has been regarded as a potent symbol of fertility and sexuality – both mystifying and feared. In the past, women have sometimes felt that their bodies do not even belong to them because they are viewed as objects by society at large. Now, more than ever, women want to feel they are in charge of their own bodies. Learning to know your body, and understanding how it functions, is an important step in this process. This section provides basic information on the sexual and reproductive nature of a woman's body, the changes that occur at puberty, and some of the other physical and psychological processes that take place on the journey from girlhood to womanhood.

Woman and Art
▶ *The beautiful symmetry of a woman's body, its rounded contours and sensual shape, has inspired great paintings, songs, poetry, and works of literature.*

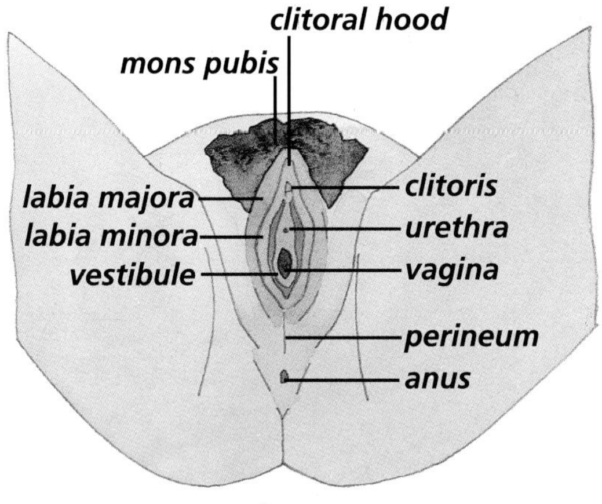

The Breasts

A woman's breasts are a symbol of her femininity, for their spherical softness is very sensual, regardless of size. The breasts are sexually responsive to tactile stimulation and they will swell slightly during sexual arousal. The nipple and the areola, the dark pigmented skin which surrounds the nipple, are also highly sensitive to touch. The nipple is made up of erectile tissue and enlarges when stimulated. While a woman's breasts are often regarded as sexual organs, their primary function is to produce milk to nourish a baby. Each breast is made up of around 20 lobes, containing numerous milk-producing glands, which are surrounded by fatty tissue. Tiny tubes – called the lactiferous ducts – carry the milk to small openings in the nipple. The breasts contain no muscles, but strands of ligament weave in between the tissues to give them their shape and support. The size of the breasts varies greatly from woman to woman, but bears no relation to the quantity of milk they can produce.

The Vulva

Vulva means visible and refers to the external female genitalia, or that which can be seen. This mainly consists of the mons, the labia majora and minora (the outer and inner "lips"), and the clitoris.

clitoral hood
mons pubis
labia majora
labia minora
vestibule
clitoris
urethra
vagina
perineum
anus

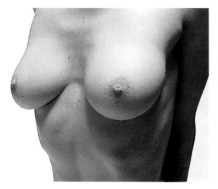 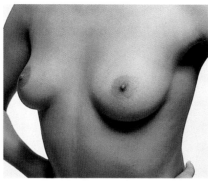 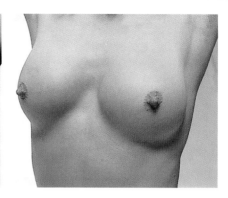

Breast Size

Breast shape and size varies greatly between women. The way a woman with a 34 inch bust (the average breast size) feels about her breasts may partly depend on the era and culture she is born in. Fashions in what is considered an attractive breast size change constantly, from the buxom and curvaceous style favoured by Hollywood in the 1950s to the small and boyish, almost androgynous shape of many of today's top models.

It is important for a woman to love and accept her body – particularly the shape of her breasts – the way it is, for it is an expression of her own unique femininity. If the breasts are large and causing discomfort it will help to wear a good support bra. Small breasts cannot be enlarged directly by exercise as they do not contain muscle, but good posture (a lengthened spine, and straightened shoulders) can lift the ribcage to give the breasts a more pronounced shape. Likewise, you can develop the underlying pectoral muscles, which may help increase the lift and support the weight. A difference in size between the left and right breast is very common.

Breast Skincare
◀ *Taking care of the thin skin which covers the breasts can help to prevent stretch marks. Rub moisturizing cream on and around the breasts to keep the skin soft and smooth.*

Variety of Shapes
▼ *Nipple shapes and sizes are also very varied. Some nipples are naturally inverted – the nipple is pulled inwards and hidden behind a fold in the skin. In most cases, inverted nipples should not prevent successful breastfeeding. If, however, a nipple suddenly becomes inverted during adulthood, it is important to consult a doctor immediately, as this may indicate breast cancer.*

Mons Pubis

The mons, or mons pubis, is also rather romantically known as the mons veneris, or Mount of Venus. It is the soft mound of fatty tissue, covered by skin and pubic hair, which protects the pubic bone from friction during intercourse. Its rich supply of nerve endings makes it very sexually responsive to tactile stimulation.

Pubic Hair

The pubic hair which covers the mons grows in a triangular shape and sometimes spreads down to the thighs. It is darker and coarser than head hair. It can be thick or sparse, and these differences can be particularly marked between races. It also thins with age. Cultural influences usually dictate whether women shave or wax their pubic hair, or let it grow. Pubic hair is one of the first signs of sexual development.

Labia Majora (Outer Lips)

The word labia means lips. The labia majora are the two outer fleshy folds of skin and fatty tissue. When a woman is sexually excited, the lips become engorged with blood and swell. They are partly covered with pubic hair.

Labia Minora (Inner Lips)

The labia minora are two fleshy folds of skin which are mostly covered by the labia majora, although they may protrude. The inner labia, in turn, cover the urethra, or urinary opening, and the vagina. There are many variations among women in the shape, size and colour of the labia minora. The labia meet to form a hood over the head of the clitoris and extend to just below the vaginal opening. They are richly supplied with nerve endings. Unlike the outer lips, they are not covered with pubic hair. The cleft between the labia minora is known as the vestibule. Ducts from Bartholin's glands, which secrete a lubricant when a woman is sexually excited, open into the vestibule. This lubricant reduces skin friction and so enables easier penetration of the vagina during intercourse.

Clitoris

The clitoris is located where the inner labia meet. In Greek folklore, the sunflower, Kleite, grew and opened when stimulated by the sun, an apt analogy for this most sexually sensitive part of a woman's body. The clitoris is made of erectile tissue similar to that of the glans of the penis, and is as richly supplied with nerve endings as the penis, though concentrated within a much smaller area. The clitoris can measure 2–5cm/ 3/4–2in, but appears smaller as only the top is visible. It is partly covered

---

Self-Discovery

Many women feel very shy about their genital area, and may never have seen it properly for themselves. In this respect, men are luckier, as they can not only see their own genitals easily, but their partner's too. To help you get to know, love and understand your body better, try this exercise to examine and explore your vulva and vagina.

Using a hand mirror will enable you to see this hidden part of yourself. Find a comfortable position, either squatting or lying on your back propped up on pillows, and angle the mirror to give yourself a full view of your external genitalia. As you look, explore each part with your hands and fingers. Notice the shape and colour of your labia, and part the outer lips to get a closer look at the inner, fleshy folds. Seek out your clitoris, and gently stroke it with a finger. Then explore the outer entrance to your vagina, allowing a finger to penetrate gently in order to feel the soft, mucous membranes of its inner wall.

A Perfect Fit
◄ *The anatomy of a man and woman is designed to fit perfectly. The vagina is shaped to receive the man's penis during coitus, and even expands during sexual arousal in order to accommodate it.*

by the labia minora and fills with blood when a woman is sexually excited. The clitoris has no obvious purpose other than to give pleasure to a woman, and with skilful manipulation during masturbation or love-making, it is instrumental to her achieving an orgasm.

Hymen

The hymen is a thin fold of tissue that partly covers the entrance to the vagina. Undamaged, it has a small central opening which allows the outflow of menstrual blood. The hymen is easily torn or stretched during strenuous activity in child-hood, by the insertion of tampons, or, in later years, by sexual inter-course. Once broken, the ragged edges of the hymen tissue ring the vaginal opening. Contrary to former belief, a broken hymen does not necessarily mean that a woman is not a virgin.

Vagina

The vagina (which means sheath) is a channel measuring 7–10cm/2³/₄–4in leading from the vulva to the uterus. The entrance to the vagina is located just below the urethra, or urinary opening. The muscular walls of the vagina are deeply folded so that it can expand during intercourse or childbirth. They are also richly supplied with blood vessels, which become engorged with blood during sexual arousal. The walls are covered with a mucous membrane which secretes a fluid that helps lubricate the vagina, especially during inter-course. These secretions are slightly acidic, which helps to keep harmful organisms in check. The vagina also acts as an outlet for the flow of menstrual blood.

Cervix

The cervix is the neck of the uterus and is located at the top of the vagina. It is a narrow, cylindrical structure, made of tough tissue and muscle, and is approximately 2.5cm/1in long. In the centre of the cervix is the os, a small opening which enables sperm to pass into the uterus and allows menstrual blood to flow out. It remains firmly closed during pregnancy, while the rest of the uterus expands to accommodate the foetus. During the final stages of labour, in response to contractions of the uterus, the cervix dilates to allow the baby to pass through into the birth canal. A special form of mucus is secreted by glands in the cervix. The consistency of the mucus changes throughout the menstrual cycle, becoming profuse, slippery and stretchy, clear or slightly cloudy around the time of ovulation, when it is called fertile mucus, and sticky, white or even absent afterwards. Fertile mucus plays an important role in reproduction by aiding the passage and survival of sperm.

Uterus

The uterus, or womb, is a muscular organ, roughly the shape of an upside-down pear, located above and behind the bladder. It is 7.5–10cm/3–4in long, on average, and weighs 60–90g/2–3oz. During the menstrual cycle, the lining of the uterus (the endometrium) increases in thickness as it prepares to receive and nourish a fertilized egg. If this does not happen, the lining breaks down and is shed during menstrua-tion. During pregnancy the uterus expands and becomes more muscu-lar to contain the developing baby. These muscles also produce power-ful contractions during labour to expel the baby.

Fallopian Tubes

The Fallopian tubes are about 7.5cm/3in long and attached at either side to the upper end of the uterus, with an opening no wider than the eye of a needle. The other end of each tube, the ampulla, is funnel-shaped and has finger-like frills called fimbriae. When an egg is released from the ovary, these fimbriae waft it into a Fallopian tube. The egg is then carried along the tube and into the uterus by the action of hair-like projections called cilia and by contractions of the tube walls. Fertilization usually occurs within a Fallopian tube. Occasionally, a fertilized egg may implant in the wall of a Fallopian tube and continue to develop, resulting in an ectopic pregnancy – a potentially life-threatening condition.

Ovaries

The ovaries are almond-shaped organs about 3cm/1¼in long. They produce the eggs, or ova, which, when fertilized by sperm, develop into a human life. The ovaries are located just behind and to either side of the uterus and lie close to the funnel-shaped ends of the Fallopian tubes. Around 600,000 immature eggs are present at the start of a woman's fertile life, although only

around 400 will develop into mature eggs. The eggs develop in special sacs, called follicles. During each menstrual cycle one egg only usually bursts out of its follicle and is collected by the fimbriae of the nearest Fallopian tube. The ovaries also produce two hormones, oestrogen, mainly responsible for female sexual development, and progesterone which causes the lining of the uterus to thicken, ready to receive a fertilized egg. If fertilized, the egg will then embed itself in the lining, where it will develop into a foetus.

Female Sexual Development

Puberty in females starts at around the age of ten, triggered by an upsurge in the level of sex hormones secreted into the bloodstream, and can take up to five years to complete. The start and rate of development of a girl's sexual maturity differs from one individual to another, but may be

influenced by hereditary factors, nutrition and health. The improvement in diet and living standards in industrialized nations is thought mainly responsible for the earlier onset of the first menstrual cycle in girls today.

The initial changes in puberty, between the ages of ten and 12, are triggered by chemical and nerve signals from a region in the brain called the hypothalamus. These signals cause the pituitary gland, just below the brain, to release hormones called gonadotrophins. These, in turn, instruct the ovaries to start releasing the hormones oestrogen and progesterone. The various hormonal changes at this time bring about a sudden spurt in growth, including increased height and muscle weight, changes in the distribution of fat around the body, and the development of the reproductive organs.

The first changes may be the budding of the breasts, one often earlier than the other, and the darkening of the pigment of the areolae. This is usually followed by the appearance of pubic hair, and then underarm hair. The uterus, Fallopian tubes and ovaries start to mature, the vagina enlarges, and the labia begin to swell. There may also be an increase in vaginal secretions, and the oil and sweat glands become highly active, often leading to acne and pimples.

The characteristic female shape now begins to develop, as the pelvis widens and fat deposits are laid down under the skin of the breasts, buttocks, hips and thighs. The first menstrual period, the menarche, occurs on average between the ages of 12 and 13 years, but usually not

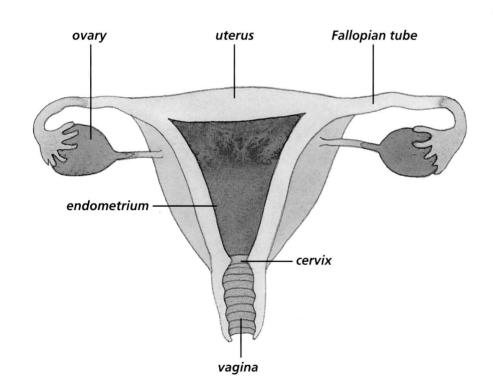

ovary   uterus   **Fallopian tube**

endometrium

cervix

vagina

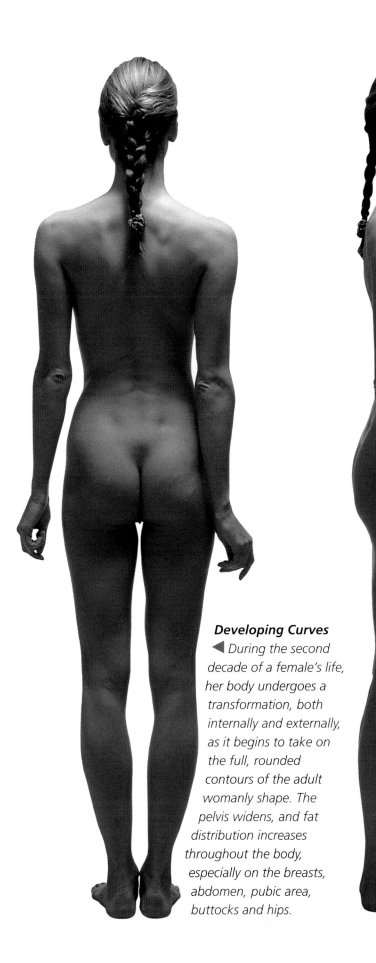

until at least a year after the secondary sexual characteristics have begun to develop. The start of regular periods marks the completion of puberty.

From Girl to Woman

An adolescent girl may welcome the dramatic changes in her body as evidence that she is entering womanhood. Equally, she may be distressed or alarmed by them, feeling that her body is out of control, or being reluctant to relinquish her childhood so soon. She is likely to go through intense mood swings, partly due to hormonal fluctuations, but also because she must adapt psychologically as well as physically to her new identity.

She is no longer a little girl and, in various ways, she may demand that her changing identity is recognized by her family. A young teenage girl may need to assert her developing womanhood, separating herself temporarily from the close bond she had previously shared with her mother. Her relationship with her father may alter as they both try to find a new way of acknowledging and adjusting to her developing sexuality. At this point, a father may stop showing his normal displays of physical affection, unsure of exactly how to relate to his daughter.

Developing Curves
◀ *During the second decade of a female's life, her body undergoes a transformation, both internally and externally, as it begins to take on the full, rounded contours of the adult womanly shape. The pelvis widens, and fat distribution increases throughout the body, especially on the breasts, abdomen, pubic area, buttocks and hips.*

Arrival of Womanhood
◀ *In the later stages of puberty, a female's menstrual cycle usually becomes more regular, on average settling at between 26 and 32 days' duration. Her breasts develop to their adult size, her pubic hair becomes thicker, and underarm hair appears. By now, her voice may have become slightly deeper. A female's growth in height slows down soon after puberty.*

A Need to Bond
▼ *On the whole, women of all ages consider intimacy, love and emotional bonding to be an important part of forming a sexual relationship*

In spite of these difficulties, the adolescent girl will need a great deal of emotional support from her parents, even though she appears to challenge them on every issue.

Sex Education
It is important that a girl is fully informed about the physical changes her body will undergo during puberty, and has adequate knowledge about menstruation, and related hygiene matters, before her periods begin.

It is not always easy for parents to discuss sexual issues with their children although, nowadays, families do tend to be more open about such topics. If the mother, or guiding parent, feels unable to discuss these subjects with the daughter (girls may also find it embarrassing to discuss sexual matters with their parents), it is important to find someone the girl can trust and who will answer her questions, or provide her with suitable books from which she can gather accurate information. Informed sex education is not a green light for promiscuity.

A teenage girl will benefit from knowing that during adolescence she is likely to feel attracted to boys, and even experiment in sexual play with them, and that sometimes her emotions and sexual feelings will be overwhelming. She needs to understand the importance of defining the boundaries of her sexual behaviour so that she is able to resist male or peer group pressure to engage in any sexual activity for which she does not feel ready. By discussing these issues with an understanding adult, she will be better equipped to take control of her body and emotions.

Studies show that adequate sex education for young people (males and females) about contraception, sexually transmitted diseases, and the complexities of emotional and sexual feelings in relationships, can help reduce cases of premature sexual intercourse and of teenage pregnancies.

Sexual Experience
Young women do masturbate, for sexual release and to explore their bodily responses, although slightly less often than males of the same age. According to research, the average age for the loss of virginity in young women in the United States and Great Britain is between 16 and 18. There are still many young women who, for religious, romantic or moral reasons,

A Growing Capacity for Sexual Arousal

▲ *As a woman's sexual experience increases, so does her orgasmic capacity. When she is fully relaxed in her body, and is aroused lovingly by a sensitive and knowledgeable partner, her sexual pleasure is almost boundless.*

or through fear of pregnancy, or sexually transmitted disease, prefer to remain virgins until they meet a man with whom they can develop a committed relationship. However, in most western cultures there is no longer the same pressure on females to remain virgins until their wedding night, and many young women will have had several sexual partners by the time they reach their twenties.

These days, women expect to compete equally with their male colleagues in the academic and work environment, and for most women marriage and children are no longer seen as their only goals. The wider availability of contraception has given women greater freedom in all areas of their lives.

Increasingly, women are choosing to live with a partner before marriage, and to delay starting a family until established in a career. It

is not unusual for women to wait until their thirties before having their first baby – and some are now leaving it until their forties to start a family – and most expect to return to work within a few months or years after giving birth.

Women's Sexual Peak

A woman's capacity to achieve an orgasm appears to increase with age and sexual experience. Women tend to reach their sexual peak during their thirties and can continue at this level for many years. In part, this may be because as a woman gets older and becomes more confident and relaxed in her sexuality, she is better attuned to what will bring her

sexual satisfaction during lovemaking. Younger women may be more preoccupied with trying to please their partners during intercourse, while, in general, women are more sexually responsive when they are involved in a secure, intimate and loving relationship.

Although women are becoming more sexually assertive and better able to initiate relationships with the opposite sex, they still suffer from society's double standards over the morality of multiple sexual experience. Whereas a man is expected to "sow his wild oats" as evidence of his virility, a woman can still be regarded as promiscuous if she has had several sexual partners.

The Man's Body

Men are conditioned to be less self-conscious about their bodies than women, but nevertheless, men still have many concerns about their physical selves which they are often unable to express verbally. Gender conditioning varies greatly between cultures but, in general, men are usually expected to sublimate their more vulnerable, gentle, and sensitive feelings and to place more emphasis on the development of physical prowess. Yet a man's reproductive system is complex and miraculous, involving him on both a physical and emotional level. This section will aim to explain the form and function of the male sex organs, and will look at a man's sexual and psychological adventure through life.

The Classic Male Image
◀ The masculine form traditionally symbolizes strength and virility, and this depiction of the athletic manly physique has been a popular theme in classic sculpture and art. The more emotional and sensual aspects of the male psyche have received far less acknowledgement.

Learn About Each Other
▲ Men and women can benefit enormously from learning about each other's sexual anatomy. It is important to understand the differences between the two – and also the similarities.

The Scrotum

The scrotum is the pouch which contains and supports the testicles, hanging down externally below the pubic bone and behind the penis. It is made up of a layer of contractile muscle covered by a pouch of thin, loose skin. While the scrotum looks like one sac, it is actually divided into two compartments, each housing one testicle. The external location of the scrotum helps to keep the sperm at their optimum temperature of two or three degrees below normal body heat. If the outside temperature drops, the scrotum is drawn closer to the warmth of the body so that the testicles are not allowed to get too cool.

Testicles (Testes)

The testicles, or testes, are the male reproductive organs. Each testicle is suspended from a thick fibrous structure called the spermatic cord. During the early stages of foetal development the testicles are located high within the abdomen, but they slowly descend until at birth they have arrived at their final position. They are composed of two types of cells – one type makes sperm, while the other produces the male sex hormone testosterone. Each testicle contains an intricate and convoluted network of coiled tubes, the seminiferous tubules, in which the sperm cells develop. Sperm then pass into a larger coiled tube, the epididymis, where they are stored until they mature.

Vas Deferens (Seminal duct)

Mature sperm are stored in the vas deferens, an elongated tube contained within each spermatic cord, and are pushed towards the urethra by muscular contractions. During a

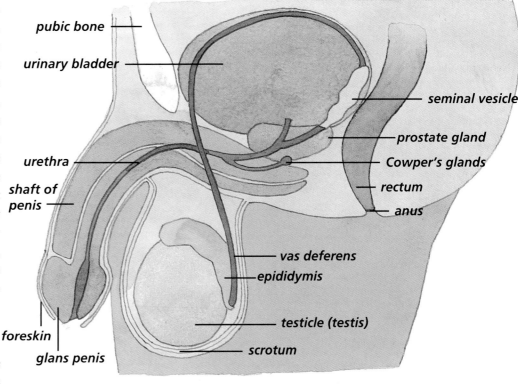

vasectomy, the male form of sterilization, each vas deferens is cut and tied to prevent sperm from leaving the testicles. After sterilization, although sperm continue to be produced, they are reabsorbed into the body. The operation does not prevent the ejaculation of sperm-free seminal fluid.

The Prostate Gland

The prostate gland, which is about the size of a chestnut, is situated in front of the rectum and just below the bladder. It secretes some of the seminal fluid, or ejaculate, which helps transport the sperm, and also produces a lubricant to keeps the lining of the urethra moist. The prostate gland can produce highly erotic sensations if directly stimulated by a partner's lubricated finger inserted into the anus, which is why it is sometimes said to be the male equivalent of the female's G-spot.

Seminal Vesicles

The seminal vesicles are two long sac-like organs located near the prostate gland at the junction of the two vasa deferentia and the urethra. They secrete about 60 per cent of the seminal fluid, which passes through the prostate gland and into the urethra via the ejaculatory ducts. The secretions from the seminal vesicles are high in sugars which will help provide the nourishment the sperm need on their long journey to fertilize the egg.

Cowper's Glands

The Cowper's glands are two pea-sized glands situated below the prostate and on each side of the bulbous portion of the urethra. Their ducts exude a clear, alkaline fluid into the urethra which helps protect the sperm by neutralizing the acidic environment of the urethra.

Penile Erection

▼ *A full penile erection, commonly known as a "hard-on", is due to blood being pumped into the erectile tissues at a much faster rate than it can escape. This causes the tissues to swell and the penis to enlarge.*

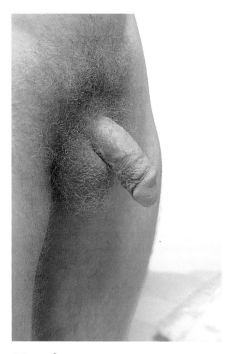
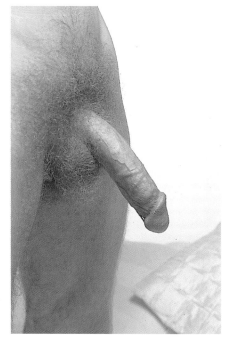

Urethra

The urethra is the channel through which both urine and semen pass out of the body. It originates at the bladder and passes through the prostate gland and the shaft of the penis before terminating at the external urethral opening, situated in the glans, or head of the penis. The male urethra is up to 20cm/8in in length – much longer than the female urethra. To prevent urine escaping with the semen, a ring of muscle closes off the bladder prior to ejaculation.

Penis

Most men would regard the penis as the most important part of their sexual anatomy and it is certainly their most erotically sensitive area. The penis consists of erectile and fibrous tissue and involuntary muscle, with a rich supply of nerves and blood vessels, surrounded by skin. The spongy erectile tissue of the penis is made up of three cylindrical compartments. These are the two corpora cavernosa and the corpus spongiosum, which surrounds the urethra. During sexual arousal, these cylinders fill with blood, causing the penis to grow erect.

The head of the penis is called the glans. The external urethral opening, through which semen is ejaculated, is in the centre of the glans. In uncircumcised men, the head of a flaccid penis is normally covered with a fold of loose skin called the foreskin, or prepuce. During erection the foreskin is stretched back to expose the glans, and this exposure is further increased by friction during coitus. The glans is very well served with nerve endings, and is the most erotically sensitive part of the man's penis. Where the skin folds back just below the under-ridge of the glans is an area called the frenulum. This is also very responsive to sexual stimulation.

A full erection of the penis can sometimes occur within seconds of sexual stimulation, although sexual arousal does not automatically lead to an erection. This can sometimes be a cause of great anxiety for men who are worried about their sexual performance.

Facts About Sperm

Sperm take about ten weeks to develop inside the testicles. Up to 30 billion sperm are produced each month and 50–100 million sperm per millilitre are present during a single ejaculation, which produces about one teaspoon of semen. In each ejaculation up to 40 per cent of sperm may be deformed or inactive. Sperm that are not ejaculated are reabsorbed into the body. Each microscopic-sized sperm has an oval head, a tubular mid-section, and a whip-like tail. The head contains 23 chromosomes – half the normal

Penis Sizes

Most men have worried about the size, shape and performance of their penis, at one time or another. This is hardly surprising since men are constantly being subjected to the concept of the mythical penis – rock hard, huge and with immense staying power. This, of course, has very little to do with the performance of a real penis, which – like the person to whom it belongs – has its good days and mediocre days. Quite often, though, men develop a distorted idea of their penis size. Comparisons with other men are inevitable but not always reliable. When men see each others' bodies, in communal showers or changing rooms, they see the full dimensions of the penises on display. However, when a man looks down at his own penis, he is going to see it from a different and rather fore-shortened angle. The best way to gauge your true penis size is to look at it sideways in the mirror.

Another anxiety for a man is whether a small penis will make a difference to the pleasure he can give a woman. It should be remembered that width is more important than length in stimulating the lining of the vagina, and thereby giving sexual satisfaction to a woman. The vagina is around 10cm/4in in length, so it is the right size for most penises. In exceptional cases, where an erect penis is very small, it may produce less stimulation. The woman, however, can still be stimulated orally, manually, and in lots of other exciting ways. The vast majority of women would say they fall in love with the man and not his penis. The skill with which a man uses his penis in lovemaking, his degree of sensuality and his sensitivity to her body's responses is what matters most.

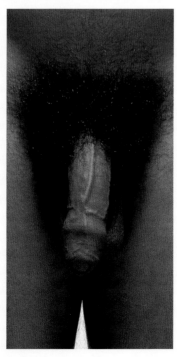

▶ *Penises do vary considerably in length, thickness and shape when they are flaccid but these differences become less pronounced once they are erect. A smaller penis will grow proportionally more than a large penis on arousal.*

human complement – including the X or Y chromosomes that will dictate the sex of the embryo after an egg has been fertilized. The midsection acts as the motor, causing the tail to lash from side to side, thereby propelling the sperm on its journey through the cervix and uterus and into a Fallopian tube in search of an egg. When conditions are right, sperm can survive for several days inside a woman's reproductive tract.

Circumcision

A circumcised penis is one in which the foreskin has been surgically removed. This is usually performed for religious reasons, particularly within the Jewish and Muslim communities, or for medical or health reasons. In the case of Jewish children, circumcision is usually carried out when a boy is eight days old. It is usually performed later with

The Circumcised Penis

▼ *Circumcision may be carried out on medical grounds, but more often it is for reasons of hygiene or religion.*

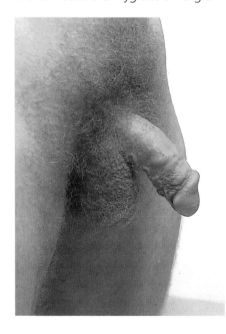

A Spermatozoon

▶ *Despite its microscopic size, a sperm is able to travel a relatively huge distance through the female reproductive tract, propelled by the whip-like action of its tail.*

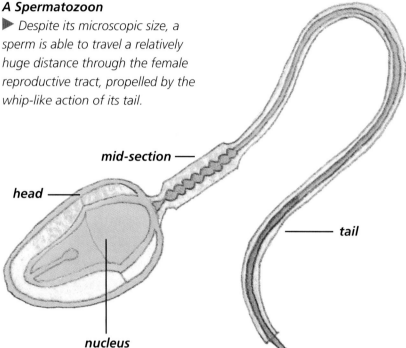

mid-section —

head —

tail

nucleus

Muslim children, between the ages of three and 15 years. In western countries, circumcision is more likely to be performed for its perceived health benefits – some people believe the removal of the foreskin reduces the risk of infection as the penis can be more easily kept clean. Circumcision is sometimes carried out for medical disorders such as phimosis, a condition in which the foreskin is too tight to retract properly, or balanitis, in which the tip of the penis becomes inflamed as a result of a buildup of secretions under the foreskin.

The Development of Male Sexuality

Puberty is the time when the male sexual characteristics become fully developed, leading to many changes in a young man's body. The first signs of puberty usually appear later in males than in females, between the ages of 12 and 14 years, although in

some individuals it may be slightly earlier or later than this.

As with girls, the initial changes are triggered by chemical and nerve signals in the hypothalamus, a region of the brain. These signals trigger the release of gonadotrophins which, in turn, instruct the testicles to start releasing increasing levels of male hormones, or androgens, such as testosterone, into the blood stream. These hormonal changes bring about a sudden spurt in bone and muscle development.

The initial signs of puberty in a boy are an increase in the size of the scrotum and testes, followed by the growth of pubic and facial hair. Sperm begins to develop within the testes, and other structures, such as the seminal vesicles and the prostate gland, begin to mature. Around the age of 13 years the penis begins to enlarge, taking around two years to reach its full adult size. The voice also begins to "break" as the larynx

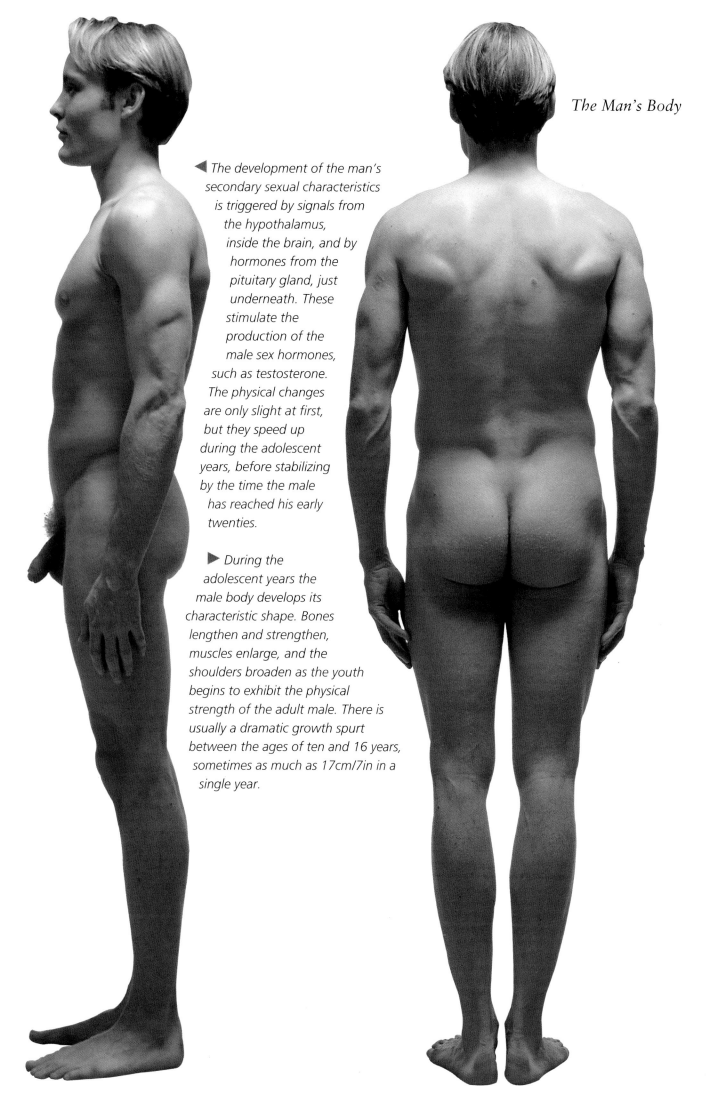

◀ The development of the man's secondary sexual characteristics is triggered by signals from the hypothalamus, inside the brain, and by hormones from the pituitary gland, just underneath. These stimulate the production of the male sex hormones, such as testosterone. The physical changes are only slight at first, but they speed up during the adolescent years, before stabilizing by the time the male has reached his early twenties.

▶ During the adolescent years the male body develops its characteristic shape. Bones lengthen and strengthen, muscles enlarge, and the shoulders broaden as the youth begins to exhibit the physical strength of the adult male. There is usually a dramatic growth spurt between the ages of ten and 16 years, sometimes as much as 17cm/7in in a single year.

Being Together

◀ *It is likely that after some sexual experimentation, a young man will want to form a more permanent and emotionally bonding sexual partnership. However, like women, men are now more likely to want to live with their partners for a time before making a commitment to marriage.*

enlarges and the vocal cords thicken and lengthen, causing the voice to drop in pitch.

Body hair appears under the arms and on the chest, and the skin becomes coarser and may darken a little. The increased levels of testosterone tend to overstimulate the oil-producing glands in the skin, leading to acne. This can usually be treated medically and will improve with age. It is not uncommon for an adolescent male to experience temporary breast enlargement. This normally subsides within a few months, though the episode may embarrass him.

Becoming A Man

Puberty can be a difficult time for a young man: he has to come to terms with physical changes in his body, in addition to defining his role as a male in society. He experiences peer group pressure, while trying to live up to the expectations of parents and teachers, yet at the same time he is trying to determine his own beliefs and goals. During this period he may start testing or challenging authority figures as he struggles to assert his own identity. At this stage of a young adolescent's development he will greatly benefit from the friend-

ship and guidance of older men who can act as role models and be prepared to advise him through this difficult, demanding, and changing period of life.

Male Sexual Experience

In addition to physical changes, a young male will probably start to experience exciting but somewhat frightening new sexual feelings. Erections occur frequently, and often at the most inopportune times. In his early teenage years, the adolescent may start to ejaculate during his sleep. These nocturnal emissions are commonly known as "wet dreams".

He will probably also engage in frequent masturbation, fuelled by his awakening desires and his growing fantasies about sex. It is not uncommon for adolescents to engage in sexual play with other boys of the same age. They may compare penises and frequency of ejaculations, and even masturbate together. For most boys this is only a passing phase, and can provide an important means of gaining knowledge about their own bodies and of comparing their development with others.

As a young man gains confidence in himself, he will start to develop an interest in the opposite sex and begin to form relationships. It is just as important for young men to be well informed on subjects such as contraception, sexually transmitted diseases, and the relationship between sexuality and emotional happiness as it is for their female counterparts.

Adolescence is usually a time of sexual experimentation and normally, while the emotions involved may be intense, these relationships do not always last long. In western cultures particularly, young men often feel under peer-group pressure to lose their virginity as soon as possible. According to recent studies of sexual behaviour in Britain, the majority of men claim to have lost their virginity at around the ages of 16 or 17 years. This, of course, is not true for all men, and many males remain virgins until they are much older.

As a boy becomes a man he has to cope with demands made upon him from many different directions. During early adulthood his prime concerns will centre around his studies or career, and establishing himself in his chosen lifestyle, but his relationships with women will also be of great importance.

Man's Sexual Peak

If a man's sexual peak is measured in terms of frequency of orgasm (either through masturbation or lovemaking) and the amount of resting time he needs between each

A Man's Sexual Experiences

▶ During adolescence, a young man may want to experiment with a number of relationships, and this can help him to build up a broad range of sexual and emotional experiences. As he grows older, however, he will be more inclined to seek his true mate.

ejaculation, he is at his most sexually potent in the years of late adolescence and early twenties. Generally, after that age his virility stabilizes, and then declines slightly in later years as he requires longer periods of recovery between each ejaculation. However, most men improve their lovemaking skills as

they get older, acquiring more knowledge about their own physical responses and becoming more sensitive to a woman's sexual needs. So, in fact, age can make a man a better lover, with more staying power during coitus. This undoubtedly enhances his sexual satisfaction, both physically and emotionally.

The Pleasure Zones

There are many pleasure zones in the sexual geography of the human body. When directly stimulated by touching, kissing, nuzzling, nibbling and licking they can awaken and heighten sexual response. Most sexually experienced adults know about the principle erogenous areas, such as a woman's lips, breasts, and clitoris, and a man's lips and penis. But a careful and caring lover also takes time to discover the more secret and mysterious pleasure sites on a partner's body.

It is important to think of your lover's body as a complete and integrated organism, of which every inch is worthy of loving attention and caresses, rather than as a map where specific areas are singled out for erotic arousal. Nothing is more of a turn-off than a text-book lover who has read all the information, and then proceeds to focus on a few selected parts of the body, to twiddle and fiddle with the expectation of scoring a sexy result.

Knowing the erotic physiology of the body is just one aspect in understanding and satisfying your lover's sexual needs. Whatever part of the anatomy you stimulate with your fingers, tongue, lips, breasts or penis, you simultaneously touch and arouse the emotional psyche of your partner.

The body's pleasure areas differ from one person to another, so the best way to discover the most erotically susceptible places on your partner's body is with foreplay, when you can lovingly, teasingly and sensitively explore each other from top to toe.

Do not be afraid to ask how and where your lover most likes to be touched, and what kind of stimulation brings the greatest sexual thrill.

You should also try to learn more about your own body's erotic responses, for this can be a changing and ongoing process of discovery.

Touch games and sensual massage techniques are also excellent ways to become familiar with one another's physical needs and responses, while regular tactile stimulation of the skin's sensory system will heighten its erogenous reactions.

Common Erogenous Zones in Both Sexes

Men and women differ in the way they respond to erotic tactile stimulation. Women tend to need more whole body touch to reach the height of sexual arousal, and are generally more sensitive to skin sensations than are their male partners.

It is highly possible for a woman to reach orgasm purely through the oral or tactile stimulation of her breasts, nipples or mons. Men, on the other hand, are greatly aroused by visual stimulation, and are much less likely to reach orgasm without direct physical contact with the penis, their most erogenous zone.

Loving Signals
▲ *Words of love, praise and affirmation, the look of appreciation in your eyes, your patience and understanding of your lover's unique sexuality, are as important to the art of lovemaking as your knowledge of a partner's erogenous zones.*

Sexual Fine Tuning
▶ *Tuning in to your partner's body is like learning to play a fine musical instrument. You need to become sensitive to all its subtle nuances.*

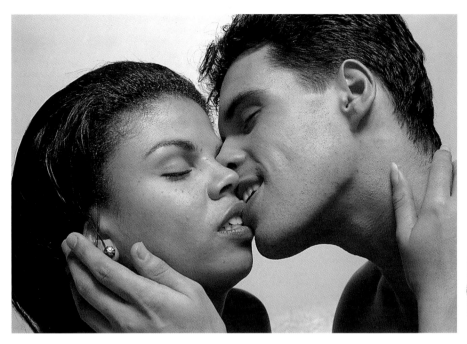

Some of these differences are the result of cultural conditioning; women are much more encouraged to enjoy their total sensuality, while men are taught to focus purely on their genital sexuality.

Most men who allow themselves to experience and enjoy a softer and more sensual approach to lovemaking will discover the sheer joy and eroticism which exists in whole body touch. Both sexes will respond well

Sexual Nuzzling
▲ *Nibbling and nuzzling the soft sensual areas of the face is very sexy. Include the ears, nose and lips.*

Passionate Kisses
▼ *Trace the fullness of the lips with your tongue, and kiss the mouth gently, allowing the passion to increase before penetrating with your tongue.*

Teasing Tongue
▼ *Stroke the belly gently as you cover it with slow and teasing kisses, then run your tongue around his nipple.*

Playful Nibbling
▼ *Toe nibbling is a playful pursuit and, especially when concentrated on the big toe, can be a major turn-on.*

to loving attention on the following parts of the body:

Head and face: Tenderly caress and kiss the forehead, brows, eyelids, tip of the nose and the chin. Comb your fingers through the hair and plant tiny kisses along your partner's hair-line.

Neck and shoulders: Nibble and kiss along the sides and down the back of the neck and shoulders to send electric shivers through the body.

Belly and navel: The belly is a vulnerable but sexually exciting area because of its close proximity to the genitals. Rub your face

softly against the belly and then blow gently over it. Cover it slowly and teasingly with kisses, and slide your tongue around the navel, before travelling slowly down to the pubic area.

Perineum: This area extends from the external genitalia towards and including the anus. It is richly served with highly erotic nerve endings and sensitive hair follicles. Stroking over the perineal skin and around the anal rim can greatly enhance sexual excitement.

Legs and thighs: Stroke the legs to awaken the sensuality of the lower half of the body. Focus on the thighs, particularly the inner leg, trailing your fingertips towards the groin. The backs of the knees are surprisingly sensitive to erotic touch. Brush your lips against the skin, and let your tongue travel over it in circular movements.

Feet and toes: Squeeze and knead the feet to activate their many nerve endings and so bring them alive. Toe sucking, and rolling your tongue over the webs of soft skin between the toes can be a powerful sexual turn-on. (Always make sure that the feet are clean and the skin is healthy first.)

The Miracle of the Skin

The skin is our largest sensory and erotogenic organ. It houses our sense of touch, and its sensitivity and importance to our survival is second only to the brain and the central nervous system. In fact, during our initial development in the womb, the skin, the sense organs, and the central nervous system are produced from the same ectoderm tissue, the outermost of the three layers that make up the early embryo form.

In this way the skin can be seen as the external, feeling surface of the internal mental processes of the brain. It has a vast network of nerve endings which responds to all manner of stimuli, from pain to pleasure. These impulses are transmitted through the nervous system to the brain.

Some areas of the skin, such as the breasts, nipples, lips, and genitals, as well as other more surprising parts of the body, are richly supplied with a high density of exquisitely sensitive and erotogenic nerve endings, sending signals of sexual pleasure to the brain and back to the entire body.

As sexual arousal grows during foreplay and intercourse, the breathing becomes deeper and the tissues get infused with oxygen. This increases the excitability of the nerves at the surface of the skin, especially around the genitalia, so that the body becomes even more sensitive to touch. It is through this process of tactile stimulation, particularly to the most erogenous areas of the body, that men and women are brought to the very peak of sexual pleasure and so reach orgasm.

A Woman's Erogenous Zones

The arms and hands: Kiss her hands and wrists tenderly and then suck gently on the fingertips. Pay attention to the soft skin on the underside of the arm, letting your mouth slowly move up towards the armpit.

Breasts and nipples: Treat them gently and with great respect. The breasts are glands, not muscles. This intimate area is packed with highly erotogenic nerve endings, which are directly connected to the emotional centres of her brain. Slowly and deliciously stimulate them with your fingers and tongue.

Thighs: Lick, kiss or stroke the thighs, especially along the soft skin of the inner thigh muscles and around the groin.

Mons pubis: The pubic area is a highly erotogenic area on a woman's body, with a rich supply of nerve endings at the base of the hair follicles. Gently rub or tug on the pubic hairs.

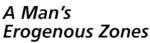

Clitoris: Every man should know more about a woman's clitoris as it is undoubtedly the most sexually important organ in her body, packed with highly erotogenic and sensitive nerve endings to the same extent as a man's penis. Focus on the clitoris only when her whole body has become sexually alive and receptive, and then caress it with your tongue and fingers to bring her to the peak of sexual arousal. Watch out for her signals indicating whether she wants you to change from gentle caresses to more vigorous stimulation.

A Man's Erogenous Zones

Chest and nipples: Stroke his chest and pectorals with your hands, and run your tongue around his nipples before sucking them gently. As with a woman, this area is sensitive to erotic arousal.

Penis and scrotum: Too much premature attention here could bring him to ejaculation too soon, as this is the most sexually charged area of a man's body. Run your hands and tongue playfully over his penis and scrotum, and cover them with tender and tantalizing kisses, before moving down his body.

Buttocks: Focus attention on his buttocks, a very sexually charged zone for men, packed with erogenous nerve endings. Knead and squeeze the fleshy area firmly with your hands.

Back of the body: Men are aroused by sensual touches on the back of the body. Stroke his shoulders and run your fingers down his spine, and then caress his calves and the back of his thighs.

Nipple Caresses
▲ Run the tip of your tongue around the areola, the dark pigmented area surrounding the nipples. Suck gently on the nipple and then dart your tongue back and forth over its tip.

Back Strokes
▲ Use long, languorous, caressing touches on the shoulders and along the spine, before making gentle stroking movements over the backs of the legs.

Chapter 3
Sex Awareness

Sexual vitality depends on both emotional and physical relaxation, and an inner sense of harmony between body, mind and spirit. Sexuality does not function as something separate from who we are, but is an expression of all the aspects of our inner and outer being. By affirming a healthy image of ourselves, through visualization, positive thinking and self-affirmation, we can transform negative thoughts which function from the subconscious mind into positive ones to affect the way we relate to ourselves and others in a beneficial way. Breathing techniques, pelvic exercises, either alone or with a partner, will help emotional and sexual tensions to release as muscles become more relaxed. Learning to love and self-pleasure our bodies is now regarded as a positive step towards gaining emotional and sexual health. Make these occasions sensual and luxurious so that you are able to explore and discover your full sexual responses.

Sexual Health Awareness

Sexual health awareness is about developing a deeper understanding of the sexual self and discovering how the mind and body interact to achieve true fulfilment. It involves a commitment to a regular health regime, to include sexual hygiene, medical check-ups and a programme of physical and mental exercises, as well as an awareness of the sexual body and of the way it changes and develops at different stages throughout life. By following a sexual health awareness programme you can learn how to become attuned to your basic physical, emotional and psychological needs, thus helping you to achieve more satisfying and fulfilling relationships and a feeling of personal well-being.

The first step towards sexual health awareness is the confidence that comes with the knowledge that your body is clean and wholesome and free from illness and disease. This will help you to feel more relaxed in mind and body and boost your self-esteem because you will be able to feel assured that you are physically appealing to the opposite sex.

Your sexual health routine should include an understanding of the way your sexual body looks and feels on a day-to-day level so that medical disorders, if they arise, are identified at an early stage, when they can be more easily treated. This approach is particularly important for a woman because the hormonal fluctuations that routinely occur throughout the menstrual cycle cause physical changes which may mask possible medical disorders unless she is totally in tune with the many different facets of her body.

Sexual Hygiene for Women

The sense of smell is powerfully evocative and so it is to be expected that many women feel self-conscious about their natural aroma. In fact, this is an exaggerated worry as a woman's basic scent is a potent turn-on for men and does not need to be masked by pungent fragrances and perfumes. Plain water and a mild unscented soap are perfectly adequate for daily washing.

Many women are over-zealous about their sexual hygiene, often scrubbing too vigorously and using highly scented, antiseptic soaps, bath salts and bubble baths. These preparations can cause skin irritation and may even lead to an allergic reaction in serious cases. It is only necessary for women to wash the external part of the genitalia, as the vagina itself is self-cleansing. In particular, douches or vaginal deodorants are to be avoided, except on medical advice, as these can irritate the vagina's sensitive lining, and upset its delicate bacterial and chemical balance. This can lead to conditions such as thrush (candidiasis).

The most important sexual hygiene rule is to always wash the bottom from front to back, to avoid spreading infection. If you use flannels, keep one solely for the genital/anal area, be sure to wash it out after use and leave it open on a radiator to dry thoroughly. A damp flannel provides a perfect breeding ground for germs.

Flush Out Infection

▶ *Cystitis, or inflammation of the bladder, is a common and distressing problem for many women and is often caused by infection spreading up through the urethra. At the first sign of an attack, you should drink a large glass of water and repeat this every three to four hours to flush out the bacteria.*

It is important to learn the look and pattern of your normal vaginal secretions so that you can recognize if an abnormal pattern develops. These secretions usually increase during sexual arousal and at the mid point in the menstrual cycle, around the time of ovulation. If you develop a discharge that seems out of the ordinary, particularly if it is accompanied by soreness or itching of the genital area, it may indicate an infection, and you should see a doctor as soon as possible.

Signs of infection include a copious watery secretion that is greenish or greyish in colour, possibly with a

fishy smell, or a discharge that has the creamy consistency of cottage cheese. Other signs include sores, inflammation, rash, pain in the lower abdomen, pain or discomfort when urinating, and blood in the urine. You should avoid having sex until the condition has been identified and successfully treated.

Some sexually transmitted diseases cause symptoms in men but not in women, although they may still lead to infertility or other serious conditions. If a sexual partner complains of symptoms such as difficulty urinating or abnormal discharge from the penis, encourage him to see his doctor and also seek medical advice yourself.

Because the urethra, the tube that carries urine out of the body, is so much shorter in women they are at much greater risk of infections spreading to the bladder, causing the painful condition cystitis. Sufferers develop a pain in the lower abdomen and find urination painful. In severe cases the urine may be cloudy and the woman may feel feverish. Cystitis can also be caused by soaps, gels, and deodorants and even by bruising as a result of over-enthusiastic lovemaking.

Always see your doctor if the symptoms are severe or persist for longer than a few days as the condition may lead to kidney infection, if left untreated. In the meantime, drink plenty of fluid, and ask your doctor to recommend a suitable painkiller. A hot-water bottle held against the abdomen may help to ease the pain. If you do not suffer from high blood pressure, drinking a solution of baking powder (sodium bicarbonate) can reduce the acidity in the urine and ease the stinging as well as helping to flush out any bacteria.

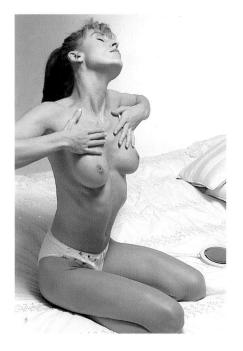

Breast Care

Caring for your breasts should be an important part of your sexual health regime. Managing your stress levels, and keeping to a diet that is low in saturated fats and refined sugar is thought to promote healthy breasts. Exercise can help strengthen the underlying muscle and so help prevent sagging, although the best way to keep breasts firm is to wear a well-fitting support bra, particularly when playing sport, or during pregnancy and when breastfeeding.

Change your bra size as often as seems necessary and be sure to try a bra on before you buy it. A surprising number of women wear a bra that does not fit properly. After washing your breasts, pat them dry with an upward motion to prevent sagging and use a moisturizer to help keep the skin smooth and supple – again using upward movements.

The breasts usually become slightly enlarged in the second half of the menstrual cycle, mainly as a result of hormonal changes, giving a sensation of heaviness and fullness. They may also feel lumpy. One third of women suffer breast tenderness as a result of these hormonal changes, which can make many activities, including sport, lovemaking and even walking up stairs, very uncomfortable. A common cause of this is

Caring for your Breasts
◄ *Breasts are a major sexual characteristic and are central to a woman's femininity. Learn to examine your breasts regularly for lumps or any signs of change, and use a rich cream moisturizer to help keep the skin supple. To avoid sagging, use an upward motion, as you would on your face.*

benign breast disease (see below), but the pain may also be due to a bruised or strained chest muscle.

Self-help measures include cutting down on stimulant drinks, such as tea or coffee, and taking evening primrose capsules and vitamin B6 (pyridoxine) in the second half of the menstrual cycle. Wearing a support bra day and night might also help. If the pain persists, or affects one side only, you should see your doctor.

Breast Awareness

Breast cancer is the most common form of cancer in women and is most likely to be successfully treated if it is diagnosed at an early stage. Many breast cancers are first detected by the woman herself, so it is important to get to know the normal shape and feel of your breasts throughout the menstrual cycle so that you can spot problem lumps, if they appear.

It is important to remember, however, that benign, or harmless, breast lumps are far more common than malignant, or cancerous, ones. The most common type of lump is a cyst in a blocked gland or duct. Such lumps are most likely to occur in the second half of the menstrual cycle and they usually subside completely after a while.

Monthly lumpiness which does not go away, especially if it is tender,

Breast Self-Examination

Get into the habit of carrying out a monthly breast examination. If you menstruate, a good time to do this is a week after the first day of your period. Undress to the waist and, with your arms at your sides, inspect your breasts in the mirror, from the side as well as the front. Look for any changes of appearance, such as changes in the outline, puckering or dimpling of the skin (like orange peel). Squeeze the nipple to check for bleeding or discharge.

Next, raise your hands over your head and look to see if any puckering or dimpling appears. Put your hands on your hips and push, again looking for puckering or dimpling.

Now, examine your breasts while lying down on the bed. Place a folded towel under one shoulder and raise your arm on that side above your head to stretch the breast. With the flat of the hand only, gently feel the breast using a circular movement and working from the outer edge to the nipple. Also feel for lumps under the armpit. Repeat with the other breast.

is called benign breast disease. This condition, although harmless, may be very painful. Another form of benign breast lump is a fibroadenoma, or fibrous tumour, which is sometimes known as a "breast mouse" because it can be moved around in the breast tissue. A malignant lump is usually not tender and is not mobile.

Because the breasts alter in size and lumpiness throughout the menstrual cycle, it is important to examine your breasts regularly so that you become familiar with these changes. All breasts have normally lumpy areas – so try to discover what is normal for you. During a shower or bath is a good time, particularly when the breasts are soapy.

In addition, at least once a month, you should examine your breasts more systematically. Aim to do this at the same time in your menstrual cycle. A week after the first day of your period is a good time, when the breasts are least lumpy and so easier to check. Look at your breasts in a mirror, in profile as well as from the front, looking for lumps, puckering or dimpling, or any changes in the size or shape.

Other signs include a nipple that has suddenly become inverted, or bleeding from the nipple, or a discharge that is unconnected with breastfeeding. Examine your breasts with your arms raised and then by your sides. If you notice any abnormalities, contact your doctor as soon as possible. If a lump does turn out to be malignant there is a far better chance of a cure if it is detected early.

Medical Screening for Women

Many conditions affecting women can be diagnosed early through regular medical screening checks. One of the most important of these is a cervical smear test which can detect cells that will become cancerous before other signs would become apparent. Treatment at this pre-cancerous stage is fairly simple and has a high success rate. During a smear test, a thin layer of cells is scraped from the cervix and smeared onto a glass slide so they can be examined under a microscope. If abnormal cells are found there will be follow-up tests and, if necessary, treatment.

Doctors recommend that women have a cervical smear test at least every three years. But those in high-risk groups should have annual tests. Women most at risk include those suffering from genital warts (or whose partners have the condition), smokers, and those with multiple sexual partners or who began an active sex life at an early age.

Smear tests are often carried out during routine gynaecological check-ups. During the examination, the doctor will look at the external genital area and into the vagina to check for signs of infection or other abnormalities. The doctor will also feel the lower abdomen to detect possible swelling or tenderness which might indicate a disorder.

Women should also have a breast examination by their doctor at least every three years, if under 40, or annually, if older. Women over the age of 50 are usually screened for breast cancer every three years using a form of X-ray called mammography. However, this method of screening is less effective in younger women because their breast tissue is more dense and any growths do not show up as clearly on the X-ray.

Sexual Hygiene for Men

While the natural musky male smell is attractive to many women, the basic masculine aroma should not be confused with the odour of an unwashed body, which is a positive turn-off. Fresh sweat has no smell, but after six hours bacteria on the skin acts on sweat causing the release

of unpleasant odours. A regular shower or bath is necessary, and it is particularly important to wash the anal and genital area daily, or more often if necessary.

Uncircumcised men should take particular care to wash the glans (head of the penis) regularly, pulling back the foreskin to ensure it is really clean. This is necessary to prevent the buildup of an oily secretion called smegma which develops under the foreskin. Smegma is a white substance produced by the sebaceous – or oil-producing – glands under the foreskin that helps it to retract smoothly. Without regular washing, smegma can build up and become a source of infection, which can lead to inflammation of the glans, a condition known as balanitis. It has also been linked with cancer of the penis and may cause cervical cancer in partners.

Men should also be alert to any signs which could indicate a sexually transmitted disease, or other serious condition. Signs of infection include pain or discomfort when urinating, abnormal discharge from the penis, or inflammation, sores or a rash around the genitals. It is important to seek medical advice immediately if

you notice any of these signs because delay can lead to a worsening of the condition and risks infertility. Abstain from sex until the condition has been identified and successfully treated.

Testicular Awareness

Just as women should learn to recognize the normal shape and feel of their breasts so that abnormalities can be detected straight away, men should get into the habit of examining their testicles regularly so that they can spot a cancerous growth or other problem as early as possible and increase the likelihood of effective treatment.

Testicular cancer is one of the most common cancers in men in the 20–34 age range. It does not usually cause any pain in the early stages and so self-examination is vital if it is to be detected. However, most lumps turn out to be benign conditions, such as a harmless cyst.

You should not notice any pain during the examination, provided you are not squeezing too hard, but if there is discomfort, especially if you notice any swelling, you should seek medical advice. There are several conditions that could cause pain and

Testicular Self-Examination

Make a point of examining your testicles once a month while you are having a bath or shower. Ensure the scrotum is well-covered with soapy lather and then roll each testicle gently between the fingers of both hands. Learn to recognize its normal shape and consistency. Carefully probe for any pea-sized lumps, or nodules, or any swelling or other changes. After your bath or shower, stand in front of a full-length mirror, hold your penis up out of the way and carry out a visual inspection of your scrotum looking for any change in size and shape. Be aware of any pain or sensations of heaviness in the groin or lower abdomen. Report any problems to your doctor.

swelling in the testicles, such as infection or injury, which are unconnected with cancer but which may still require treatment.

A simple testicular self-examination (see above) takes only a few minutes and is best carried out during a warm bath or shower while the scrotum is well-covered with soapy lather. The scrotal skin is most relaxed at this time and the lather will make it easier to slide your fingers over the testicles to search for changes in consistency. After your bath or shower, look at your genitals in a mirror to detect any change in size and shape.

Psychological Exercise

A major step towards finding a partner with whom you can truly relate as an intellectual, sexual, and emotional being is to have confidence in your own mental outlook, physical attractiveness, and emotional status. Before you can develop your self-esteem you must first identify and eliminate the negative patterns of behaviour formed by past experiences and replace them with positive and self-enhancing thoughts and attitudes.

Negative patterns of thought and behaviour can often become etched into the unconscious mind as a result of unhappy childhood experiences, broken relationships and unfulfilled hopes and desires. These harmful facets of the human psyche represent a heavy burden, holding us back in our attempts to form loving liaisons based on mutual respect and esteem. Yet we are often totally unaware of the unwelcome mental baggage we are carrying around with us.

The effect that the mind has on our psychological make-up can be likened to an iceberg. It is only our conscious mental processes that we are fully aware of yet these actually play a very small part in the development of our psychological profile. It is the unconscious, an unseen force lurking below the waterline of our awareness, that has the most profound influence on our behaviour patterns, our self-image and

Contemplative Contentment
▶ *Take time to meditate each day to help you unravel the tensions caused by the daily stresses and strains and to restore your spirit to a state of equilibrium. Find a quiet place where you will not be disturbed, and light candles to enhance the meditative atmosphere. Then sit with your back straight, and breathe naturally, focusing your awareness on your breathing as you inhale and exhale.*

our ability to form lasting and meaningful relationships.

Negative patterns of thought that have formed in the unconscious can damage our self-esteem and hinder our attempts to form lasting relationships. By following a daily pattern of psychological exercises we can get in touch with our unconscious selves and repair the damage caused to our sense of self-worth.

Breathing and Meditation

To form a loving and giving relationship with another person you must first learn to be at peace with yourself. Pressures at work, the demands of friends and relatives, as well as the constant reminders of international

tensions, make this increasingly difficult. However, it is vital for your mental equilibrium that you try to set aside some time each day for quiet contemplation in order to relax your mind and body completely.

You have to cut yourself off totally from the turmoil of the outside world until you are able to restore your physical and emotional nature to a state of peace and harmony. You will then be able to return to the pressures of the daily routine feeling revitalized and replenished in body, mind and spirit.

The first step on this road is to learn the correct breathing techniques. Breathing powers the brain cells so that you become more open and alert, it provides the vital nutrients required by the tissues and removes harmful wastes. Correct breathing will recharge your batteries when you are feeling tired and will soothe you when you are feeling anxious or under stress. Don't force your breathing. Inhale and exhale through your nose, letting the air flow smoothly down into your abdomen and feeling it spread throughout your body, replenishing its cells. Close your eyes and focus on your breathing, feeling the rise and fall of your abdomen as you breathe.

Breathing can then combine with meditation to help you relax totally and get in touch with your inner being. Seek out a quiet place to sit and meditate for 20 minutes and make it a daily routine of relaxation. To enhance the contemplative atmosphere, close the curtains, turn down the lights and let candlelight cast a gentle glow.

Make sure you have a comfortable, straight-backed chair to sit on so you can maintain a good upright posture, or sit cross-legged on a cushion on the floor, keeping your back straight. Take a few minutes to relax and then start to breathe regularly, as above. Clear your mind of all thoughts and just concentrate on your breathing, focusing on the slow and regular movements of your abdomen. Now direct your breathing to all areas of the body, relaxing each part in turn with every exhalation. Work slowly from your toes to the top of your head, paying special attention to the legs, pelvis, back, shoulders, arms, neck and head.

By developing these meditation skills you will find a way to get in contact with the innermost reaches of your mental processes and help your psyche to be more receptive in preparation for the next stage of your programme of mental self-improvement – to develop a loving attitude towards yourself.

Positive Thinking

Negative feelings about your physical or psychological self, and indeed whether you are even worthy of forming a good relationship, can act as a self-fulfilling prophecy, either

Accentuate the Positive

▶ *The first step towards finding a loving and fulfilling relationship is to have a positive attitude towards yourself. How can you expect someone else to love you if you don't love yourself?*

blocking attempts to enter into new liaisons, or ensuring that any relationship that develops is full of disharmony and discord and so bound to fail. By following a psychological exercise programme each day you can eliminate negative thoughts and accentuate positive ones. You will not only feel good about yourself but also encourage others to feel the same way about you too, fostering a sense of love and equilibrium in any partnership that develops.

A low self-image can often become deeply ingrained as a result of the negative messages we have received from friends, relatives and loved ones, particularly in our early formative years when we were at our most vulnerable and impressionable. Therefore, if you are to develop a positive image of yourself you must first find a way to counteract these negative feelings.

The Love of Laughter

▲ *Never underestimate the importance of smiling and laughter to lighten up your life. If you make the effort always to look for the joyful aspects of every situation, rather than being suspicious of happy feelings, you will encourage others to share your sparkling mood.*

The first step is to try to identify those aspects of your thoughts and feelings about yourself that embody your negative mental patterns and to write them down as a list on one side of a piece of paper.

These may be, for example: "I am not attractive", "I am not sexually desirable", "I am not worthy of a relationship", "Nobody could love me", "My relationships don't last". Next, on the opposite side of the paper, write down the positive affirmations that counteract these negative images. Write "I AM attractive", "I AM sexually desirable", "I AM worthy of a relationship", "I CAN be loved", "My relationships WILL last".

Say these things to yourself every day and this continual reinforcement of your positive

nature will change the negative patterning of your subconscious mind, creating a direct effect on your conscious actions, and your attitudes to others.

Visualization Techniques

When individuals have endured a very painful experience in a relationship, or have been left deeply scarred as a result of psychological trauma, or a broken family background, it can leave them feeling disillusioned with themselves and lacking confidence in their ability to form loving relationships. In such cases they will often have to reach deep down inside their subconscious to undo the damage that has been caused.

One way to achieve this is to use the technique of positive visualization. Sit in front of a large mirror, and make yourself comfortable. You need to be very relaxed, so use the deep-breathing and meditation techniques you have already learnt to get into a relaxed and receptive frame of mind, ensuring that you keep your eyes closed.

Once you feel physically and mentally at peace, cast your mind back to a time when you felt truly

Eliminate the Negative

◀ *You can turn negative thoughts into positive ones by following a programme of exercises for making positive affirmations. Write down those thoughts and judgements you have on yourself, and then counteract them with positive affirmations. Repeat this regularly to yourself to counteract the negative patterning of your thoughts.*

loving towards another person, recalling the situation in minute detail. Try to remember where you were, who you were with, and what had happened to make you feel this way. Recapture the feelings of love that you experienced at the time and fill your mind and body with them.

Now, open your eyes and look at the image of yourself with the feelings of love, tenderness, warmth, and joy you have just re-evoked. Think about the various aspects of yourself that you most admire; not just the physical characteristics that you are happiest with – your attractive eyes, perhaps, your shapely legs, or your long hair – but also the personality traits that you think are most worthy of appreciation – maybe your intelligence, loyalty, perseverance, or perhaps your affectionate tender nature.

Once you have begun to see yourself in this new and affirming light, concentrate on those aspects of your character that you would like to improve. Perhaps you would like to be more relaxed, or more energetic, more forgiving, or more loving. Repeat this exercise every day. You may not get spectacular results immediately, but slowly these positive affirmations will print themselves over the negative patterning that existed before.

By enhancing this positive self-image, you give out a confident, contented aura that encourages others to think highly of you as well, and so increases your chances of forming a successful and fulfilling relationship.

Once you are in a relationship, it is important to continue with these exercises to reinforce your positive thinking patterns and to counteract any discordant feelings that might arise. You can use these techniques with your partner to reinforce each other's self-image and your loving feelings towards one another.

Take it in turns to make positive loving statements about each other while gazing deeply into your partner's eyes. Combine this with mutual breathing and meditation sessions to help bring you closer on an emotional and spiritual level.

Seeking Friendship

To achieve true contentment, it is important to feel fulfilled on all levels. If you are in a committed relationship it is all too easy to look to your partner to satisfy all your emotional and psychological needs. In fact, though, it is rarely possible for one person to gratify another's wants and desires in this way. For example, it might be a very loving and contented partnership on a domestic level, but there may also be major intellectual differences, perhaps one of you is interested in opera or philosophy and the other prefers to talk about sport and listen to pop music.

If you keep looking to each other to fulfil your needs on every strata it can quickly drain the relationship, leading to disharmony and conflict. For this reason it is vitally important to have a wide circle of friends to act as a natural resource from which you can

Fulfilment of Friends

◀ *It is important to have a wide circle of friends outside of a sexual relationship. Friends can provide communication, empathy, and support that comes from shared interests and a similar outlook, and can often satisfy needs that cannot be fulfilled within the sexual relationship itself.*

empathy to your situation. Men and women can more easily relate to their own sex and have a common outlook, and a meeting of minds, which could rarely be achieved with a partner, no matter how close. Women are usually much better at forming these sympathetic, same-sex relationships, but men, too, can benefit from having friends that they can relate to on an emotional level and who will provide insights and experiences from which they can learn.

Discovering yourself is an ongoing process and one that can never be fully achieved even if you devoted your entire lifetime to the task. But there are a wide range of self-improvement books that help you achieve greater insights into your mental and emotional condition and enable you to fulfil more of your potential. Books on relaxation, visualization, meditation and positive thinking, for example, can help to reveal dormant abilities and find new ways to accentuate your latent active and creative sides, while at the same time eliminating the destructive and negative aspects of your nature.

gather all the mental and spiritual stimulation you need and also to share parts of yourself that perhaps do not flourish within the partnership.

These friends should include members of the same sex to satisfy other aspects of the relationship that your partner cannot give you. The nourishment that comes with this form of close bonding can be very important. In any relationship, certain issues crop up, whether of a sexual, or emotional nature, that you cannot not talk over with your partner, or indeed any member of the opposite sex. In these situations you can greatly benefit from talking to someone of the same sex who will have a natural

Expand Your Mind

◀ *Self-discovery is an ongoing process. Take time to study self-improvement books and learn to expand your consciousness so that you can release all the potential that is lying dormant deep inside your psyche.*

Exercises for Sexual Fitness

Physical exercises that concentrate on the key sexual areas of the pelvis, lower back, buttocks, abdomen and thighs can release the tension in body and mind that prevents you achieving your full orgasmic potential. These exercises allow you to achieve the strength, suppleness and mobility you need to explore and express fully the physical aspects of lovemaking, and when combined with correctly focused breathing techniques, they open up energy channels in your body which will enhance your enjoyment of sex, and enable you and your partner to achieve a feeling of greater spiritual harmony and union.

Sex is fundamentally a physical activity, so if it is to be enjoyed to the full it is important to ensure that the muscle groups, tendons and joints that come into play during healthy vigorous lovemaking are supple and well conditioned. The positions and movements involved in the various forms of sexual intercourse put muscles and joints under pressure in a way that is totally different from that encountered during routine daily activities.

Unless you keep your body supple and pliant you are liable to suffer muscle cramps and strains during sexual intercourse as you and your partner try to achieve the different angles and changes of position you are seeking in order to obtain mutual sexual satisfaction.

By conditioning the areas of the body that are most actively involved in lovemaking – most notably the muscles of the buttocks, abdomen, thighs, lower back, and pelvic floor – you will extend your range of motion and enhance your ability to move smoothly and with control, enabling a wider variety of pelvic movements and allowing more comfortable lovemaking.

When you are sexually fit you have the suppleness, mobility, and enthusiasm to throw your mind and body into the passion of the moment and even to explore new positions and hitherto undiscovered heights of ecstasy.

By relieving tension you are also helping to fight the stress that often prevents you getting into the relaxed and giving mood needed to achieve a satisfying sexual encounter. Tension in the pelvis, legs, lower back, and abdomen restricts the flow of sexual energy and vitality and reduces your total enjoyment of lovemaking. Repressed feelings here can upset the wholeness and unity of the body and act as a barrier between the mind, the emotions and the physical responses. Exercises combined with breathing techniques, that you can carry out alone or with your partner, will release the tension in these key areas, and help to release the flow of sexual energy so that you can achieve your full orgasmic potential.

Gentle Warm-Up

As with all physical exercises, ensure you are fully warmed up before you try these routines to reduce the risk of minor strains and sprains. Exercise is best carried out after a warm bath or shower so that relaxing warmth is

Pelvic Swing

▼ Stand with your feet a shoulder-width apart, knees slightly flexed. Place your arms by your side with your palms open forwards. Breathe in and draw your pelvis back.

▼ Breathe out and swing your pelvis forwards, allowing arms, hands and genitals to swing up. Repeat this for up to five minutes as a continuous pelvic motion.

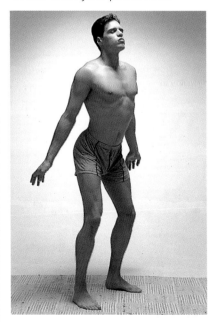

transmitted deep into the muscle fibres. Put on some loose, comfortable clothing, choose a room that is draught-free and fairly warm (but not too warm), and ensure you have a soft floor surface to lie on.

Start off the session with some loosening movements and gentle stretches to free the muscles and tendons. Follow this up with ten minutes of vigorous activity, such as brisk walking or a quick jog. Alternatively, try a simple warm-up routine such as marching on the spot while circling your arms above your head. Remember to fill your lungs with air when you start an exercise to ensure your body gets all the oxygen it needs, and then expel your breath on the exertion to rid the body of the waste products it has accumulated.

Pelvic Circles

▼ *Stand with your feet a shoulder-width apart and knees slightly flexed. Place your hands on hips. Mentally focus inside to the inner shape of your pelvic bowl.*

▼ *Rotate your pelvis slowly in wide circles – ten times to the right and then ten times to the left. Breathe in to the movement and consciously allow any tension to relax.*

The following simple routines can help release tension in the abdomen, lower back and pelvis.

Breathing

Correct breathing is a vital part of these exercises. Your breathing is directly affected by your emotional state as a result of external worries

Deep-Breathing Exercise

◀ *Deep breathing brings oxygen to the cells to nourish the body, and eases emotional tension by relaxing the muscles, making you feel more alive and vital. Your partner can kneel behind and encourage the tension to melt by placing his hands softly over the key areas of the chest, diaphragm and abdomen. Breathe into each area in turn, focusing awareness into every inhalation and exhalation.*

and pressures. When you are tense and under stress your breathing becomes rapid and shallow and your body cannot get all the air it needs for normal healthy functioning.

By focusing on your breathing you can draw the air deep down into your abdomen to fill the lungs to capacity. This saturates the blood with life-giving oxygen, which is then pumped round the body to restore the tissues and replenish the energy reserves depleted during physical activity. When you breathe out, aim to empty your lungs completely to rid your body of the waste products that have built up. This slowly releases the emotional tension, leaving you feeling relaxed, more alive and vital.

Pent-up feelings of anger, anxiety, or fear can also lead to tension in the key energy centres of the body – the chest and abdomen. Inhalation and exhalation can be combined with the healing power of touch to help you direct your breathing into each part

Solo Pelvic Release Exercise

▼ *Lie down comfortably on your back and place your hands over your abdomen. Close your eyes and breathe slowly and deeply into your belly, then slowly breathe out, emptying your lungs as you do so. Notice your abdomen softening and expanding with each inhalation, feel it fall back with each exhalation. Imagine the whole area is relaxing with each outward breath.*

in turn, to unblock the energy channels and release the sexual tension.

Place your hands softly over the chest and abdomen and imagine that the warmth and contact of your hands is melting these areas.

Encourage the tension to drain away as you focus your awareness into every inhalation and exhalation. You can do these exercises by yourself, sitting or lying down, or encourage your partner to sit behind you resting his hands gently on your chest and abdomen.

Strengthening the Pelvic Floor

You can greatly enhance your sex life by learning exercises to strengthen the pelvic floor. This is the collection of muscles and ligaments at the base of the abdomen that supports the bladder, vagina, uterus, and rectum. Childbirth and ageing can weaken this part of the body, reducing control over the vaginal and pelvic muscles and blunting the nerve responses. A weakened pelvic floor can also lead to serious medical problems such as a prolapsed uterus and urinary incontinence and is often the underlying cause for women who are having difficulty achieving an

Genital Release Exercise with Partner

This exercise releases sexual tension in the pelvic and genital area and increases vitality. Lie down comfortably on your back, with your feet on the ground and knees raised. Your partner gently supports your head. Place your hands over your chest and abdomen to encourage breathing and aid relaxation. Repeat this exercise for up to five minutes, then rest for five minutes – feel the vibrations in your legs and body and acknowledge any rising feelings.

▲ *Breathe into your chest and abdomen. Imagine your breath to be reaching your genitals. Breathe in and out.*

▲ *Place your arms by your side. Breathe in – draw your thighs together. Imagine your in-breath to be pulling your legs in.*

▲ *Breathe out – let your legs flop open – to open up the genitals and relax the thigh muscles and groin. Then breathe in again.*

Squats

▶ *Squat on your haunches, placing your feet wide enough to support your body. Let your buttocks drop down, and relax your anus. Feel your entire pelvic floor relaxing. Breathe in four to five short breaths (don't exhale). With each inhalation, draw up and tighten the pelvic floor muscles, as if pulling your vagina up step by step. Then give five short out-breaths (don't inhale) releasing your pelvic floor muscles step by step. Do this ten times to tone the pelvic floor muscles.*

orgasm. Regular pelvic floor exercises will ensure that these muscles and ligaments remain taut and well toned, so that you have adequate structural support for the uterus and vagina, and will be able to continue to enjoy sex.

Many women also find that by toning up the muscles of the pelvic floor they are able to climax more freely and to experience stronger or more intense orgasms. Improving the strength and flexibility of these muscles will extend your range of movement and make those positions that involve squatting over your partner, or wrapping your legs round him, easier and more comfortable to adopt. Your vagina will also be able to grip your partner's penis more firmly during lovemaking, which will enhance the enjoyment for both of you.

The following exercises will tone and strengthen the pelvic floor. They are particularly important after childbirth, but all women will derive some benefit from them. You will particularly notice the effect during lovemaking when you find that your vagina is better able to clasp your partner's penis – but be careful not to squeeze too tight! You can discover your pelvic floor by imagining you need to urinate but are trying to hold it back. The part of the body that tightens as you do this is your pelvic floor. In addition to the exercises in this section, there is a simple pelvic floor exercise that you can practise at any time, as no one can see you do it. Slowly contract the pelvic floor muscles, ten times, pulling the muscles up inside in slow stages each time. Breathe normally as you do this exercise. Practise two to three times daily for at least a month. Another exercise you could try on your own is to place two fingers inside the vagina and try to squeeze them by contracting the muscles.

Pelvic Curls

This exercise is good for strengthening the pelvis and thighs – it aids whole-body vitality, improves posture, strengthens support for the vital organs, and relaxes the lower back. Do this exercise five times. Lie with your back on the ground with the whole of the spine touching the floor – including the small of your back. Let the ground support your weight. Keep your knees bent and place the soles of your feet flat on the floor, a shoulder-width apart, supporting your legs. Put your arms by your sides with your hands palms-down on the floor.

▲ *Breathe out and roll your spine upwards, using your buttocks and lower abdominal muscles to curl your tailbone up off the floor. At the same time tighten your buttocks and inside thigh muscles.*

▲ *Now breathe in and roll your spine down to the floor, uncurling your tailbone and relaxing your buttocks and inside thigh muscles.*

Self-Pleasuring

Nowadays, masturbation is regarded by most sex experts as a normal and even beneficial sexual activity. However, until recent times, masturbation was a taboo subject. It was considered immoral, termed a "sin", and young people were warned that it would make them mad, blind, infertile, or ruin their chances of sexual happiness in marriage. Not so long ago, the word "masturbation" was defined as "self-abuse" in a standard dictionary. That view of masturbation has now radically changed.

Attitudes to masturbation began to alter in the late 1940s and early 1950s, when the Kinsey reports on male and female sexuality stated that, according to their studies, 94 per cent of American men and 40 per cent of American women masturbated to orgasm. More recent research suggests that, while the figure for male masturbation remains the same, female masturbation is now considerably higher, though still less than for men.

Masturbation, which is the self-stimulation of one's own genitals for sexual pleasure and orgasm, is clearly, then, a normal part of human sexual activity. None of the dire warnings that were made about it were found to be true. In fact, the Kinsey report concluded that the only harmful side-effects of masturbation were the anxiety and guilt it might evoke in those who practised it.

Masturbation is now seen more as "self-pleasuring" than abuse. It is a valuable way for males and females, young and old, to learn more about their bodies, and to enjoy their sexual and orgasmic responses. It can be a useful way to release sexual tension, but more importantly, it gives men and women the chance to enjoy sexual pleasure and body sensuality, regardless of whether or not they are currently in a relationship.

These days, masturbation is one of the basic tools used in sex therapy, and clients are often encouraged to masturbate in the privacy of their homes as one of the key methods of discovering and encouraging their sexual and orgasmic responses and of overcoming their anxieties, guilt or other problems surrounding sexual issues.

Art of Self-Pleasuring

Masturbation is often carried out in a speedy and rather unsensual fashion, with the aim of achieving a climax in the fastest way possible by focusing the manual stimulation solely on the genital organs. This method has its uses, especially if the aim is to obtain a quick release from sexual tension. However, to turn it into the art of self-pleasuring, you should learn to feel at ease with the situation so that it can become a way of making love to yourself in a wholly sensual way.

Try to create some time for yourself that is dedicated to self-pleasuring. Ensure that you have complete privacy and that you won't be interrupted. Warm your bedroom and light some candles, if it is dark, to create a sensual ambience. Have a bath so that you feel relaxed, and then soothe your skin with a lotion. Play some music that will help you feel sexy, and then lie naked on your bed. Begin to stroke and caress your whole body, including your genital area, but do not at this point focus

Vary Your Strokes

▶ *Experiment with different strokes, pressures and speeds of movement, sliding your hand up and down the whole shaft of the penis, from the base to above the ridge of its head, or focus more on applying pressure to the erotically-sensitive frenulum.*

specifically on it. If you have an imaginative mind, allow your fantasies to unfold, but also remain totally involved in the physical sensations happening in your body as you touch and stimulate yourself.

Self-Pleasuring for Men

Most men, when they masturbate, concentrate the stimulation solely on the penis. Instead, try to let your hands also stroke your chest, belly, thighs, scrotum, perineum and buttocks, sweeping them over your penis as they move from one part of your body to another. If you choose, fantasize that your dream woman is stroking your body, or indulge yourself in whatever imagery works as a powerful aphrodisiac for you.

Uncircumcised men should draw back the foreskin to expose the glans while masturbating. The most erogenously responsive area is usually around the frenulum, on the underside of the shaft, just beneath the head of the penis. Experiment with pressures and strokes, speeds and rhythms, delighting in all the different sensations that you can create.

As your sexual feelings rise, let yourself go, breathing deeply and

moving your body, thrusting your pelvis, and making sounds to express your growing excitement. If you feel you are approaching ejaculation, slow down to prolong your self-pleasuring, then build up the tempo towards climax again.

For a truly sensual experience, try to let this pleasuring last for 15 minutes, or even longer, before you climax. As you approach an orgasm, abandon yourself totally to the sensations. Then rest awhile, touching your body and relaxing deeply.

Self-Pleasuring for Women

Women tend to be more naturally sensual in the way they masturbate, and also quite inventive in their style of touching and stimulation. As described above, turn your self-pleasuring into an erotic feast. Prepare your bedroom to make it warm and inviting, so that you can luxuriate in the act of touching and exploring your body. First, though, why not take a bath enhanced by the aroma of aphrodisiac essential oils.

Ylang-ylang, sandalwood, jasmine, rose, basil, patchouli and black pepper are all oils that are sensually and sexually evocative. Choose up to three of any of these oils, mixing a maximum of seven drops in the water, and then relax in the warmth and fragrance of the bath.

When you have dried yourself and used moisturizer on your skin, lie on the bed and allow your erotic fantasies to take over. Touch and stroke your body, including your genital area, thighs, breasts and nipples. As you become mentally and physically aroused, apply different pressures and strokes of your hands and fingers to your pubic and genital

Enjoy Your Body
▲ *Many women touch and caress their whole bodies while they are masturbating. Try stroking and caressing your most erogenous zones, such as your breasts and nipples, to experience a new intensity of sexual arousal.*

area. You can begin by gently arousing the whole area with a circular motion, placing the heel of your hand on your pubic bone and resting your fingers against your vulva.

As you become aroused, part your vaginal lips with your fingers, and stroke all over the inner folds, around the opening of your vagina, and the area surrounding your clitoris. You may want to pull back the hood of the clitoris to apply pressure on it directly, but if this kind of stimulation feels too intense, rub the skin above and beside it instead.

Experiment with different strokes, vibrations, pressures, and rhythms, finding out exactly which sequence of movements is the most erotic for you. Increase the pressure and speed of

Fingertip Caresses
▶ *Stroke around your vaginal lips and clitoral area, sometimes letting your fingers caress the outer edges of the vagina itself, or slipping into it. As you approach orgasm, increase the pressure and speed of your strokes.*

your touches as your arousal builds, and then, as you approach your climax, maintain a more regular tempo, sustaining pressure on your clitoris throughout your orgasm. Let yourself go into the orgasmic contractions, allowing them to pulsate through your whole body. Moan, sigh or cry out, and move your pelvis to enhance the powerful sensations of your orgasmic release.

For even more arousing sensations, men and women can apply a water-soluble lubrication to their genital area while masturbating. However, avoid oil-based products such as petroleum jelly.

Sex Toys

Many forms of sexual aids can play an important role in helping you to discover your sexual self, and to fulfil your full orgasmic potential. They can enable you and your partner to find new and more exciting sexual sensations and to reach greater heights of orgasmic ecstasy. For some women, in particular, sex aids or masturbation may be the only way that they can achieve sexual release, and therefore have a vital part to play in lovemaking.

Sex toys, or sexual aids, have been used to enhance sexual arousal for thousands of years. Love eggs have been known in China since ancient times. These are small oval or circular objects, often of wood or china, which are inserted into the vagina to produce erotic sensations as the woman walks around. They are available today, although modern love eggs are usually hollow, containing smaller balls or weights inside, and are joined by a length of cord.

Aid to Self-Exploration
▲ *A vibrator can be used if you are not currently in a sexual relationship. Run it around your vulva, or place it just above your clitoris. It can help you explore your orgasmic potential. A vibrator is useful for women who have never been able to climax, as it is certain to produce an erotic response, and this can be used as a basis for further sexual exploration.*

A better known example of a sex aid is the dildo, a kind of artificial penis, which may be fashioned out of wood, china or steel and can be used by both men and women. Some forms of dildo are attached to the groin area by straps so that they can be used by women during intercourse with a partner of the same sex, to emulate the male sexual role, or to perform anal sex on a man. Men, too, can strap on a dildo to obtain what is, in effect, a permanently erect penis.

The modern, and more sophisticated, version of the dildo is the vibrator, which is battery powered and contains a small vibrating motor. The vibrations created by the motor can be intensely arousing, particularly for a woman, because they are more efficient at stimulating the sensory nerve endings in the skin that produce sexual excitement and orgasm than normal skin-to-skin contact.

During penetrative intercourse, for instance, sexual stimulation is

---

Hygiene

Never share sex toys, and always keep them clean by washing them regularly in hot soapy water. A vibrator can be covered with a condom which is thrown away afterwards. If you use a vibrator for anal stimulation, always wash it before inserting it into the vagina, to avoid spreading infection, or keep a vibrator solely for this purpose.

---

brought about by the friction caused by the penis rubbing along the inside of the vagina and against the labia and clitoris. This triggers the nerve endings at a steady rate and may lead to orgasm. The vibrator, however, can stimulate the nerve endings at a much faster rate, so an orgasm is almost guaranteed.

Sexual Self-Discovery

For a woman to explore her body thoroughly, to find its most sexually sensitive areas, and to reach her orgasmic potential, a vibrator can be an invaluable aid to self-discovery. Vibrators have helped many women to achieve an orgasm for the first time, particularly in those whose enjoyment of sex is hindered by feelings of shame, guilt or embarrassment instilled in childhood.

The intensity of the stimulation from a vibrator can also overwhelm those psychological blocks that may be preventing some women from achieving satisfaction, forcing them to surrender to the pure animalistic pleasure of self-gratification. They can then build on this experience by incorporating the vibrator into their sex sessions with a partner until the remaining mental barriers have been eliminated entirely. Because of guilt feelings, some women may even be reluctant to touch themselves directly to achieve sexual satisfaction, but able to overcome this aversion with a vibrator.

For other women, the inability to achieve sexual fulfilment may be due to their lack of understanding of their

Vibrating Waves of Pleasure

▲ *Introduce a vibrator to sex sessions with your partner. He can use it on you to produce multiple sexual sensations. It will send shock waves of pleasure through your vulva while he kisses and licks your nipples, driving you into a sexual frenzy.*

own sexuality. Here again, a vibrator can be used to discover which parts of the body are erotically sensitive: not only the most obviously erogenous zones, such as the nipples, vagina or clitoris, but other areas, such as the thighs, belly, earlobes, and arms.

You may feel happier if you are alone for your first experience with a vibrator. In that case you should aim to create the right atmosphere in which to explore your body so you can really relax and let yourself go. Choose a time when you will not be disturbed, lock the door, take the phone off the hook, and turn the lighting down low. Revel in your sexual fantasies and let the vibrator do the work. You can play the vibrator over the inside of the thighs and over the mons before slowly running it along the inside of your labia.

Some women may find that the stimulation is too intense if the vibrator is held directly against the clitoris for very long, but if placed just above or alongside, the erotic sensations it produces may be sufficient for them to climax. If you prefer you can

insert the vibrator into your vagina, as a surrogate penis, either moving it in and out to simulate intercourse, or just letting the vibrations have their effect by themselves.

Some women may find that they need additional lubrication if they are going to use the vibrator inside their vagina. Lubricating cream or gel smeared over the labia and clitoris also enhances the sensation when stimulating these areas as well.

Vibrators for Men

A vibrator can heighten a man's sexual response too, although he will probably need some additional manual stimulation to achieve orgasm. For some men, the glans, or tip, of the penis may be too sensitive to take this degree of stimulation for long. However, other men may find it is sufficiently arousing to enable them to reach orgasm, and it has been successfully used to cure impotence in many cases.

The whole shaft of the penis is responsive to the vibrations, particularly the underside and the frenulum. But a vibrator can also be used to discover other highly charged areas on the man's body. The base of the penis is particularly sensitive to the vibrations, and applying the vibrator to the perineum, the area of skin between the anus and the genitals, enables the pulsing effect to reach down to the prostate, a gland that

Erotic Charge

◄ *Use it on your man to show him just how erotically sensitive the male skin can be. Play it over his thighs and buttocks, working teasingly towards his anal area. Rest it on the highly charged zone between his legs, just in front of the anus, for an electrifying experience.*

can produce intense sexual feelings itself when stimulated. Pressure applied to this area can sometimes produce an erection, without using any other stimulation.

Mutual Fun

A vibrator is not only useful for self-pleasure, or for those who are temporarily on their own or without a sexual relationship: it can also be used during intercourse to heighten the sexual response. The man can slide it over his partner's thighs and breasts, or around her vulva. A woman can use the vibrator to stimulate her man's thighs and buttocks.

Vibrators are available in a wide variety of shapes and sizes, from sex shops and through mail order catalogues, so it is worth spending time deciding which type is best for you. Many are skin-coloured to look like an erect penis, with a veining effect down the side. They may be made of soft latex to make them feel more penis-like, and some also oscillate up and down or from side to side.

Some vibrators may be perfectly smooth, or covered with a ribbed or grooved pattern, to increase the stimulation, and they can often be adjusted to produce a powerful throbbing or a delicate pulsation. They can also be very noisy, so check before you take one home, if the sound of the vibrations is likely to be a source of embarrassment.

Chapter 4
The Art of Romance

Learning to signal your availability for love and romance is an art. The way you dress not only affects your self-esteem but also projects a certain image to draw to you the kind of person you most wish to attract. Knowing the nuances of body language helps you to be more aware of what your actions are saying. When you meet that special person, you begin a tentative and hopeful journey into the first stages of romance and courtship. How you behave towards each other at this point forms the basis for your future relationship. It is a time when you will need to affirm your feelings for the other, while not overwhelming him or her with your needs. Becoming aware of your hopes and expectations will help you through this difficult period of transition as the new relationship deepens into a more intimate bond.

The Language of Clothes

The clothes you wear can say much about your emotional state and feelings of confidence. Both men and women use clothes to broadcast aspects of their personalities, or to create a certain persona with which to impress other people. That slinky "little black number" can bring out aspects of a woman's character that might otherwise have remained dormant. "Power dressing" inspires respect in others and so gives the individual's own confidence a major boost. In comfy leggings, or jeans and a sweatshirt, on the other hand, a person presents a more relaxed and easy-going image.

Dress to Express

Women often wear more revealing clothes when they are feeling confident about their sexuality. Some researchers claim this is most likely to be around the time of ovulation, when a woman is at her most fertile. However a woman can feel sexy at any time, and the clothes she wears will often reflect this mood, accentuating her most attractive characteristics.

It is a common misunderstanding, though, for a man to assume that a woman dresses purely for the effect her clothes will have on the opposite sex. Very often a woman chooses a certain style, even one that is overtly appealing, because she enjoys feeling attractive in her own right and expects to have the freedom to express it. A woman who chooses to wear a figure-hugging dress or even a revealing mini-skirt may be doing so because she favours the style, wants to feel good about the way she looks, and may be just as concerned about making an impression on her female friends as on men. In other words, if a woman is wearing clothes that reveal her body, it does not necessarily signal that she is wanting or expecting to receive uninvited male attention.

Nowadays, a women has a greater sense of her personal freedom, and her wish to express her sexuality without being perceived as a sex object means that men must decode

Party Time

▲ *This short, figure-hugging dress says the woman is in the mood for some fun and is not ashamed to broadcast the message. The dress is shaped to reveal the sensual curve of her neck, while the high heels accentuate the length of her legs. By choosing black she is also showing she feels confident and in control.*

her availability signals without simply basing them on the way she is dressed. This can be difficult to grasp for a man who is conditioned to believe that a woman's desire to look attractive is only designed for a male response. These days, if a woman wishes to attract the attention of a man, she is likely to give more direct signals to him. Men, then, can no longer afford to make automatic assumptions on a woman's intentions simply because she is dressed to kill.

The ability to be able to change the style of the clothes to match the mood is a positive one, and gives a woman a greater flexibility in being able to express herself as a more all-rounded person rather than being fixed into a specific image. On the whole, a woman will probably be more clothes-conscious than her men friends, or her partner, but it is important for her to select her clothes to suit her colouring, height and size rather than try to emulate a particular style simply because it is fashionable.

A woman's size is not a barrier to her looking good if she takes the time to pick the clothes which flatter her particular body shape. She should forget about trying to copy any top-model look that happens to be in vogue. Feeling comfortable in what she wears is the most powerful way for a woman to be attractive, and

Power Play

▲ *This is a style of suit that means business. Sex is definitely secondary to ambition. However, there are enough feminine touches – the open neck and length of skirt – to show that the wearer has not sublimated her sexuality. She is saying, "I have got where I am because I am a woman – not in spite of my sex."*

most men respond to a woman who is relaxed and confident in herself, rather than only to the clothes that she happens to be wearing.

While revealing clothes can be fun to wear, and can certainly make a woman turn heads, sometimes the look can have a reverse effect on a man and actually scare him off. He might perceive the woman as a predatory man-hunter, and if he is not confident in his own sexuality, he may feel unable to cope with what he imagines will be her demands.

A Casual Approach

A woman may prefer to dress in such a way that she camouflages her more obvious sexual attributes, because she prefers men to be drawn to her because of her personality rather than her obvious feminine assets. She may prefer to wear comfortable clothes, like a shirt and jeans, that do not reveal too much of the shape of her body. In doing so, she feels more able to relate to men on an easy, equal and friendly basis rather than an immediately sexual one. This does not mean that she has switched off her sexual signals, but she is drawing attention to herself as a complete person with a mind and personality, as well as a feminine body.

Dressed to Impress

A man's clothes are likely to reflect his financial status and the power he commands as much as his sexual availability. A business suit, like a uniform, can indicate dominance and assertiveness and so conveys an air of

Easy Does It

▶ *In tight white jeans and denim top, open at the neck, this woman can present herself as undeniably feminine but is making it clear she is meeting the man on equal terms. Any relationship must be serious and include an appreciation of her as a person, not just a sex object.*

confidence and achievement. For some women, this aura of power is very sexually attractive, particularly if they seek a partner with whom they will feel secure and who is a successful and reliable provider. So a well-cut suit from a famed fashion designer, suggesting financial security and career success, could have definite appeal to these women. Even a man's casual clothes will often have an expensive branded trademark if he likes to dress to impress.

When a man is feeling sexually confident his clothes are likely to reflect the fact. Most men who keep themselves fit look good in jeans and T-shirts and although this is a common masculine attire, it is usually very attractive to women. Many find that the sight of well-shaped buttocks, accentuated by the cut of a tight pair of jeans, is an extremely powerful turn-on. Men, like women, have increasingly broken the gender mould when it has come to dress, and a lot of men like to experiment with softer textures such as silk shirts, and brighter colours, moving away from the more traditional choice of dull grey and blue. This gives them the opportunity to express the more flamboyant, artistic or sensitive sides of their nature.

Both men and women dress to please and attract the opposite sex, but there is far greater freedom of expression nowadays for them to explore and project their own personality through what they wear without being inhibited by the constraints of gender conditioning.

Under Your Clothes

The choice of underwear a woman picks to put on before going out on a social or business engagement can make a major difference to the way she feels about herself. What items of clothing she has next to her skin, and that only she knows she is wearing, can do much to enhance her confidence and sense of attractiveness.

The colours can also affect her own mood, and definitely those of a lover if he sees her when she gets undressed. For instance, a red bra-

Frankly Scarlet
▼ *Sexy red underwear makes an unmistakably bold statement about you. It says you know what you want and nothing is going to stand in your way.*

and-panty combination can send a passionate message. In fact, for an overtly sexual statement you can't beat scarlet. It states that the woman is sexually confident and that she knows what she wants and plans to get it.

Black lacy underwear makes a sophisticated but feminine statement, and is flattering to any body shape. It is sultry and sexy while being practical, and shows the woman feels confident and in control. Sexy silk underwear in virginal white creates a wonderful contrast when worn under a smart but severe business suit. The soft material on the skin will feel very sensual and feminine. Silk underwear, in particular, is so smooth and teasingly flimsy that it gives a woman the daring impression that she is wearing nothing at all.

In contrast, sporty underwear that is comfortable and supportive helps a woman feel relaxed, knowing she can move easily and that her body looks and feels firm and secure.

Lacy Days

▲ Silky virginal white underwear will make you feel sexy and special – no matter what the day holds in store.

Nice and Easy

▶ Sporty and comfortable, this combination is not designed just for exercising to keep trim: it can make you feel relaxed and well supported under leisure clothes.

Body Language

According to psychologists, up to two-thirds of communication between humans is non-verbal. The way you sit or stand and the gestures you make broadcast a powerful message to the people you meet. While some of these signals may be given consciously, most body language is involuntary, either instinctive behaviour, or unconsciously learned through watching others. Even if you try to hide it, this secret code can reveal the way you truly feel. Understanding these subtle signs can indicate whether the person you feel drawn to is going to reject your overtures – or already feels the same way about you.

Our innermost thoughts trigger chemical and emotional changes in the body and we respond on a physical level by unconsciously altering our posture, expression and mannerisms. These responses may be subtle movements of the eyes and mouth, or more obvious statements, such as the way we fold our arms. Individually the signals may not amount to very much, but they all represent clues, like pieces in a jigsaw, that can fit together to reveal a picture of our true feelings.

Our body language is most expressive when we are with a member of the opposite sex. Men and women may not always be conscious of their feelings, but if they are genuinely attracted to another person, their bodies will broadcast the message loud and clear. Some responses are due to the fact that sexual attraction causes the body to release chemicals such as adrenaline, the "fight or flight" hormone, which causes the heart and breathing rate to quicken and so prepares a person for sudden hectic physical activity.

This leads to feelings of tension and restlessness, makes the mouth go dry and produces other signs associated with nervousness and embarrassment, such as a flushed face and sweating. These reactions are impossible to suppress.

Other human actions have their origins in evolutionary history. When birds follow a pattern of behaviour designed to attract a mate it is called a courtship display. We can see echoes of this avian mating ritual – the brightly coloured plumage, distinctive head actions, and changes in movement – in the behaviour of humans as they try to find a partner.

Yet the human mating game is far more sophisticated than that in the animal world, and as society becomes more complex, so does non-verbal communication. Body language now must cope with the subtle interplay of relationships between busy working men and women, both in their social lives and while pursuing demanding careers. As a result, the messages of body language are becoming increasingly difficult to decipher – and therefore more open to misinterpretation.

Confused Signals

Women complain that men often misread their signs. One reason for this may be that much of a woman's body language is concerned with creating a good impression generally,

Negative Signals

▲ *These body postures signal protection and defence. The arms are folded, closing off the emotional centres – the heart and belly – there is a distance between the couple, their eyes are averted and they are wearing bored expressions. There is no interest, and no chemistry.*

Opening Up
▲ *The body language here is starting to convey availability. Their bodies are leaning towards one another, and their arms and legs are in a more open posture, showing they are beginning to feel sexually at ease. A knee is extended to make that initial, exploratory touch.*

Making Contact
▲ *Their bodies are now getting energized as they feel safe enough in each other's company to really open up. They are smiling and making eye contact, his arm is on the back of the chair, ready to enfold her, and her hand is resting lightly on his knee.*

perhaps to a client, or business colleague, or to male and female acquaintances. In crowded work or social situations it may not even be clear who, if anyone, has caught the woman's interest, or she may give conflicting signals because she is unsure of herself or has other things on her mind. Her signals may not even be aimed at a single individual.

A woman who is unsure about the response she will get may look at everyone else in the room rather than the man she is attracted to, apart from an occasional glance. This is a signal that men often misread as indicating a lack of interest.

Differences in background can also lead to confusion. For example, a woman raised in an overly protective environment, or one where contact with males has been limited, may give out seemingly provocative signals when talking to men. She might be shocked to discover her behaviour was seen as a sexual invitation. On the other hand, the signals given out by a woman who is well used to male attention may be too discreet. Careful to avoid giving a false impression, her subtle signals might appear remote or even unfriendly.

A woman's natural fluency in body language means she can often spot when another female is attracted to a man before he can. He may even be unaware of being the focus of a female's attention, in the office or at a party, for example, until his partner points it out to him.

Men, too, must be careful about the signals they broadcast. As women tend to use delicate non-verbal cues with members of their sex, they can mistakenly believe that men are equally subtle and so get a false impression. What seems to be a brush-off may simply be a sign that a man is preoccupied with his thoughts.

Alternatively, a man may be thought to be showing genuine interest in a woman when, in fact, he is just being friendly, or going through the motions of flirting without any real intention of taking it further. To avoid such misunderstandings men and women must make an effort to decode the signals and so discover how the opposite sex really feels about them.

Complete rejection is usually easy to comprehend, but there are other more subtle signals which may suggest doubt or shyness. So never try to read body language in isolation or be too quick to jump to conclusions. It is important to weigh up all the signals before making a judgement. A man might be indicating a lack of interest if he evades your eye while talking to you, or he may just be shy.

A slumped posture could be a sign of rejection or that a man is feeling depressed and is having difficulty shaking the mood off.

At times, what seems like rejection might actually indicate confusion. If a woman sends out conflicting signals, seemingly interested but also defensive, it might be because her body is saying one thing but her mind is over-riding it. Such a situation may arise when a woman is in a long-term relationship with one man but is strongly attracted to another. She may be playing for time because she is not yet ready to reveal how she truly feels.

If your instinct tells you that a man is attracted to you, but he is not responding, there may be reasons for his negative body language. He may be recovering from a relationship in which he was badly hurt and so is wary of getting involved again too soon. He may already be in a relationship and so unable to show his feelings openly, or he may be incapable of making a commitment. It may even be that he considers you to be totally unattainable, even though he desires you.

Negative Signals

A round-shouldered stance, whether seated or standing, indicates that a man or woman is not feeling at ease. This message is often reinforced by a typical protective posture – arms folded defensively, knees held tightly together and legs or ankles crossed – in a subconscious desire to guard vulnerable parts of the body.

Sometimes a woman will sit or stand with her legs tightly entwined, with one foot locked behind the calf of the other leg, and she may place her hands protectively in her lap, unconsciously indicating that her genital area is off limits.

A man may signal rejection by turning right away from the other person, but in social situations it is usually only the lower half of the body that indicates the true state of affairs. For example, a man's head and torso are turned towards the woman and he appears to be concentrating on what she says, but his legs and feet point towards the exit door, indicating where his thoughts are leading him.

Men and women also use eye language to indicate rejection. These messages, known as "cut-off signals", indicate the desire to withdraw from a situation through lack of interest, or shyness. A woman will often glance round the room, as if

Getting Physical

▲ *His arm is around her shoulder and they are holding hands. The body language here is communicating intense interest and intimacy, mixed with tension, as their attraction to each other increases.*

calling out for someone to rescue her. It is an unspoken plea to be taken away from her companion, or for others to join the group, and so diffuse the situation.

Men and women may indicate stress through rapid blinking, or a blink that lasts longer than normal. They may also signal their unease by glancing rapidly to and fro, as if looking for someone, unable to settle their gaze on you.

Our social conditioning makes it difficult to be deliberately rude to people we meet, no matter how much we may dislike them. To avoid causing insult we are sometimes forced into telling white lies. This causes a conflict between what we say and how we feel, which is reflected in our body language. Small children automatically put a hand to their mouths when they tell a lie. In adults the gesture is more subtle. A person who is being evasive will often rub his nose, or hold a hand up to his cheek in a unconscious attempt to hide the falsehood.

If a man stands with his arms crossed and his thumbs pointing upwards he is communicating that someone is getting too close for comfort and is invading his body space. A similar defensive gesture is to sit with one arm placed across the body at waist level.

Accentuate The Positive

While body language is mostly involuntary, simple changes may improve the way you appear to others. If you are nervous or insecure you may give out negative signals, such as folding your arms, even when you want to be friendly. There are positive steps you can take to make yourself more inviting to other people, particularly members of the opposite sex.

It is vital to relax, particularly when meeting a man or woman for the first time. When you are tense your muscles tend to stiffen and this limits your repertoire of facial expressions and makes your movements seem jerky, awkward and ungraceful. It also makes you seem much older. You can reduce the tension in work or social situations, for example, by learning a relaxation technique such as deep, regular breathing whenever you feel nervous.

A natural smile, on the other hand, relaxes the facial muscles and has an instant effect on those around you, immediately putting them at their ease. If the smile is genuine, a small group of facial muscles will make the skin form characteristic little crinkles around the eyes. These muscles are impossible to control consciously. In contrast, a false smile looks stiff and lasts longer than is natural.

It is also important to adopt an erect posture. Sitting or standing in a slumped, round-shouldered way creates a negative impression. For women in particular, it tends to be seen as a defensive posture that suggests you have put up barriers and are not inviting anyone to take the trouble to get to know you. Try to adopt a more open posture and you will seem more approachable.

A man should aim to hold the woman's gaze directly, without furtively glancing away, even if he is feeling nervous. Otherwise he can appear rather shifty. His gaze should be friendly, rather than deeply penetrating, which can appear fierce. An open, steady look that is softened with a smile can work wonders in smoothing the way to an introduction.

A major turn-off is a look that seems to linger over a woman's body, studying every curve. A man's urge to look at a woman's body is natural, but he should do it in a respectful and appreciative way otherwise she will feel as if she is under a microscope.

The man who is most popular with the opposite sex is the one who makes each woman he talks to seem special by concentrating his gaze exclusively on her, without surreptitiously glancing at other females.

Relaying Availability

Men have a more limited non-verbal vocabulary than women when it comes to signalling interest in the opposite sex. Men often think they are making the opening moves in the mating game and so have less need of subtlety. In fact, it is a woman's more expressive body language that encourages the man she has chosen

Basic Attraction
▼ *The sexual signals are clear as they lean towards each other. His legs are wide apart, exposing his genital area. Her back is arched and her bottom is pushed out – it is a perfect example of primate sexual posturing.*

to make that first approach. Females have such a wide range of body postures, movements, and actions in their sexual armoury that males are often powerless to resist.

The way that males and females signal their availability is – initially – very similar in both sexes. When men and woman feel strongly attracted to someone they have seen for the first time, in the office or at a party, for example, the first sign is usually a change of posture. They will immediately sit or stand much straighter,

Mirror Images

Psychologists say that an important sign of whether a couple are forming a rapport is a type of behaviour called "mirroring". Here the man and woman unconsciously copy each other's actions or posture. For example, at a party if two people are sitting on a sofa deeply engrossed in conversation, the man may turn sideways and lean towards the woman, perhaps resting an arm on the sofa back. Almost immediately, this action is likely to be copied by the woman. If the woman crosses her legs the man will cross his too, or they will both raise their wine glasses and take a sip of their drinks at the same time. To observers these copy-cat actions will seem like mirror images.

Power Games
◀ *At first glance this couple look as if they are getting on well, but the pose is quite defensive. The woman is presenting herself, with her chest thrust forward, but her pulled-back pelvis indicates a withholding of her sexual energy. He is the opposite. His pelvis is forward, indicating sexual willingness, but his chest is pulled back and his arms are folded, suggesting emotional withholding. This is a classic "here I am but you can't have me" posture. They are playing power games as each suspects the other of wanting something that they are not willing to give in return.*

Little Girl Lost

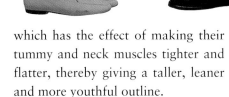

◀ *She plays helpless and vulnerable, her defenceless posture signalling "I need to be rescued". He plays the macho super-hero, with puffed up chest, always in control, coming to her rescue. She fits right into his ego pattern, but no doubt has an agenda of her own.*

which has the effect of making their tummy and neck muscles tighter and flatter, thereby giving a taller, leaner and more youthful outline.

A woman may arch her back so that her breasts are pushed out. She will often tilt her head back or to the side, exposing her sexually sensitive neck and making it seem longer and more elegant – a universal symbol of beauty. Preening actions, such as smoothing the dress down and patting the hair, are typical gestures at this stage, and, if walking, the

sway of the hips may become more exaggerated. If a woman is holding an object such as a wine glass, or cigarette lighter she may begin to stroke it rather suggestively while she looks at the man who has caught her interest.

A man may push his shoulders back and thrust his chest out, too, making his shoulders seem much broader, and his torso more muscular. Some sexually aggressive males may stand with both hands arrogantly placed on the hips and the chin jutting forward. If they are fairly assured of success they may lounge back in the chair with their hands behind their head. These gestures are designed to enlarge the man's outline, so making him look bigger and more powerful, and to create an air of confidence.

If men and women are strongly attracted to each other they may stand with their legs wider apart than normal. In women this stance makes such a powerful sexual statement

that it is regularly used by fashion models to make clothes look sexier. A relaxed, open stance also makes a woman seem friendlier and more approachable, so inviting the man to make contact.

At a party, a woman may sway in time to the music and glance at the male of her choice, inviting him to suggest that they dance together. This can be such a subtle gesture that men often feel that they instigated the approach without any prompting from the woman.

Male body language tends to draw attention to the genital region as the most overtly sexual signal. For example, a man will often sit with his legs spread apart to display his crotch, or he will stand with his pelvis thrust forward. One or both thumbs may be hooked into his belt or the waistband of his trousers, with the fingers pointing downwards towards the genitals to give extra emphasis. This pose is particularly common among adolescent males who have not learned a more subtle approach. A less blatant way of indicating the genital area is to stand with one hand inside a trouser or jacket pocket.

A woman's eyes will open much wider, giving her a welcoming and yet rather vulnerable appearance. She will look for an early opportunity to move closer to the man, even if she is currently engaged, perhaps talking to a close friend or an important client. If this is not immediately possible she will often turn towards him slightly to reduce the distance between them. If he is close by, this may draw him into the group, so providing an opportunity to initiate a conversation.

She may glance over her shoulder, or lower her eyelids and glance sideways until the man notices, and then quickly look away. If a woman lacks self-confidence she may never look at the man directly but only give side-long glances. A more overtly sexual gesture is to toss her head, flicking the hair out of her face, or she may run her hands through her hair, or lift it up behind her head.

Close Contact

Another sign of sexual interest is that a woman's feet will be pointing towards the man, often with one foot extended. She may touch him or brush against him, and keep her hand in contact with his for an extended time, when accepting a glass of wine or a light for her cigarette, for example. She may even allow her breast to touch the man's arm, as if unaware of the contact, and keep it there for a few moments.

Sitting down, her body will be turned towards him, signalling her interest and excluding all others. A woman will often sit with one leg tucked under the other and the knee pointed towards the man, and she may slowly cross and uncross her legs, or squeeze them together, tensing her leg muscles.

The man's body will also point towards the woman who has taken his fancy. This may start with just one foot aimed towards her, while his head and body are still directed at the person he is talking to. However, he will begin to turn his head towards the woman, to draw her into the conversation.

As his confidence builds he will move more of his body round to face her directly and will hold the woman's gaze for slightly longer than would normally be the case. He may lean across the woman, or move

A Meeting of Equals

▲ *Both are meeting on equal terms. Their open, balanced bodies indicate a willingness to communicate, without defences or preconceived expectations.*

round to exclude other group members who may be competing with him for her attention.

Displacement Activity

The special chemicals released in the body by sexual attraction cause a form of fidgeting and restlessness that is known as "displacement activity". This is the body's way of dissipating the nervous tension we feel when aroused by a member of the opposite sex. A man may straighten his tie, smooth his hair, or tuck his shirt in tighter. He may play with cuff-links, or remove imaginary pieces of lint, or specks of dust from his clothes, or he may be keep putting his hands in his pockets and taking them out again. The tension will make his mouth go dry, so he will need to clear his throat and lick his lips, and may run a finger around his collar, which will seem to have grown uncomfortably tight.

Women also show this displacement activity, indicating that a powerful sexual urge is being suppressed. Typical signals include playing with her jewellery, or twirling a lock of hair round a finger. She may swallow more than usual and may even wrap her arms around herself in an embrace. Other signs of attraction include gently stroking the thigh, and sliding a foot in and out of her shoe, or letting the shoe dangle from the toes.

More subtle sexual signals come into play once a man and woman are close together. A very feminine gesture is to hold a drink or a cigarette, for example, with her wrists and palms turned upwards or towards the man. This is a gesture that few males perform, except those who unconsciously want to appear more feminine.

Her head may also be angled to one side in a pose indicating rapt attention to his conversation. When she is speaking her tone of voice will become softer and lower in pitch. A husky female voice is considered sexy because it emulates the breathless quality of a woman who is very sexually aroused.

A woman's facial expressions also become much more eloquent and intimate. Her smiles will be broader and more frequent, and she will be quick to laugh at the man's attempts at humour – whether she finds them amusing or not.

A woman's lips represent a powerful sexual symbol. Some researchers believe the female mouth gives secondary signals about her genital area. The pouting open-mouthed look made famous by sex symbols such as Marilyn Monroe, the use of bright red lipstick, and the way a woman moistens her lips with her tongue to make them glisten, all emulate the female genitals, which open, redden and become shiny with her natural lubrication when she is sexually aroused.

The Language of Eyes

The eyes also provide an important indicator of sexual attraction. When a man sees something pleasurable, such as a beautiful woman, his eyes will dilate – as they would if he

had walked into a dimly lit room. This is a purely automatic response and cannot be faked. A woman's eyes also dilate when she is attracted to a man –

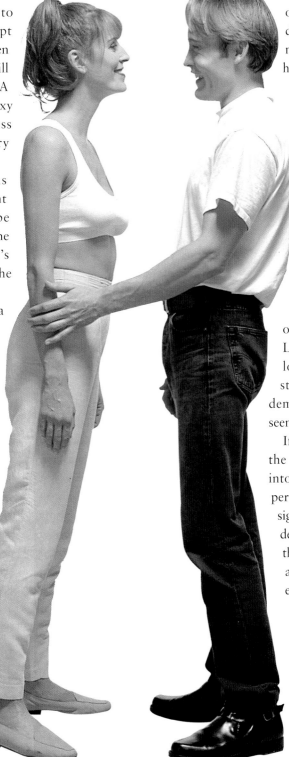

a sign men look for instinctively. One reason that a candlelit meal has long been associated with romance is that low lighting makes the pupils dilate, suggesting sexual interest. The women of Renaissance Italy used an extract of the deadly nightshade flower to dilate their pupils artificially and so make them appear more alluring, hence the plant's other name – belladonna, or "beautiful lady".

A female's eye language is particularly expressive, perhaps because of the important role that eye contact plays in establishing a bond with new-born babies. When a woman is with a man she finds attractive her eyes will grow wider and she will raise her eyebrows, to give an open and attentive air. Initially, the woman will look at the man often, but for brief moments only. Later on, she will hold his gaze for longer periods of time, but will still occasionally lower her eyes, demurely, to avoid making herself seem too forward.

If the relationship develops, both the man and the woman will stare into each other's eyes for extended periods of time. This is the clearest sign of all that a sexual rapport has developed between them. It is as if they exist in their own little world, apparently unaware of anyone else in the room.

Touching Moment
◀ *A light touch on the arm acknowledges closeness but is not invasive. The gesture does not come from a loaded or defensive stance, so it leaves the other person room to respond.*

First Encounters

The first moments in a relationship are very important. You are both nervous, unsure of yourselves and of how the other will react, yet desperately eager to create the right impression. You are aware that there is something special between you – the butterflies in the pit of your stomach and the light-headed feeling confirm that. But you are also worried that a careless move or a thoughtless word can spoil the mood and cause irrevocable harm to this budding relationship. Fear not, you must seize the moment. Remember, "Faint heart never won fair lady" – or man.

How a man and woman interact when they meet for the first time can set the seal on a relationship, or may crush a fledgling romance before it can take flight. A certain gaucheness now is understandable and acceptable. A slip of the tongue, a clumsy action – like knocking over a wine glass, or tripping over your feet – is to be expected when you are nervous about the way you will appear.

You are both eager to seem attractive, informed, interesting and sexy, but try to keep control of yourself – and the situation – and not let your tongue run away with you. You are keen to create a good impression, but don't start babbling on about yourself and stop the other person from getting a word in. At best, this can make you seem rather self-obsessed and conceited and may even appear that you have no interest in him or her but are simply looking for an available audience.

To avoid creating this impression, you should take every opportunity to draw the other person into the conversation. If you have been talking about a movie you saw recently,

Magic First Moments
◄ *The meeting place for that special first date will be special wherever you choose. But make sure it is somewhere you can talk and really get to know each other. A simple walk in the park will give you the time and space you crave, without the fear of irritating interruptions.*

ask your companion what he or she likes to see. If you have a favourite sport or pastime, try to find out about the other person's interests.

This approach is particularly important if your companion seems tongue-tied, perhaps through shyness or because he or she is unsure of the situation and anxious not to make a wrong move. Try to find areas of shared interest and keep to those, avoiding controversial topics, or subjects that seem to bore or irritate the other person. This will help you to discover whether you are compatible and may build a springboard from which you can launch the next stage of the relationship.

The First Date

No matter how well this first interaction with your new companion has gone, the relationship can still be nipped in the bud unless one of you plucks up the courage to ask the other for a date. Traditionally the man has been expected to make this first move. But now that women want to become more assertive in a relationship, this rule need no longer apply. Indeed, many men would be extremely flattered to be asked out by a woman.

However, no matter how confident some women are about other aspects of their lives, they may be reluctant to initiate the first approach. In that case they should steer the conversation in such a way that the man is encouraged to suggest a date. For example, a woman might mention in passing that there is a movie she has been keen to see, or she could ask if he knows anything about a rather cute little restaurant that has just opened. Whoever makes the suggestion, the

Give the First Date a Chance

Avoid choosing a night-club or pop concert for the first occasion. The noise and the crowd will make it difficult for you to hear each other, let alone talk, and you will probably have learnt little more about each other by the end of the evening than you knew at the beginning.

If you choose a movie, allow plenty of time to chat beforehand and conclude the evening with a visit to a bar or a restaurant so you have another opportunity to get to know each other.

Remember, though, the most idyllic settings are usually the simplest. If you are in reach of the coast, there is nothing like walking along a sandy seashore, as the setting sun casts golden reflections in the sea, to create an atmosphere of enchantment in which a relationship can flourish.

You could take a stroll in the park together – when there is an autumnal carpet of russet leaves covering the ground, or as the first buds of spring are peeping into view. Whatever the season, it is up to you to create the magic mood to match the moment. If the love affair develops these early trysts will always have an important place in your memories.

venue should be chosen with care on this all-important first date. You are still in the process of finding out about each other and need to select somewhere that will let you relate in an intimate atmosphere that is free from distractions.

The First Touch

Now that you are sure there is a developing bond between you, try to open up and reveal something about yourself, your hopes and aspirations, as well as your likes and dislikes. But don't just communicate your feelings verbally. Body language continues to play an important part in the way a couple interact, even after the initial meeting.

On this first date, try to avoid creating barriers, such as placing a handbag or umbrella between you, or folding your arms across your chest. Walking with your hands behind your back can also be taken as a defensive posture – that you are withdrawing into yourself. People react differently when courting, according

to their personality type, perhaps appearing very restless or withdrawn. Watch out for signs of tension or anxiety in your companion, such as tightly crossed ankles, or fidgeting with jewellery or cutlery, and look for ways to put her or him at ease.

Public Gestures

A simple touch of the hand can be very comforting, if it is done lightly, in a non-threatening way. Allow your fingers to brush against his, or take her hand in yours and give it a little squeeze. But don't make a sudden grab for the other person's hand before they are ready or it can be viewed as a show of power rather than a sign of affection.

By holding hands as you walk along you are providing a clear sign of your feelings. Many men are reluctant to display such a simple show of affection in public, yet to women it can mean a great deal. Women have often said that it was when their partner first held their

Holding Hands

▲ *Don't just hold hands palm to palm in the conventional way – intertwine your fingers, or give the hand a little squeeze, and gently stroke the highly sensitive skin on the inside of the wrist. These actions carry powerfully charged messages that can increase the electricity of the moment.*

hand in public that they realized the depth of their love.

If, perhaps out of shyness, the man does not make this move, it gives the woman an opportunity to take the initiative. This touching gesture from her reveals her feelings for him and can give his confidence a tremendous boost.

A comforting, protective arm round her shoulder is a simple enough gesture, too, but says far more than words can ever do. But the timing has to be right – watch for an instinctive flinching or tensing up on her part to indicate you have moved too soon. If

you sense this, don't remove your arm too quickly as this will show you have noticed her reaction and may embarrass her. Instead, wait a few minutes to take your arm away and then try again when your instincts tell you the gesture will be appreciated. If the relationship develops as you hope, you will soon be moving onto one of the most significant aspects of a new romance – the first kiss.

Sealed With a Kiss

It is natural to be over-anxious about the first kiss. Advertisements on television and in the glossy magazines

are designed to make us feel insecure about the way we smell and taste to others. Provided you have followed the basic rules of oral hygiene you can rest assured that your companion will be feeling just as insecure, and with as little reason.

However, if you are going to have a meal it is a good idea to avoid foods with really pungent aromas, such as garlic or onions, unless you know your companion is going to be eating the same thing.

A really confident, extrovert male may throw his arm round a woman and kiss her passionately on their first date. But with most women this rather proprietorial gesture is likely to lead to embarrassment and even hostility. Her body language will indicate this. She will tense up and look away, while her hands remain at her side showing no sign of returning the gesture. A better approach is to kiss her gently on the cheek, perhaps accompanied by the lightest of touches on the arm or shoulder.

Once you detect that a rapport has developed between you, the time will come to show your affection with a kiss on the lips. Unless you are sure that your partner is in the grip of an all-conquering passion – and that you feel the same way it is best to keep this first mouth-to-mouth kiss as light and affectionate as possible. Again, the man is usually expected to make the first move – although there is no law that says this has to be the case.

A man will be looking for a sign from his companion that his advances will not be rejected. As he slowly edges forward he will notice whether she stays in the same place, or edges back defensively, or whether she mirrors his movements and leans forward too. She may lift her face to meet his and purse her lips slightly. If a woman closes her eyes as she kisses a man she is showing a clear sign of trust and affection, but this may not come until much later in the relationship.

Kissing can remain friendly and affectionate like this, or it can build up to become passionate and arousing. It takes sensitivity to know when the change is appropriate. It is not a good idea to plant a wet slobbering kiss on the lips, or to stick your tongue in someone's mouth before there is a tacit invitation to do so. At the same time, too much hesitation and uncertainty can be equally off-putting.

If you are beginning to explore a sexual relationship with a new friend, let the kissing experience build up its own momentum. Try to stay relaxed so that your mouth and lips remain soft and yielding. That will help you to avoid the embarrassment of clashing teeth that so frequently occurs during the teenage days of early sexual exploration.

In many ways, the sexual kiss reflects the sexual act itself, because it involves a close and intimate exchange of physical contact, and in the case of deep kissing, a mixing of body fluids as the tongue enters the warm, moist mouth. The contact of mouth, lips and tongue, all highly sensitive and erogenous areas, can be an initial and safe way to discover whether there is a sexual chemistry and compatibility between you.

It Starts With a Kiss

▼ *When two people become sexually attracted to each other, the first mouth-to-mouth kiss usually signifies the change in the relationship. Let your partner's response dictate whether the kiss remains a light contact of the lips, or a passionate embrace with urgent thrusting tongues exploring each other's mouths.*

The Art of Wooing

Buoyed up by the success of that first romantic meeting, you feel as though you are floating on air, and the signs are that your new friend feels the same. No matter how well that first date seemed to go, the start of a new relationship is a nerve-racking period filled with opportunities for mistakes and misunderstandings. At this critical juncture, your next steps may decide whether you will part merely as friends or whether the relationship will develop into a lasting love affair. If both sides are honest and say how they feel, there is more chance that the relationship will be successful.

This is an anxious time as you wonder whether the person you have fallen for also feels the same way about you and would welcome another meeting. Waiting for someone to telephone to arrange another date can be agonizing, so, if you have had a good time, pick up the telephone and tell her how much you enjoyed the evening.

Suggest a second date within the next few days to judge whether your feelings are reciprocated. If you get the brush-off you must be philosophical; there is no easy way to deal with disappointment other than to hope to meet someone else soon. But if your companion is keen to see you again give plenty of encouragement.

It is important to nurture the friendship by keeping in contact and setting regular dates to meet. Try to vary the venues and activities to keep the relationship fresh and alive. Look for shared interests and try to capitalize on them by arranging activities you can take part in together. For example, if you both enjoy jogging, or have just talked about starting an exercise programme, arrange regular running sessions together. If you both enjoy the movies, set aside one night a week to see the latest releases.

Even if your pastimes are very different, try to take an interest in the other person's pursuits. It won't hurt you to attend a classical music concert or a football game occasionally, and you may even enjoy it.

At the same time, try not to be over-enthusiastic. Give your new friend the space to continue with his or her own life and to maintain other friendships. This will avoid giving the

Keeping In Touch
◄ *If you have enjoyed the evening, say so. A call from you will dispel any nagging doubts she may have about the success of your first date and a call at other, unexpected, times will show you have been thinking of her.*

impression that you are trying to push the relationship on too quickly. If you spend time away from each other, it will ensure your days together are even more vibrant.

Keeping Romance Alive

Just because you are getting to know one another, don't take the relationship for granted and let the romance of those heady early days begin to slide. Look for ways to show your feelings, for example by giving a present when you next meet. This should be a simple token of affection and not an expensive gift loaded with expectation, as though you expect something in return. Flowers, especially red ones, the colour that more than any other signifies love, still represent one of the most romantic statements a man can make. A woman, too, should play her part in the art of wooing by presenting the man with little gifts, such as a bottle of his favourite wine. As well as being a touching gesture in itself, this shows she has taken the trouble to discover his tastes.

Showing consideration and an awareness of the other person's moods and feelings can also enhance the loving feelings between two people. For example, a simple gesture such as helping a woman on with her coat, or complimenting her on her hair or dress, shows you really care.

Notice that your friend is tired after a busy day at the office and suggest that you cancel the date you had planned that evening, or leave early, even though you may have been looking forward to it. Your companion will really appreciate the fact that you are so finely attuned to his or her emotional wavelength and are willing to put another's best interests before your own.

Shared Interests
▶ *Find an interest that you have in common, such as jogging, and make it a regular part of your weekly schedule. Finding a sport or pastime you can share is the quickest way to cement a friendship.*

Food of Love

Once the relationship is at a stage where you feel confident enough to do so, it is natural to want to invite your new friend to your home for a meal. A sultry candlelit dinner is still one of the most romantic settings for a couple during the early stages of a relationship. It provides just the right ambience to open up to your new friend.

This does not have to be an exclusively female gesture. Males are just as capable of preparing a meal and a woman will be enchanted by this sign of a man's thoughtfulness. Cook only what you can comfortably handle. If the menu is too elaborate you will be tired before the meal starts and are likely to be spending all your time fretting about the next course, rather than enjoying your friend's company. You may also feel resentful if he or she shows less appreciation for your efforts than you think you deserve.

The atmosphere, rather than the food, is the most alluring aspect of the dinner, so aim to set the right mood. Low lighting is important to create the feeling of closeness, so you can relax and reveal your innermost thoughts. But don't rely on candles alone for the lighting. If the room is too dark it can seem forbidding rather than comforting. The room should be pleasantly warm but not stifling, or you will both feel sleepy rather than

Language of Flowers
▼ *The simplest message often speaks volumes and a gift of flowers, whether as a large bouquet or a single red bloom, is unmistakable. It shows that you care about her, without hinting that you might expect something in return.*

romantic, so leave a window ajar to ensure there is adequate ventilation.

A vase of fragrant flowers adds a spring-like touch, and romantic music playing softly in the background will help enhance the mood, but make sure it is quiet enough for you to hear each other without raising your voices. Your aim is to create an island of intimacy, cut off from the cares of the outside world.

This is a time to talk and share and be as one with each other. How much of yourself you reveal in these intimate encounters is entirely up to you, but it is better to be as open as possible, rather than hold back and risk creating an emotional distance between you.

Expectations

This can be a crucial time in a relationship. The food, the wine, the warm, moodily lit romantic atmosphere, can make your dinner date seem the sexiest companion in the world. Once you have opened up to your "significant other" on an emotional level you will be better able to judge whether you want to take the relationship on to a more physical stage.

Whether that means passionate kissing and heavy petting, penetrative sex, or any of the sexual possibilities in between, this is a very personal decision that individuals must make themselves, according to their own moral codes and social mores.

The question of when to sleep together for the first time has always been fraught with ethical and practical worries. In the past, the main concern has been the fear of pregnancy. The greater availability of effective contraception has largely removed that fear for many couples

A Thoughtful Gift
▲ *A romantic gift should show some thought and consideration for the other person. A bottle of his favourite wine suggests that you have taken the trouble to discover his preferences.*

(although, on religious grounds, it may still not be an option for other people) but this concern has been replaced by the risk of HIV infection.

It is not unusual for some couples to have sex on the very first date, while others prefer to reserve sex until after marriage, or ensure that it is part of a clearly committed long-term relationship. For most modern couples, however, the change of pace from simple friendship to sexual intimacy is likely to occur at some point between these two extremes. It might

Candlelight Romance

▲ *A romantic meal can set the seal on a developing love affair. Bathed in the warm glow of candlelight you can lose yourselves in the magic of the moment and enjoy just being with your companion, free from the cares and distractions of the outside world.*

be after a second or third date, or it may be that a couple will not feel they know each other well enough to take this step until several weeks or even months have elapsed.

However you feel about the issue, it is your decision and you should not feel pressurized into having sex before you are ready, nor should you coerce others to do so.

No matter how aroused you become, you will need to remain highly attuned to your partner's signals, ready to slow the tempo, or stop altogether, if there are any signs of nerves, or hesitation. A man, in particular, is making a very grave error if he assumes that his sexual technique is so irresistible he will be able to get a woman into a state of sexual arousal in the face of her obvious signs of reluctance.

A woman's right to say "no" to sexual intercourse must always be respected, regardless of whether a couple have had sex on previous occasions, or have been enjoying a highly arousing session of kissing and petting, and no matter how passionate her sexual signals may have seemed beforehand.

Her cooling off need not imply that the woman is a "tease" or that she has suddenly lost interest in the man, merely that she is not in the mood or is not yet ready to let the relationship develop to that stage.

Just as men have always been expected to make the opening moves in a sexual encounter, a woman should also be free to take the initiative and invite the man to stay overnight if she chooses. And if the man declines, for whatever reason, or no reason at all, this should not be taken as a rejection or a lack of sexual interest. It may simply be that he is not ready to make that commitment, or is tired, or has drunk a little to much alcohol, and is worried that his sexual performance will prove to be a disappointment to her.

A sensitive lover is one who can read his companion's mood and knows how far to go. Constant oblique references to sex, or overly passionate kisses when the other person is clearly not responding, are more likely to make them feel cold and resentful, rather than sexually aroused.

When two people are attuned to each other's needs and desires, eager to give pleasure as well as receive, and ready to consummate the relationship with a physical display of their love – the sky's the limit.

Chapter 5

Basic Techniques

The physical expression of your love is a profound way to show the depth of your feelings for each other. Yet lovemaking can embrace many forms – from the first moments of undressing each other to the sensual touching and caressing of foreplay; from erotic oral-genital stimulation to full penetrative intercourse. The way in which you express your love and sexuality should be an unfolding journey of mutual discovery, experimentation and pleasure. It is important, however, that neither partner should feel coerced or obligated, nor that needless health risks are taken, so an awareness of safer sex practices is an important factor. Then, this can become a truly caring and sharing experience, in which the man and woman exchange active and passive roles, if they choose, but without the need for sexual domination or competition. If viewed in that spirit, a loving couple will be able to experience the very heights of sexual ecstasy.

Safer Sex

Nowadays, the phrase "safer sex" is generally used wherever sexuality is written or spoken about. Safer sex practices help lovers to care for their own and each other's health while enjoying an exciting and joyful sex life. The term "safer sex" generally refers to all sexual activity which avoids the exchange of body fluids, such as semen, vaginal juices and blood, between partners. It is a way of modifying sexual practices to help prevent the risk of infection from the HIV virus and other sexually transmitted diseases (STDs). (See the section on Sexually Transmitted Diseases for information on HIV/AIDS and other STDs.) Safer sex practices apply to all members of the community, both homosexual and heterosexual.

Safer sex is essential to the art of love at the present time when the HIV/AIDS virus continues to spread through the world's heterosexual and homosexual population. HIV can remain in an otherwise healthy person for many years without causing symptoms, and any sexual acts that involve contact with the person's blood, semen or vaginal fluids can put lovers at potential risk of catching the disease.

Safer sex means taking adequate precautions against the exchange of these body fluids, and in abstaining from high-risk sexual activities which allow this to happen. For instance, the sensual and erotic massage programmes described in this book are examples of safer sex practices.

If you are making love with your partner in any way that involves penetrative sex, then you should consider using condoms. If used correctly, condoms reduce the risk of the spread of the HIV virus and other sexually transmitted diseases. Initially, you may feel that condoms inhibit the spontaneity of lovemaking, but by simply knowing they are the best method available of protecting yourself and your partner, you

Getting Attuned

▶ *Kissing, cuddling and hugging are safer sex practices through which new partners can discover if they are physically and sexually attuned.*

Return to Romance

◀ *Many men and women have longed for a return to old-fashioned courtship. As awareness grows around safer sex issues, romance is coming back into fashion. The wish to form monogamous relationships is popular again. Many couples now prefer to become better acquainted with each other before embarking on full sexual intimacy. Casual encounters or multiple sex partners are definitely not a good idea in terms of safer sex, and this provides an excellent excuse to modify sexual behaviour if you have previously allowed yourself to be pressured into casual sexual encounters.*

can begin to consider them as an integral part of the lovemaking. Safer sex, like massage, is a way of showing how much you care for the well-being of the body, mind and spirit of both yourself and your lover.

How To Discuss Safer Sex

Anyone who is contemplating a sexual relationship, or who is already involved in one, should consider safer sex. However, since sexual issues are invariably difficult to discuss, you may find it embarrassing to raise the subject of safer sex practices or to reach an agreement about it with a new partner.

The best way forward is to develop a clear and responsible attitude towards your own health and sexual practices, rather than relying on anyone else's responses. This clarity will enable you to stand firm on your decisions, and may also help your partner to resolve his or her own conflicts.

Adopt a clear but sensitive approach. You can affirm your attraction to your partner and add something like, "I would love to make love with you, but first I need to tell you that I always follow safer sex practices," and then outline what this means to you. Explain that, to you, safer sex is a way of showing a caring attitude.

If you meet a negative response, be patient but firm. Your partner may believe, mistakenly, that safer sex practices are relevant only to people who belong to high-risk groups. He or she may insist that they have had only a few sexual partners and, therefore, present no risk. The truth is, it is often impossible to know the sexual history of all the other people

Find Time to Talk

▲ *Try to discuss safer sex issues at the point when you realize the relationship is going to become sexual, rather than leaving it to the last moment when passion and feelings are running high. Also, giving yourselves time to know each other better allows you to build up trust, discuss your past sexual histories honestly with each other, and to decide if you are ready to make this commitment.*

who have been linked in a sexual chain of partners.

For instance, a previous lover may have had a relationship with someone who, at another time, had sex, unknowingly, with a person from an HIV high-risk group. Making love only once with someone who carries the HIV virus can present sufficient risk of becoming infected yourself. People can be HIV infected without knowing it and remain in good health for a very long period of time, showing no outward sign of the infection. Also, there are other sexually transmitted diseases which need to be considered.

Some women, in particular, find it difficult to assert themselves over sexual issues. Old attitudes persist despite the dramatic changes in sexual mores and gender roles over the last few decades. Women are still

generally more conditioned than men to please others, and often feel shy to take the initiative on safer sex issues, particularly if there is resistance.

As a woman, you may be worried that you will be deemed too sexually forward if you produce a packet of condoms at the opportune moment. Remind yourself that you have as much right to self determination over your sexual health as you would, nowadays, expect to have over your choices of contraception. If you are a sexually active woman, there is absolutely nothing wrong with your having a supply of condoms, or other barrier methods which protect you against sexually transmitted diseases, or with your decision to use them during lovemaking.

At the end of the day, however, both men and women have to make the decision for themselves on

Basic Techniques

Caress with Confidence
▶ *Close physical contact which does not involve the exchange of body fluids is perfectly safe. You can caress and explore each other's bodies with peace of mind.*

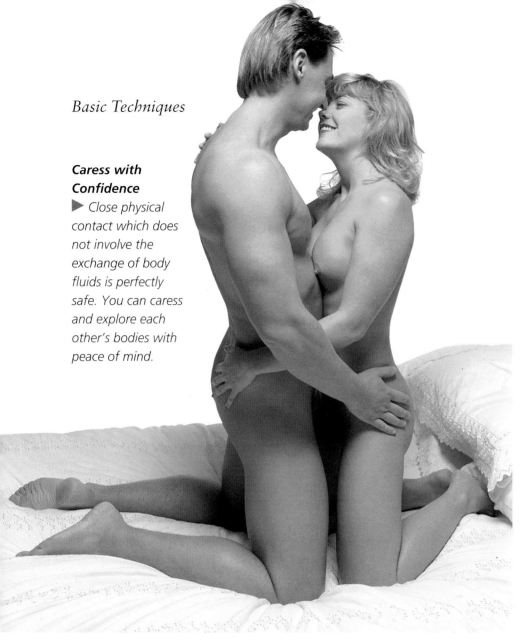

whether or not to use safer sex practices. This decision should be based, partly, on your own sense of self-worth and value for your health.

The bottom line is: if you want to use safer sex methods and your potential lover refuses, for whatever reason, you will need to delay any sexual activity involving the exchange of body fluids until you have reached a mutual agreement; or even be prepared to forgo a full sexual relationship with that person.

Long-Term Relationships

If you are already in an established relationship, you may believe that you do not need to consider safer sex issues. This is so only if the relationship is truly monogamous and you are both absolutely sure of the safety

of each other's sexual and drug-related past. For the various reasons mentioned before, it is virtually impossible to know the whole truth because you can rarely vouch for the sexual history of all previous partners who have been linked by sexual activity. As a couple, you should examine and discuss all the implications involved before making a decision on whether or not to start or abandon safer sex practices.

The HIV Test

The HIV antibody can take up to three months to develop and be detected in a blood test after the virus has been transmitted. HIV testing is one possibility for couples who are willing to commit and be monogamous with each other and want a

sexual relationship without using safer sex practices. There are, however, quite contrasting professional views as to whether this is an advisable or necessary step to take.

In any event, it is not a decision to be taken lightly, and all people testing for HIV should first receive proper counselling as to its advisability in their particular situation. This help can usually be obtained from health specialists attached to the STD clinics or specialized hospital departments. The decision to test for HIV must always be an individual one, and no one should allow themselves to be coerced into taking it.

Risky Behaviour

While considering safer sex issues, it is important not to become over anxious or alarmist. The HIV virus has a low infectivity rate, cannot survive long outside the human body, and is spread only when it enters the bloodstream through the exchange of body fluids. You cannot catch it from sharing utensils such as cups, knives and forks with an infected person, or from normal physical contact such as hugging or holding hands.

Transmission of the virus from sexual activity is only possible if either you or your partner are already infected.

However, it is essential for all sexually active people to become well acquainted with the facts of the disease and to put into practice safer sex methods whenever there is even the slight risk of infection.

The following activities are considered to present the highest risk:
Anal intercourse without condoms:
The blood vessels in the rectum can easily rupture with the friction of sexual activity, creating a high

risk of infection if one or other partner carries the virus.

Vaginal intercourse without condoms: Vaginal fluids and semen can both contain the HIV virus, as can the menstrual blood flow. Broken blood vessels, and small abrasions either in the vagina or on the penis can allow the virus to enter the bloodstream.

Multiple partners and casual sex: The more sexual partners someone has, the greater exposure to the risk of infection of all STDs, including the HIV virus. In the case of casual sex affairs, it is unlikely that you will know the full sexual history of that person.

Sharing needles: Although this is not a sexual activity, anyone who has been an intravenous drug user and has ever shared a contaminated syringe or needle with another person has a high risk of HIV infection. That person's sexual partners are also at risk if safer sex precautions are not used.

The following sexual activities carry less but some risk:

Oral sex: The HIV virus in semen and vaginal fluids will normally be destroyed by stomach acids if ingested. However, the risk of infection increases if the partner giving fellatio (when the woman gives oral sex to the man) or cunnilingus (when the man gives oral sex to the woman) has any small cuts, sores, or ulcers in the mouth, or bleeding gums. To minimize risk, condoms should be used during fellatio and latex barriers can be used during cunnilingus.

Intercourse with condoms: The use of condoms and other barrier methods reduces the risk of disease transmission by 98 per cent, so long as all the safer sex precautions are used. The risk lies in not following the proper procedures for barrier method protection, or in the accidental tearing of the rubber causing a spillage of semen or vaginal fluids.

Sharing sex toys: You should not share a sex toy with your partner because of the risk of cross-infection.

Safer Sex Activities

This term refers to all physical contact that does not involve the exchange of body fluids or create broken skin or bleeding. This still leaves many delightful ways to enjoy your sex life.

The following suggestions should present no risk so long as there are no open sores or cuts to the skin which could allow cross-infection. To be extra safe, cover any open wounds on the skin, however small, with adhesive plaster.

Cuddling, hugging and caressing: These are all perfectly safe and wonderful ways to make physical contact.

Kissing: Mouth to mouth or dry kissing is fine. Deep or "French" kissing and saliva exchange is only minimally risky if there are open

Safe and Exciting
▲ *Safer sex need not mean boring sex. Couples can explore and enjoy a whole range of exciting sensual and sexual practices. By stroking, massaging and caressing each other you will become more familiar with your partner's body and its unique erogenous responses.*

Enhance Your Pleasure
▲ *Kissing, licking, nuzzling and touching are all safer sex practices which can only add greater pleasure to your sexual relationship as well as extending your range of foreplay techniques. As your relationship develops, you will learn how your lover likes to be caressed.*

cuts, bleeding gums or ulcers in the mouth.

Licking, nibbling and sucking: Go ahead and enjoy yourselves, but ensure that you do not bite so hard that you break the skin.

Masturbation: Self-masturbation is fine. So is mutual masturbation, so long as you take care that body fluids, such as semen and vaginal fluids, do not penetrate the skin. Keep all skin abrasions covered.

How To Use Condoms

Learn to regard the use of condoms as a natural addition to your lovemaking techniques. There are a few tips to make this easier. Don't wait

In Place Before Penetration

 *The condom should be in place on the man's penis before any kind of penetrative sex takes place as pre-ejaculation seminal fluid can also contain the HIV virus.*

Choosing Condoms

Condoms are also popularly known as "rubbers", and "French letters". Once you and your partner decide that safer sex is caring sex the use of condoms can have a really positive place in your lovemaking. Condoms are about 98 per cent reliable when used as a barrier method during penetrative or oral sex to protect against infection of sexually transmitted diseases, including herpes and HIV.

Nowadays, there are many varieties of condoms to choose from, and you can experiment with different brands. Flavoured condoms can make protected oral sex more enjoyable and palatable, and coloured ones add to the fun. Some condoms are already lubricated and covered with spermicide, while others are not.

You should always use a water-based lubricant, such as KY jelly, and not an oil-based one, such as petroleum jelly, which can interact with the rubber and damage it. Lubricated condoms are less likely to tear with friction. Always check that you are using a suitable condom and lubricant. Look for the use-by date on the condom packet as the rubber can deteriorate with age, and always store condom packets away from direct sunlight, heat, perfumes and sharp objects.

In the United States, condoms from certified manufacturers will have an expiration date and lot number. They will have passed stringent tests by the International Standards Association. In the United Kingdom, check for the Kitemark guarantee on the packet, though it is important to be aware that this is usually a statement of suitability for vaginal sex rather than anal sex. Especially strong condoms are now made for anal sex.

---

until you are too fired up with passion before debating whether or not to use a condom. Discuss and agree on this issue as soon as you know you are going to make love. Keep the condom packet on you, close to the bed, or under the pillow, so you know where to find it at the crucial moment. The suggestions listed below can ensure that your condom usage will bring you maximum safety and pleasure.

❖ Open the packet carefully and ease the condom out, taking care that you do not snag it on your jewellery or fingernails.

❖ At this point, do not start to unroll the condom. Make sure you have the condom round the right way, with the rolled up ring on the outside, and just squeeze its tip between your index finger and

Penis Must Be Erect

▲ *Wait till the penis is erect before putting on the condom, otherwise it can easily slip off.*

thumb to dispel air. (Most condoms have a teat at the tip to collect the ejaculated sperm.)

❖ The man can either put the condom on by himself, or his partner can do it for him as part of their foreplay. Ensure the penis remains erect while putting it on.

❖ Unroll the sheath down to the end of the penis. If there is no teat, then leave about 1cm/¹/₂in spare at the top to collect the semen.

❖ The vagina should be moist before penetration, for the woman's comfort and to avoid tearing the condom with dry friction. You can smear a little water-based lubricant over the outside of the rubber, or either of you can carefully insert extra lubricant inside her vagina, if necessary.

❖ While making love, check to see if the condom is still in place, as it can sometimes slip off. After ejaculation, the man should hold the base of the condom securely with his fingers while he withdraws his penis from the vagina before he loses his erection. This will prevent the condom coming off and causing a spillage of semen in or around the vagina.

❖ Wrap the used condom securely in tissue and dispose of it safely. It is advisable not to flush it down the toilet. Never re-use a condom.

Keep It In Place

▶ *Once in place, the ring of the condom should fit comfortably at the base of penis and remain there during the whole of the lovemaking session. If the penis becomes soft during lovemaking, hold the ring of the condom with your fingers to keep it in place until the full erection has resumed.*

Ways to Stay Aroused

▼ *The woman can keep her man in a state of arousal by manually stroking the shaft of his penis, and saying sexy things about him, as he rolls down the condom. If the female partner is putting the condom on her partner's penis, he or she can stroke it so that he stays erect.*

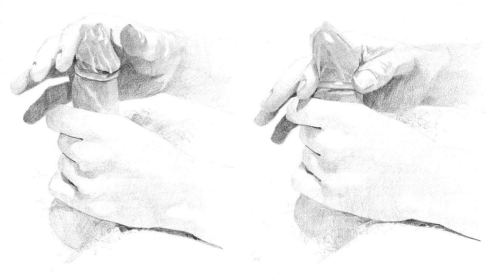

Other Barrier Methods

In addition to the male condom, there are other barrier methods that can be used for safer sex practices. The female condom, which lines the vagina, is claimed by its manufacturer to be 98 per cent effective against the transmission of sexually transmitted diseases, provided it is used correctly.

Alternatively, there are latex barriers, which are also used in dentistry where they are known as dental dams. These are small sheets of thin rubber which can

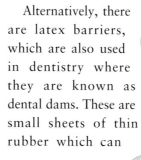

be placed over the vulva to make oral sex or cunnilingus safer. They act to prevent vaginal fluids or menstrual blood from passing into the mouth which can present a risk to your partner if he has open cuts, sore or bleeding gums, or mouth ulcers.

Latex barriers can also be placed over the anus to prevent the spread of disease if either of you enjoy "rimming", the name given to oral anal stimulation. Latex barriers can be obtained from medical suppliers, and sex aid suppliers may stock flavoured and coloured varieties.

Undressing Each Other

Whether your relationship is new or well established, there is always a delicate moment of transition when it moves into a more intimate and sexual dimension and you both know that you want to make love. Men and women have developed all sorts of signals, both subtle and overt, to convey to their partners that they are ready for sex. So now is the moment to get undressed, to expose and reveal your bodies to each other, to explore one another and to become naked in body and desire.

Getting undressed with your lover is an important part of foreplay, an art in itself, a vital scenario in the theatre of love. Of course, you can tear off your clothes, or each other's, throw them into a heap and leap into bed. Sometimes, when passions are running high, that uninhibited approach is all part of the fun. Or you may be shy about your body, have judgements about it, and end up trying to get undressed surreptitiously in the bathroom or under the bed clothes. Getting undressed and being naked in front of a lover can be very traumatic for some people.

You may prefer to take off your own clothes and present yourself naked in front of your partner. But if you are shy, and your relationship is new, then you could choose to get undressed alone, and slip on an attractive dressing gown before returning to the bedroom.

Dressing For Undressing

For the bold and uninhibited and for couples who like to bring fantasy into their love lives, why not try a tantalizing strip-tease for your partner. However, undressing each other, slowly and lovingly, letting each part of the body reveal itself when the moment feels right, is a romantic way to become unclothed in your prelude to making love.

If the love scenes in movies are anything to go by, undressing your partner is guaranteed to be a smooth and graceful operation. Clothes slip like silk off the skin, buttons undo

themselves and, most certainly, the bra fastener pops open with the greatest of ease.

It is rarely like that in real life, and most people have had embarrassing moments of fumbling and fiddling with fasteners, zips that stuck, or jeans and skirts which simply refused to budge past the thighs. If any of these situations happen then you may need to give your lover a hand or take off the awkward item of clothing yourself.

You do not always know when you are going to make love but if you have a suspicion that sex is on the agenda, dress with undressing in mind. Simplify your clothing so it can be removed easily, and avoid wearing items which leave marks on your skin. Don't be caught out wearing your oldest and most ragged piece of underwear, your woollen thermals, baggy Y-fronts, string vests, socks with holes, or immovable bra. What you have on next to your skin should add to your allure, and that applies both to men and women.

If you have time to prepare, put on soft lighting. Low-light lamps or candlelight will spread a more flattering and romantic glow in the room, softening your skin tones and body shape. Background music can help you to relax, so have your favourite tapes close at hand.

Strip-teasing

▼ *Try to make the act of undressing part of your love play. Slowly undressing each other and allowing your mutual nakedness to reveal itself, stage by stage, will intensify your desire for one another. As each item of clothing slips from the body, pay your partner a compliment, mentioning not just the obvious sexual areas, but also the eyes, hair, mouth, skin, hands, feet and so on.*

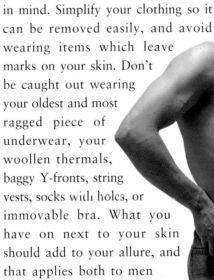

Opening Moves

▶ If you have been petting, hugging and kissing each other, you may need to signal that you are ready for more. It is sometimes a relief for the man when the woman decides to take the initiative, giving him signs that she wants to go further. Slowly undoing his belt buckle and trouser zip should really do the trick!

Slow and Steady

▲ Now it is his turn to make a move. Take things slowly and let your mutual anticipation of pleasure build up gradually. Open the buttons carefully one by one, and joke about it if one gets stuck. Telling her just how much you have been looking forward to this moment of love will help to put her at ease.

Touching and Kissing

▶ Getting undressed should be part of the whole lovemaking experience rather than a means to an end. As the clothes begin to slip from her body, continue to touch and kiss her.

Keeping Active

▼ She is going to need to move around so that you can remove her outer clothing with ease. Part of the fun of undressing each other is to constantly exchange the active and passive roles. As her body becomes more exposed, stay sensitive to her signals so that she feels happy and relaxed about what is happening.

Baring It All

Removing the top layer of clothing is an art to master, but even more sensual skill is needed when you start to take off each other's underwear. You are going to be naked and vulnerable and also, very turned on. There is something very erotic about starting your foreplay with your underwear still on. At this point, you know you want to make love, but the presence of this scant clothing against your skin makes the whole situation more tantalizing. It creates an exciting sense of seduction as if you are saying to each other: "I want you and I know you want me but let's not take anything for granted."

Some couples like to make love while still wearing an item of clothing because a half-exposed body is more exciting to them, or they find certain types of underwear or lingerie inspire their sexual fantasies and hot up their sex lives.

The Esquire Report, *Men on Sex* reveals that many men find it more arousing to see their partners partially clothed rather than totally naked. The reason given was that it added to the air of expectation and anticipation even in a long-term relationship.

Also, keeping some clothes on encourages you to extend your time of foreplay, allowing you to embrace, kiss and caress longer before intercourse which gives your bodies more time to warm up and tune in to each other's mounting sexual feelings. If either one of you is shy or nervous about being seen naked or of making love, the lingering presence of these clothes will give you the extra time you need to relax.

Fun of Unfastening

▲ *Wearing a front-fastening bra will make the undressing manoeuvres easier for him. If it closes at the back, lean into his body and snuggle up to him, whispering some sexy words while he focuses on the job in hand.*

Sexy Texture

▲ *As you stroke and touch one another, the brush of the cloth against your breasts and genitals can be very arousing. Only you will know the point when you are ready to remove all your clothes.*

Getting Undressed

Jane, aged 42, a nurse: "I've always been a little shy about undressing in front of a man, and I prefer to make my appearance in the bedroom already undressed but covered with a slinky, silk kimono. I feel most relaxed about it when I'm involved in a deeply trusting relationship, then somehow, if I feel relaxed, sensual and sexy enough, my skin just seems to ·have a special glow and I lose my inhibitions."

Lucy, aged 26, a production assistant: "I'm all for the bodice-ripping stuff and getting on with it the first time around. If I undress too slowly, then I'm afraid the man is going to be checking out my body too much. My fantasy, though, is to find a relationship with a man I trust enough, and who knows my body well enough, that I can undress for him by doing a slow strip-tease."

Ernie, 32, a photographer: "I prefer mutual undressing because it is less threatening. It's more playful and the power is shared. I find it very sexy."

Don, aged 28, a courier: "When I am going to have sex with my girlfriend, I like it best if we undress slowly and start doing it with some of our clothing on. I think it adds something 'naughty but nice' to the whole thing. It adds a bit of extra excitement as if we shouldn't really be going the whole way – though we both really know that we are."

Voyage of Discovery

► As her bra falls from her body, and her breasts are exposed, cradle them in your hands to acknowledge their soft, sensual beauty. Touch and stroke her naked belly, letting your fingers slip under the panty line with just a hint of exploration.

Brief Encounter

▼ Your man will be thrilled if you show your desire for him by removing his underpants. Roll them down slowly over his buttocks, allowing him to touch you while you do so.

Unpeeling Her Panties

▲ When you remove her panties, try not to do so with indecent haste! She'll enjoy the feeling of having them peeled away from her like the skin of a forbidden fruit. Edge them down little by little, stroking and squeezing her buttocks gently. In certain positions, you can pull her close to your body to kiss and caress her at the same time.

Naked Passion

▲ Once the clothes are removed and there's nothing more to hide, your foreplay enters into a new and exciting stage. The whole body is available for all the touches of love that you can lavish on each other. Take some moments just to be there with each other, savouring and enjoying your own and your lover's nakedness.

Sensual Play

The term "sensual play" is probably more apt than "foreplay" to describe all the many wonderful, caring, romantic, sensual and sexual activities that a man and woman can engage in to express their attraction and love for each other. "Foreplay" usually refers to those sexual techniques that lovers can use to arouse each other to ensure satisfactory intercourse and orgasm. As such, it implies an activity with a goal in mind, something that comes before the real thing, a little like the hors-d'oeuvres before the main meal – a nice taster but not quite substantial enough in itself.

While this section mostly focuses on sensual play in the context of love-making, it can actually start from the moment two people become attracted to each other. It manifests in body language signalling a desire to become more intimate with each other. It includes holding hands, cuddling, hugging, kissing and the exchange of sweet words.

It plays a part in the way partners choose to spend time together – dancing to music, going to the theatre, walking in the woods, arranging candlelit dinners, and the exchange of small but meaningful gifts. Sensual play acknowledges the special relationship, both sexually and emotionally, that you have developed with your chosen partner, whether that person is a new or long-term lover. It is not a set programme of techniques but more a response to, and an acknowledgement of, the whole person – body, mind and spirit – which makes you and your partner unique and special to each other.

It is important to give it the time and space it needs, both outside and inside the bedroom, for it will nurture and enhance your relationship, so that it remains caring and sensual, warm and erotically alive.

Comforting Contact

▼ *Sensual contact may be as simple as a cuddle for comfort and closeness, a massage for relaxation, kisses to show affection, caresses to soothe or pamper, or moments spent looking tenderly into each other's eyes. All of these can be the start of a sexual journey, but they can also be relished purely for their own sake.*

Kissing

Kissing is one of the most intimate aspects of sensual foreplay and love-making because, in addition to being sexually arousing, it reveals the degree of affection and tenderness which exists between you and your lover. Attitudes towards kissing change from culture to culture, and in some parts of the world it plays a very small role, if any, in the sexual relationship. Most of us, though, regard it as a highly personal part of our lovemaking which reflects emotional closeness. From our earliest memories, kissing is associated with warm and caring contact, and some people find it easier to have full penetrative sex for purely physical sensation and release than to kiss mouth to mouth without a certain depth of loving feeling.

Kissing usually plays a big part in the early stages of romance as a way of exploring sexual compatibility and expressing attraction and tenderness. However, it can become a sadly neglected activity once the relationship has become firmly established and is taken for granted. One of the most common

Kiss and Tell

Jacqueline, aged 28, a secretary, has been married for four years: "To be honest, kissing is the best part for me. If my husband doesn't kiss me enough, I just don't get that turned on. When he takes the time to kiss me properly, I feel he is appreciating me rather than just my body."

Roger, aged 27, unemployed, has a long-term girlfriend: "I used to be an action man, you know, straight to the point. When I met Louise, she was keen on lots of kissing and foreplay. I started to really enjoy it too, and sometimes now we just kiss and cuddle for ages before going on to anything else. It's great."

Avril, 31, a model, is currently single: "I love kissing, but I hate it when I've just met someone and he tries to stick his tongue in my mouth straight away. I prefer to be seduced into a full French kiss, and even then, only after the first few dates. How a man kisses me tells me a lot about how he is going to make love to me."

Fred, 62, a taxi driver, has been married for thirty-two years: "We are from the old school, and we didn't have a full sexual relationship until we were married. We were courting for several years and it was very romantic, but all we did was pet and kiss. Those kisses were lovely and so full of promise. Even now, we make sure we kiss each other every day."

complaints made by women in long-term relationships is that their men do not kiss them often enough, either as a purely romantic and affectionate gesture, or as part of their sexual lives. Too often, a sexual relationship can settle down to the basics, where arousal techniques are focused purely on intercourse and orgasm, while the subtler expressions of love and tenderness, such as kissing, are regularly overlooked. Let kissing remain an important part of your physical interaction outside the bedroom, as well as an integral part of your foreplay and lovemaking.

Tender Touches

▶ *Kissing during a sexual episode can change from being tender and sweet to deep and passionate. It can start with the gentle brushing of the lips over the face. Kissing the forehead is an especially caring and affectionate gesture. So is planting little kisses on her nose and cheeks.*

Tease with Kisses

▶ *Playful kisses are also exciting. You can lift his face towards yours and teasingly kiss him all around his chin and jaw, moving down to the erotically sensitive areas of the neck and throat.*

Savour the Moment

▼ *Having taken your time to enjoy the sensuality of lip-to-skin contact, let eager anticipation grow as your mouths come closer together. As your lips meet, close your eyes to savour this deliciously intimate moment.*

Gentle Kisses
◀ When you first begin to kiss, let your mouths and lips relax together so that they become soft and yielding to one another. Don't rush into a deep, passionate kiss too soon. The longer you can delay before inserting your tongue into your partner's mouth, the more sensual and stimulating the kissing will be as it slowly begins to build up into an erotically charged embrace. Try kissing all around the edges of the lips, then run the tip of your tongue over them, as this can also be very sexy.

Passionate Embrace
▶ The chemistry between you both will heat up once the tongue enters the mouth – but don't thrust it immediately towards the throat. Instead, roll it languidly over the teeth and trace the moist contours of the mouth's interior. Then, let your tongues move and dart together to initiate a sexual rhythm, setting the pace for what is to follow. The act of kissing each other, gently and slowly, or passionately, can involve you both so deeply that you can begin to feel as if you are dissolving together. It can keep you attuned and responsive in both body and mind, while increasing your sexual arousal.

Thrusting Tongues
▶ During intercourse, kissing can become very exciting if it imitates the movements of coitus. As you hold each other tight, your lips may meet with a new sense of urgency and your tongues will seek each other to dance together to the tempo of the pelvic thrusts.

Be Spontaneous

Sensual play is tremendously important to your emotional happiness and your sexual life. Forget the pre-conditioned programmes and learn to pleasure each other's bodies in ways that acknowledge the needs of the heart, mind and emotions of your partner at any particular moment. Also, become more aware of your own physical and emotional needs which will require different degrees of tactile stimulus depending on your own shifts in mood.

Acknowledge that there are times when either of you may want to be hugged and held, kissed and stroked, but may not necessarily be ready for full sexual intercourse. Couples often hold back from comforting physical contact because they are afraid it will lead to sexual intercourse for which they are not ready. If either you or

your partner are under stress and simply not in the mood for sex, or if you have an infection or disability that would make intercourse unwise or undesirable, there is no need to abstain from loving physical contact. In its broadest sense physical contact answers a huge spectrum of human needs, sexual and non-sexual, as well as a certain sensual state which exists between the two.

Becoming Sexually Alive

Play with each other's bodies in such a way that you enjoy each touch for its own sake, and try not to worry about achieving an orgasm, because that will create a subtle tension. Every person has different sexual responses, so explore with each other what turns you both on.

There is no specific programme of foreplay techniques that will be able

Hygiene Matters

Sensual foreplay means close physical contact with every part of your body, so take special care of your hygiene so that your body is fresh, clean and smelling good. Nothing is quite such a turn-off as unpleasant body odours, bad breath, smelly feet or dirty nails. Bathe or shower beforehand, alone or – even better – together, and try adding a few drops of luxuriant aphrodisiac essential oils, such as jasmine, ylang-ylang, patchouli or sandalwood, to the bath water. If you have eaten a spicy meal, garlic or onions beforehand, smoked a cigarette, or drunk alcohol, make sure that you clean your teeth and rinse out your mouth.

Some people enjoy "rimming" in foreplay, the term used for anal stimulation. If you do practise this, make sure you wash your fingers before inserting them into the vagina as you risk spreading bacterial infection to its delicate tissues. Taking special care about your hygiene is a statement of your self-esteem and also shows you care about your partner.

Sensual Celebration
◀ Sensual play can achieve something greater and more holistic than foreplay. It can be a wholly satisfying experience in itself, an expression of love, and a celebration of the playful, sensual and erotic capacity of the human body.

to guarantee sexual success. What pleased and thrilled a previous partner may not be as exciting or acceptable to a new one. Also, sexual responses vary, not just from person to person, but at different psychological and biological stages of life and even day to day.

Learn to recognize your own sexual needs and those of your partner, and enjoy experimenting so you do not fall into boring patterns. It is not always easy to guess what a partner wants at any particular time, so be prepared to talk to each other about your likes and dislikes.

When something feels good, say so or make appreciative sounds. If it does not feel good, there is no need to criticize. Just say to your partner something like: "I would really like you to do this to me," and then be prepared to explain or demonstrate exactly how you want to be touched. Rather than focusing your whole attention on the most obvious sexual areas, such as the genitals or breasts, read the section on erogenous zones to appreciate how the whole body can be responsive to erotic touch. Enjoy the exploration so that you can turn your foreplay into a delightful variety of sensual play.

Making it Last

◀ *Take time to include sensual play as foreplay so that lovemaking lasts longer and is more luxurious, making every cell of your body come alive and more responsive while letting yourselves become emotionally open and relaxed with each other. In this way your sexuality can envelop your whole being.*

Stoking the Fires

▲ *Sensual play includes all forms of touch, such as stroking, caressing and holding, or oral contact, such as kissing, nibbling, sucking and licking. It can involve every part of the body. Sucking on his fingertips or rolling your tongue around them will certainly fire up his imagination.*

Fun and Foreplay

▲ *Humour is an important part of foreplay. It takes away the seriousness of performance-related sex and helps you both unwind and relax so your bodies feel completely at ease with each other. Play fighting, gentle bites, giggling, making sounds, rolling on the bed together can all be part of the fun.*

Touching the Whole Person

There are no rules to sexuality except what feels good or right to the people involved. There are times when the passion is high and the "quickie" way of having sex is exciting and welcome to both parties. More often, though, extended loving foreplay is important to a sexual relationship, because it enhances the emotional bond, and helps the man and woman become sufficiently aroused so that the ensuing lovemaking is compatible and deeply satisfying to both people.

This is particularly important for a woman, who needs more time than a man to become sexually aroused, and whose sexual responses are heightened when she feels emotionally and physically cherished. Also a woman's whole body is erotically sensitive to loving touches, not just the most obvious erogenous zones, such as her genitals and breasts.

It would be a great mistake, though, to believe that foreplay is primarily a "woman's thing", and that it is something a man should learn to do just to satisfy his partner and be deemed a good lover. Men are sensual beings too, and can also enjoy full body stimulation, loving and playful strokes, kissing, licking and all kinds of erotic tactile contact.

A man who is relaxed in his sexuality will enjoy extended foreplay for its own sake, for his pleasure as well as his partner's. It will help him to be less genitally orientated so that he can feel all kinds of wonderful sensations throughout his body. He is then more emotionally in tune with his partner.

If he relaxes into full body sensuality, a man can be more spontaneous and less programmed to performance. He will be less anxious about all the sexual pressures to which men are invariably subjected, such as performing well, maintaining an erection, fear of a premature ejaculation, fear of emotional vulnerability, concern about whether his woman will have an orgasm before he ejaculates, and so on. Sensual play will be an emotionally nourishing experience for him too.

Text-book lovers, male or female, may achieve the sexual responses they seek from their lover, but the partner will know that the touches and techniques are more mechanical than loving, and geared to an ulterior motive. He or she may feel personally abandoned or used, even while being turned on. Most women dislike the experience of having a man zone in on their breasts or clitoris, and having them rubbed or stimulated purely to achieve sexual stimulation.

Similarly, a sensual man may not be keen on having a woman grab for his crotch as a way of achieving an instant turn-on. Bodies are not separate from the feelings of the person within them. They are not machines to be geared to results, regardless of their intrinsic emotional and subtle responses. Sensual play gives time for both men and women to warm up and tune in to each other, on both somatic and psychic levels.

Tools of Arousal

▲ *Any part of the body can become a sensual tool in foreplay. The sweep of your hair, the soft brush of your nipples and breasts against his body, or the warmth of your breath on his skin will be extremely arousing to him. Trailing your fingertips or nails lightly over his skin will heighten its sensitivity. Try to involve your whole body in sensual play, so that even while kissing one part of his body, you are aware of the impact of your thighs, belly, and pubic area as they press gently against him.*

Body Worship

▼ *A woman's whole body, not just her most obvious sexual areas, is an erogenous zone. Take time to let your kisses and touches worship her total sensuality. Focus your attention not just on the front of her body, but on her arms, legs and back. Cover her back with a carpet of kisses, following its sensuous curves and lines. Then stroke and gently squeeze the muscles in her buttocks and thighs so that they become warm and erotically alive.*

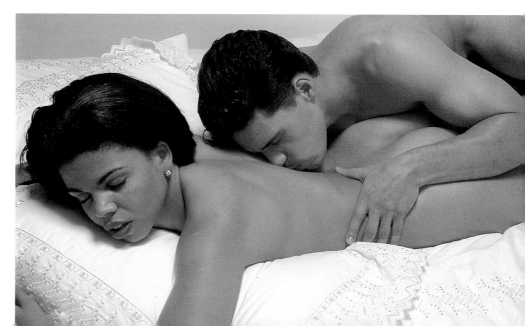

Loving Touches

► *Your man will also enjoy having your touches and kisses on the back of his body. This can include massaging the legs, kissing and licking the highly sensitive soft skin at the back of the knees, stroking, pummelling and squeezing the buttocks, and lightly scratching your fingernails over his skin to excite sensory nerve endings. In this way, the whole body will be suffused with sensual feelings.*

Tongue and Toe

▼ *The feet and toes are remarkably sensitive to tactile stimulation if your partner is not too ticklish. Rubbing and massaging the feet can be followed by deliciously erotic toe sucking. Run your tongue around her toes, sucking on them playfully one by one. Special attention can be given to the big toe which, according to zone therapy, has a special connection with the pituitary gland, which regulates the sex hormones.*

Wave of Passion

► *Your extended foreplay should give you time to relax together emotionally, as well as becoming sexually aroused. If you enjoy it for its own sake, rather than proceeding headlong*

towards a goal, you can savour moments of tenderness and touching purely to enhance your intimate connection. Do not be afraid to let your states of arousal rise and fall like waves in the ocean. Once you are in harmony, both physically and emotionally, you can ride those waves together, letting one peak of excitement ebb to give way to another. Touching, stroking, caressing and eye contact will keep you closely attuned to each other.

Sexual Arousal

Extended foreplay allows the whole body to become flooded with sex hormones so that the correct physiological changes can occur to ensure harmonious lovemaking. For a woman, sufficient arousal will allow her vagina to undergo changes which enable successful and comfortable penetration during intercourse. The outer and inner lips of her vagina will swell and secrete lubricants, to give off her own special sexual scent. The shape of her vagina will change, so that the outer third becomes narrower and better able to grip the penis to

ensure adequate friction, while the inner two-thirds of the vagina expands. It, too, will secrete a sexual lubricant as she becomes excited. Her clitoris also enlarges, as it becomes engorged with blood, and its nerve network becomes erotically sensitized.

As a woman's arousal increases, her breasts may increase slightly in size, and her nipples become erect. If the sensual play which has preceded intercourse has acknowledged her whole person, then physically and emotionally she should feel vibrant and receptive and ready to receive her man.

Loving and sensuous foreplay benefits the man because it can take the sexual charge away from his genital area so that it streams through his whole body, enabling him to become more relaxed and better able to enjoy full body pleasure without the fear of ejaculating too soon. If intercourse is to be the result of the foreplay, when the excitement grows the right tactile stimulation will enable him to achieve a full erection. As his arousal increases, the scrotum skin thickens, and the testes draw up closer to his body. In some men, nipple erection during arousal is also common.

Secret Zones

◄ *A woman's body has many surprising and hidden areas of sexual sensitivity. Sensual play allows you to unravel its mysteries, so that you both can discover new and exciting pleasure places. The underarm and armpit can be very responsive to your loving attention. Try rolling your tongue languidly over its soft skin while gently stroking her breast.*

Breast Care

▶ *A woman's breasts are one of her most erogenous areas, but their responsiveness to tactile stimulation may vary, depending on her mood or the phase of her menstrual cycle. Always be sensitive to them and to her responses, and do not zone in on them before she is ready for such intimate contact. Gentle palpation of the breasts can feel great, but remember her breasts are glands and not muscles, so handle them with care.*

Increase Arousal

▼ *When your woman is sexually aroused, you will notice changes to the shape of her breasts as they begin to swell; the areola darkens and the nipples become erect. Licking and trailing your tongue around the areola at this point will be highly exciting to her, increasing her eager anticipation as your lips move closer to her nipple.*

Chest Massage

▼ *Many men love to have their nipples kissed, licked and stroked during foreplay. In some men, just as in women, the nipples will also become erect when they are sexually aroused. Stroking, kissing and massaging his chest can help him contact his more emotional and vulnerable feelings as well as increasing his whole-body sensuality.*

Peaks of Pleasure

▲ *When sexually excited, the nipples seem magically connected to her whole nervous system, sending waves of pleasure down through her body to her genitals. Kissing, licking, sucking and flicking your tongue over the nipple will bring her to a peak of arousal. Pay loving attention to both breasts, moving from one to the other, and tell her how beautiful and special they are to you.*

Basic Techniques

Warm and Welcoming

▼ *The soft roundness of her belly will welcome your loving kisses as your lips move down her body. This vulnerable area needs your attention so it can become charged with sexual energy. Kiss it tenderly all over, run your tongue teasingly around the navel, and warm the skin with your breath. Work slowly down to her pubic area. Stroking and rubbing her mons with your fingers and tugging gently on the pubic hair will enhance clitoral stimulation. Kissing along her groin can also produce wonderful sensations.*

Guiding Hand

▲ *Ask your man to show you exactly how he likes his penis to be touched. Stroking, rubbing and kissing his penis is all part of your sensual play. Being comfortable about touching this important part of his body will enhance your mutual satisfaction in lovemaking.*

Understanding Each Other

Even in close relationships, both men and women can be remarkably shy about discussing their sexual needs with each other, including what turns them on and what turns them off. This is partly because the sexual ego is very fragile and it is easy to feel rejected or to take any comments, other than highly positive ones, as criticism.

Talking about sexual issues requires delicate negotiation, being able to choose the right moment, a willingness on both sides to experiment and explore new methods, and a readiness to change old patterns. The latter can be particularly difficult if your methods have worked perfectly well on previous occasions or with another partner.

However, by not disclosing your sexual needs and preferences, there is a danger that you may become resentful and gradually withhold your sexuality altogether from your partner, or deaden your sensory responses so that your sexual life becomes more of a functional duty rather than a joyful celebration of your relationship.

Sexuality should not be imposed on the other person regardless of how he or she may feel. Much of the pleasure can be in the mutual exploration of each other's bodily responses. It is a two-way interaction, involving many subtle nuances and variations. You can jangle along together, or you can compose a symphony of love, touch, sensuality and eroticism which will always hit the right note, depending on your changing needs and moods.

How most men and women touch and want to be touched in their most erotically charged areas – the penis and clitoris – reveals quite opposite male and female needs. A man will often long to receive firmer touches to his penis during manual stimulation, while a woman generally prefers a more subtle approach to the stimulation of her clitoris, usually after she has become aroused. You can help each other by showing exactly how you like to be touched.

Many men and women experiment with genital touching during masturbation and usually perfect their technique in doing so. (See Self-Pleasuring, and Mutual Masturbation.) Watch each other masturbate, or guide your partner's hand or fingers with your own, showing the different pressures and strokes that you most enjoy and that are most likely to help you reach your peak of arousal.

Thighs and Sighs

▼ *Don't focus your attention solely on her clitoris, but regularly return your sensual touches to other parts of her body, especially the areas close by, so that the erotic sensations can stream through her body. The insides of her thighs are a very erogenous area. Cover the soft skin with kisses, bringing your lips a little closer each time to this most intimate part of her body.*

Just Connect

▼ *Foreplay can bring you both to a state of arousal, where intercourse is the desired conclusion. As sensual play, it can also be complete in itself without penetrative sex. Just pleasuring each other, exploring every part of the body with loving oral and tactile stimulation, can create a deep and mutual sexual and emotional connection, whether or not it eventually leads to orgasm or sexual intercourse.*

Clitoral Stimulation

Most women dislike having their clitoris roughly handled; it is an exquisitely sensitive part of their sexual anatomy. Correct stimulation of the clitoris is very important to a woman's sexual satisfaction and to her achieving an orgasm. Too much, too soon can be irritating and even painful.

Once your woman is aroused by more loving and sensual foreplay, and she is naturally producing her vaginal secretions, stroking, rubbing, licking, flicking the tongue back and forth and gentle sucking on the clitoris can create euphoric sensations throughout her whole body. However, she may not want you to focus stimulation directly onto her clitoris for a prolonged period of time, but would prefer if you also touched and palpated the surrounding areas, such as the vaginal lips and mons. Also,

from time to time, return your attention to other parts of her body which will be pulsating with pleasure and demanding your caresses.

If you are using your fingers to stimulate the clitoris, then lubrication is important. It is best to spread some of the sexual juices from her vagina onto her clitoris. Otherwise, use your own saliva, or, if necessary, an appropriate cream, gel or oil (make sure it is hypo-allergenic as the tissues here are very sensitive and delicate – scented creams should never be used).

Vary your rhythm, vibrations and movements, but remain alert to her responses, which she will indicate by the movements of her pelvis, and her sighs, moans, and words of encouragement. Do not be afraid to ask her what, exactly, she likes best.

Penile Stimulation

A man most definitely wants his penis to be handled with care, but he may well prefer firmer pressure and strokes than he is actually getting from you. Many women err on the side of being too timid in the way they handle their lover's penis. Ask your man to show you exactly what he likes. Watch him stimulate himself, and then let him put his hand over yours to move it up and down the glans and shaft. This way you can learn whether he likes short or long strokes, rapid or more sensual ones.

Remember, though, if you want to extend your foreplay, do not overstimulate his penis at this point, or you can bring your man to orgasm too soon. During sensual play, kissing and licking the penis and testicles tenderly, flicking your tongue over them, and saying appreciative things about this treasured part of his body, will make him feel especially good.

Oral-Genital Sex

Oral-genital sex can be one of the most enjoyable and sexually arousing options available to people who seek pleasure and fulfilment from a sexual relationship. The term refers to the sexual activity in which men and women stimulate each other's genitals by use of the mouth and tongue. When a woman receives this from a man it is called cunnilingus, and when a man receives this from a woman it is called fellatio. The degree to which a couple may include oral sex in their lovemaking will vary from one sexual episode to another and between one couple and another.

Many people like to include oral sex as a special intimacy to aid arousal in their foreplay, but prefer to attain orgasmic satisfaction through coitus. Others like it to be a complete sexual experience in itself, through which both sexes are able to achieve a deeply satisfying orgasm and emotional and physical intimacy, with or without intercourse.

A woman, who is more inclined to reach orgasm through clitoral and vulval stimulation rather than vaginal stimulation from the penis alone, can find it particularly beneficial to her arousal and subsequent sexual satisfaction. The soft moistness of the tongue and its sensual movements suits the delicate clitoral area very well, and is more likely to excite her and less likely to irritate than having a dry finger rubbed against the area during manual stimulation. If her partner is prone to ejaculate before she has reached her own peak of arousal, he can use his tongue to help her reach an orgasm.

The majority of men take special pleasure in receiving fellatio from their partners. Depending on the particular situation, a man may enjoy it purely as a method of arousal and then want to proceed towards full penetrative intercourse, or he may hope that his woman uses her mouth to bring him to orgasm.

Although oral sex is highly arousing, some men who have a tendency to ejaculate prematurely find that oral stimulation gives them greater control over their orgasmic processes than if they had vaginal sex without it. In other circumstances, the very thought or sight of seeing a woman performing fellatio, or the erotic sensations created by her tongue and mouth on his penis can very quickly bring a man to the peak of arousal. In this case, if the couple are looking forward to an extended period of lovemaking, it would be better to avoid overstimulating his penis through oral sex methods.

One of the most delightful aspects of oral sex is that it provides the opportunity for lovers to take it in turns to surrender themselves totally to simply giving or receiving loving and highly erotic attention. Some couples save oral sex for a special treat, perhaps only on a birthday, or on holiday, or to mark a romantic

Spread Your Loving Touch

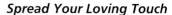 *She will be more receptive and eager for oral sex if she feels able to trust in your love for her and is already aroused by your mutual sensual play. Don't let her feel as if her clitoris and vagina are the only areas of her body you are interested in. Before, during and after cunnilingus, acknowledge her whole body and pay special attention to the areas surrounding her genitals, such as the belly, mons and thighs.*

anniversary. In a relationship that includes oral sex, only the couple involved will know from experience, when and how to use it to enhance their love life.

Cunnilingus

Your sexual partner is the best teacher in showing you exactly how to please her. Woman all have different responses, so experiment together and let her guide you with soft sighs, encouraging words, and pelvic movements to discover how your mouth and tongue can thrill her.

Most women would prefer to be aroused through sensual play, loving strokes, kisses, and whole body attention before they receive any direct stimulation of the clitoral area. This gives a woman time to produce and secrete her own love juices, so her vulva becomes receptive, warm, wet and welcoming.

Women often complain that men either neglect the clitoris or they zone in on it before they have become aroused, which can be irritating and painful. Before you begin to perform cunnilingus, kiss and excite all the areas adjacent to her genitals, then gently nuzzle and lick over her mons and vulva.

Her Arousal Blossoms

▲ *Nuzzle into her mons and vulva, seducing it with the warmth of your kisses. As she relaxes and becomes increasingly aroused, her vaginal lips will begin to swell and lubricate and produce her exotic sexual scent. When she is ready, this area will begin to open to you like a flower in the morning sun.*

When she is aroused, her clitoris will swell, as will the lips of her vulva. You can gently part her lips, and begin to thrill her with your tongue. Change your strokes and pressures and pay special attention to the areas surrounding her clitoris as this can be even more arousing. Let your tongue playfully stroke around the vagina, even thrusting a little into it. (Never blow air into her vagina. This can cause an air embolism and may be dangerous.) Change the

rhythm and action of your tongue, as too much sustained pressure can be irritating. You can also suck gently on her clitoris, and flick your tongue over it from side to side.

Be alert to her signals so that you can judge whether she wants you to take her all the way to orgasm, or would prefer to change to another activity. She might want to return the favour, or to take your penis into her vagina so that you can both orgasm in coitus. Cunnilingus can bring some

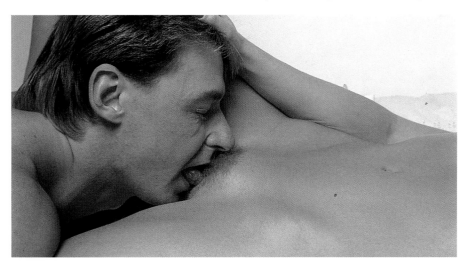

The Pleasure Builds

◀ *She will treasure you as a lover if you really learn to love this intimate part of her. Apply stimulation to her clitoris only after she is fully aroused, but don't focus directly on it all the time. She may find it more pleasing to have the areas surrounding the clitoris stroked by the moist softness of your tongue. Slowly build up the pressure, or speed up your strokes, but let the tempo vary. Be alert to her signals of pleasure.*

women into a multi-orgasmic state, so she may just want you to continue.

For other women, the clitoris becomes extremely sensitive after an orgasm. In that case, she probably won't want you to continue to stimulate it and may even move your head away. If you are sensitive to her cues, you can take her all the way to a state of ecstasy.

Fellatio

If you are performing fellatio on your man, it is probably a good idea to place one hand around the shaft of the penis so you can control his thrusting movements. In this way, you can overcome the fear that you might inadvertently choke. Your man should always let you remain in control of the movements, and he should refrain from thrusting deeply into your mouth, no matter how excited he is.

Teasing Touches

▼ *Work your way slowly and sensuously down his body towards his genitals, bringing the whole surface of his skin alive with your breath, lips, tongue and touches. Linger over his belly, kissing teasingly around the pubic area, and moving inch by inch closer to his genitals.*

Begin by nuzzling, fondling, kissing and licking his pubic area, penis and scrotum and stroking his perineum so he becomes more aroused and his erection increases. Then run your tongue over the most erotically sensitive parts of his penis – the top and around the ridge of its tip (the glans) – and along its shaft, flicking your tongue from side to side or up and down. Focus special attention on the underside of the penis as this part is particularly sensitive to stimulation.

Experiment with the movements of your tongue, changing its pressure and rhythm, and encourage him to tell you what he likes. Men generally prefer a strong, firm pressure on the penis, and sometimes complain that a woman's touch is too light and timid. He will enjoy you fondling his scrotum too, but remember that here you need a light touch as this is his most

delicate area. Once you have taken his penis into your mouth, ensure that your teeth don't make contact. Cover them with your lips – remember, his greatest fear is that you will bite or nip it by accident.

Prolonged fellatio may make your jaw ache, so rest your mouth if you need to, continuing the stimulation by hand in the meantime. Try to put yourself in your man's body and imagine what sensations he must be feeling and let your imagination guide you. (Despite the fact that fellatio is commonly referred to as a "blow job", never blow into your man's penis as this can be harmful.)

Ask him to let you know if he is going to orgasm – or be alert to his signals. It is up to you to decide whether you want him to ejaculate in your mouth, or would prefer to move on to another stage of lovemaking. You may be very willing to go all the way during fellatio, feeling that you are imbibing the very essence your man into yourself if you swallow his semen. It can bring you great pleasure because you know he will feel loved and totally accepted by you and that, in itself, can be deeply arousing.

You may, however, be willing to do this only if you feel secure and very much in love with your partner. It may be that you simply cannot stomach the idea of swallowing seminal fluid, even though you may feel fine about performing fellatio, or even of having your man ejaculate in your mouth. In that case, keep some tissues close at hand so that you can discreetly dispose of the seminal fluid from your mouth.

If you don't want him to ejaculate in your mouth, you can manually stimulate him to orgasm. Let him

come on another part of your body, rub his penis between your breasts until he ejaculates, or guide it into your vagina so you can carry on to intercourse.

Concerns and Objections

Many couples feel that oral sex is an integral and natural feature of their sex lives and, for some, it is the best part of it. Oral sex has always been an option for men and women in sexual relationships and the practice is recorded in ancient texts such as *The Kama Sutra*. However, at different times in history, and in different cultures, it has been considered deviant behaviour. In the early part of this century a request for oral sex could be considered grounds for divorce. In some states of America it was outlawed.

Research now shows that the majority of sexually active people have participated in oral sex at some point in their lives, though statistics indicate that more men than women enjoy it or put it at the top of their list of favourite sexual practices. This may have something to do with the fact that men are not always so skilled in performing oral sex to their women's satisfaction.

Women, too, can have deep anxieties about the smell, taste and appearance of their vaginal area. They may be against the idea of putting the penis into their mouths for fear of choking, or repulsed by the idea of swallowing seminal fluids if the man ejaculates.

Oral sex is a normal, healthy activity in an intimate relationship. However, if you do not want to do it, you should not consider yourself lacking or abnormal in any way. It is a very personal choice. You should never try to pressurize your partner, or be forced against your will into performing or receiving oral sex, or any other sexual activity, if either one of you objects, even if you participate in it on some occasions but are just not in the mood right now.

It is an extremely intimate activity, and should only be performed with total mutual consent. A partner's refusal to participate in oral sex may be rooted in deep moral or religious convictions and is not necessarily a rejection of the other person. Everyone has their own sexual boundaries and limits, and while many loving couples feel secure enough to abandon all or most of their sexual inhibitions, some individuals may genuinely need to set rules.

Discuss these issues honestly with each other because understanding and accepting each other's truths is an important part of a loving and intimate relationship. Some people, particularly women, can only participate in oral sex activities if they are deeply in love and feel the relationship is a committed one. They may come to enjoy oral-genital contact once the sexual relationship has become established and secure. Patience can often be rewarded.

Some of the objections people have to oral sex may be based more on fears, misconceptions and misinformation, such as that it is "dirty" or harmful, or they may have anxieties about the genitals being ugly, or smelling or tasting unpleasant. Such

Good Vibrations

▶ *When you are ready, take his penis into your mouth, to whatever depth you feel most comfortable. You can suck on his penis or vibrate your tongue over the shaft.*

Sexual Exploration

▼ *Many men love the sensation of having their scrotum gently stimulated by loving licks and kisses. Move his penis gently to one side and explore the whole area with your tongue, while stroking his thighs and buttocks and perineal region with your other hand.*

anxieties can usually be alleviated with gentle understanding, exploration and support. Reading sex manuals like this one, or speaking to a psycho-sexual counsellor can also help to alleviate unnecessarily inhibiting anxieties or phobias.

Smelling and Tasting Good

As a woman, probably your biggest concern about receiving oral sex is whether those intimate parts of you are going to taste and smell good to your man. Normally, your natural, special, musky, and earthy sexual scent and taste will be very appealing to him. Those men who are squeamish about vaginal secretions and

When To Abstain From Oral Sex

The chapter on Safer Sex explains the risks involved in HIV/AIDS transmission during oral-genital sex practices. If you are unsure about your own or your partner's health, or know little about each other's sexual history, then fellatio should be performed only when using a condom or, in the case of cunnilingus, a dental dam.

You should not participate in oral sex if you have an active cold sore around your mouth, or a genital herpes sore, or any other kind of infection or sexually transmitted disease, until it has been treated and cleared up. Oral sex is not advisable during a menstrual period because of the risk of blood-transmitted infections.

smells will probably avoid oral sex altogether, or move on quickly. The taste and smell of your sexual secretions can be affected, however, if you have eaten lots of spicy or garlic-flavoured food.

The secretions sometimes become more acrid or metallic tasting just before a menstrual period. Try sexual honesty, and ask your partner to let you know if the taste suddenly changes and he would rather abstain. If you notice a strong smell or discharge from your vagina, you may have an infection. In that case, put oral sex on hold and seek a medical check-up.

The normal amount of seminal fluid in each ejaculation is about a teaspoonful, and for those who are weight conscious, it contains about five calories. It has the constituency of raw egg white and tastes a little salty. Except in the case of infection or sexually transmitted disease (in which case oral sex should be avoided), there is no evidence to prove that swallowing semen is harmful in any way to a woman, providing she is a willing participant in the act.

Sixty-Nine

The name sixty-nine refers to a form of oral sex in which the man and woman take up a head-to-tail position to mutually pleasure each other. It is sometimes known as soixante-neuf – which is French for sixty-nine. It can be performed with one person lying on top of the other, but facing the opposite direction, so that both mouths are close enough to the genitals to apply simultaneous oral stimulation. In this position, it is usually preferable for the woman to be on top of her man because of the probable weight difference.

Another more comfortable position to take is with both partners lying on their sides, facing each other, but in opposite directions. The upper leg should be opened away from the genital area. Each partner can then place his or her head on the other's lower thigh so that mouths and tongues are close to the genitals.

Soixante-Neuf

▼ *The sixty-nine position is worth experimenting with and adding to your sexual repertoire.*

While the sixty-nine position in oral sex can lead to wonderfully erotic sensations, and can be taken all the way to mutual orgasm, it is often preferred as a part of foreplay, rather than as a full orgasmic experience in itself. One disadvantage of the practice is that it is quite difficult to really relax and enjoy the sensations you are receiving at one end of your body, while being actively involved at the other. You may also climax at different times.

If you do achieve an orgasm while receiving this kind of oral stimulation, you won't necessarily be able to control your responses or muscle contractions, and it is highly unlikely in these moments that you will be able to continue returning the favour.

Other Positions

Couples can be fantastically inventive with sexual positions once they feel relaxed about each other's bodies and are in the full flow of arousal. Here are some other suggested positions for giving and receiving oral-genital stimulation – though the chances are, you will create some more that are uniquely your own.

One partner can lie down with the other partner kneeling over the face, so that the genitals are close to the mouth. From this position, the active person can also stroke and squeeze the buttocks to give added stimula-

Kneel and Play
▲ She can sit on an armchair with legs spread over the arms while you kneel in front of her and adorn her vulva with succulent kisses, licks and all manner of exciting forms of oral play. In this position, she can relax completely, abandoning herself to overwhelming whole body sensations.

Sexual Hygiene
Careful hygiene precautions should be taken by both men and women before intimate sexual contact but there is no reason to believe that the genital area is a dirty, taboo or unclean part of the body just because it is "down there". Adequate bathing, or even washing each other's genitals in the shower before making love, should suffice. Special care should be taken to ensure the anal area is also clean before any intimate contact to avoid the risk of spreading infection or passing on a sexually transmitted disease. If there are any signs of irritation or discharge, sores or abrasions in the genital area of either sex, then abstain from any kind of genital contact and seek medical advice.

Armchair Arousal
◀ She can support herself while sitting back in an armchair or on the edge of the bed, while you arouse her with your mouth, and stroke her buttocks and thighs at the same time.

tion. If a woman is performing fellatio from this position, she should ring her man's penis with one hand so she can have full control over how much enters her mouth. The man should be careful not to thrust too hard.

Compatibility

There are no rules about the positions you take or the things you do while making love, except one – that both of you should feel physically and emotionally satisfied by the experience. Often, at the beginning of a relationship, you need time to gauge what gives pleasure and feels good, which movements work harmoniously and what pace and rhythm feels right. Lovemaking tends to improve as you get to know one another's preferences and responses. You then begin to fall in tune with each other in much the same way that musicians or dancers do when they continually practise their art together.

What will increase your sexual compatibility is not an array of impressive techniques, nor a unique sexual position, but intimacy and tenderness, and the willingness to learn from, and be open to, each other. The way you make love may change from one episode to another because the act of intercourse should reflect the mood and feelings of the moment, rather than following a pre-conceived pattern. Passionate love-making may feel exhilarating on one occasion, yet on another, a vulnerable and tender approach will suit your needs better.

Well tried and tested formulas of lovemaking may need to be jetti-soned if new lovers are to remain spontaneous with each other. What worked well in a past liaison may simply not be appropriate to a new sexual relationship. Everyone's timing, arousal levels and bodily responses are unique – unravelling those mysteries together is the key.

Sharing and Caring
▶ *Sexual intercourse is not just about body positions and movement, or skills and techniques – it involves the heart, mind and emotional being of each person concerned. Love and intimacy, and a sense of comfort, appreciation and sharing, are the main ingredients necessary to ensure that coitus satisfies and nurtures both parties.*

Time to Explore

▼ *With a new sexual relationship, allow plenty of time for sensuality, exploring your partner's body during foreplay, so that you get to know each other's physical responses. Being in tune with one another leads to compatible lovemaking.*

Whole-Body Contact

▲ *During intercourse, tactile contact should not be confined to the genitals alone. For example, the female partner can use her breasts and hair to caress the man's chest as she sensually sways her body from side to side. Continue touching and kissing the whole body throughout lovemaking.*

Enjoying the Afterglow

◄ *After making love, you can lie in each other's arms, bathed in a glow of contentment, rested, relaxed and nourished by the experience. For some people, these are the happiest moments of all.*

The Basic Positions

There are a number of lovemaking positions in common practice that most couples feel comfortable with. These allow both the man and woman to express themselves sexually in different ways by taking more active or passive roles in the lovemaking, and thereby eliciting a variety of physical and emotional responses. An equal and balanced sexual partnership is capable of sharing the more dominant and submissive roles quite easily, allowing a natural transfer between the two, either within one episode of lovemaking, or on different occasions.

Exploration, experimentation and a sense of humour are important to keep a sexual relationship interesting and alive. Once you feel comfortable and secure with each other, it is worth trying something new to add variety, fun, and excitement to your lovemaking.

Here, we sum up the basic lovemaking positions, and then on the following pages of this chapter, some of the more popular sexual positions assumed by couples in coitus will be discussed in greater detail. In other sections of this book you will find more adventurous positions that you can add to your lovemaking repertoire, as well as ideas on spontaneous and fun lovemaking.

Man on Top
▲ The most commonly practised position for lovemaking is when the man assumes the more active role and moves on top of his partner. This allows face-to-face intimacy and full, front-of-the-body contact. The nature of this position means the man takes the more dominant role, while the female role is more submissive.

Woman on Top
◀ The woman-on-top position enables the couple to swap the more active and passive roles and allows them to experience and express other aspects of their sexuality. The woman has more freedom to move and is better able to control the depth of the man's thrusts and the stimulation she may need to reach orgasm.

Sitting Position

▶ *In this sitting position, the couple can feel equal in their sexual roles as it allows them to embrace each other closely and feel intimately bonded. While their movements are somewhat limited, it is a perfect lovemaking posture for more meditative intercourse.*

Kneeling Back to Front

▼ *This is a variation of the woman-on-top position in which she kneels astride the man's hips with her back turned to him. While it does not have the intimacy and contact of a face-to-face position, it can allow both partners time to surrender deeply to their own sensations of sexual pleasure. The man can also stroke the woman's back and buttocks, or squeeze the buttocks gently to give her extra erotic stimulation.*

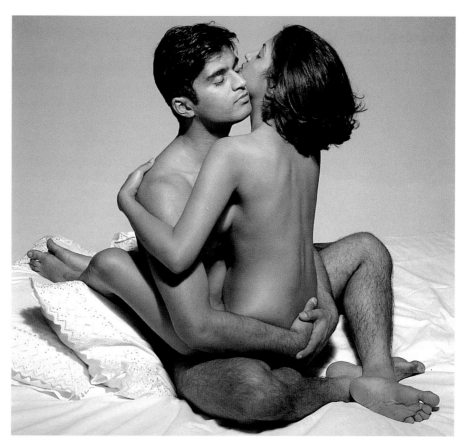

The Man-on-Top Position

Intercourse in which the man assumes the more dominant role, on top of the woman, is one of the most commonly adopted sexual positions. However, as an automatic choice it has been challenged in more recent times because sexually liberated women are just as eager to share the active role in sex.

It is popularly known as "the missionary position", a name first given by Pacific Islanders who witnessed the "strange" marital activities of white missionaries – the wife on her back with her husband on top. The islanders preferred to make love with the woman squatting over her man – a position which allowed her to express her sexuality fully. Certainly the "missionary position" would have been the obvious choice whenever the man assumed the dominant role in the partnership, or the woman regarded her sexual role purely as a duty.

That it still remains a popular choice for sexually emancipated couples is probably because it is a very intimate position, in which partners remain face to face and in eye contact, allowing the exchange of tender and arousing kisses, and words of love. In addition, it offers close physical contact between the most erogenous and vulnerable parts of the body, the pubis, abdomen, chest and breasts.

A woman who, on other occasions, enjoys exploring and expressing the more active part of her erotic nature may also enjoy relaxing sexually into the more submissive role, and letting her man take charge. While this position obviously suits a man who prefers to be the active sexual partner, he should also be prepared to explore other postures if his partner so desires.

The advantage of this position for a man is that he has more command over his pelvic movements. His penis is at a comfortable angle to enter the woman's vagina, and he has better control over the depth of its thrusts, which enables him to regulate his pace and rhythm so that he is able to gain the maximum stimulation needed to reach orgasm.

Preparing for Penetration

▼ *When sensual play progresses to intercourse it is a moment of physical and psychological transition for the man and woman. Both need to be ready in body and mind for this deeper level of intimacy and penetration, so it is important to stay in touch with your own and your partner's responses. Don't rush into penetration if either of you is not quite ready for it. If both are fully aroused by the touches, kisses, words and embraces of foreplay, the woman's vulva will have swelled, and her vagina will be secreting its juices, in readiness to receive the penis; the man's penis will be erect and firm, and able to enter her. Emotionally, both should be open and available to each other, as they enter into coitus. To check that the woman is sufficiently lubricated to accept his penis, the man can stroke his fingers over her vulva and vaginal opening, or simply ask her if she is ready for penetration. She may indicate by words, sounds or touch that she wants him to enter her. He can then guide his penis into her vagina.*

Slow Entry

▼ In this basic man-on-top position, the man is between the woman's legs as his penis begins to penetrate her vagina. She lies on her back, and opens her legs wide to give him room to enter her. Slow and careful manoeuvring will ensure the penis remains in the vagina and does not slip out, which can happen if either tries to move too rapidly before both bodies have adjusted their fit to each other. Many women love a slow entry, when the tip of the penis enters and lingers teasingly just within the vaginal orifice. This can give her further time to relax, emotionally and physically, so that her vagina is flooded with the total desire to be filled. She can also reach down to caress his scrotum and the shaft of his penis, which is waiting to enter.

Slow Motion

◀ The man can begin thrusting with shallow actions, moving his pelvis slowly and gently back and forth, and allowing more time for attunement. On arousal, the first part of her vagina constricts, enabling it to grip the penis securely, adding to the pleasurable sensations of friction. However, if the man is in a state of high arousal, he needs to be careful not to overstimulate the erotically sensitive tip of his penis if he is prone to ejaculating too quickly.

Making it Comfortable

For the woman, the main disadvantages of the man-on-top position are the restrictions to her own pelvic movements and, unless her partner is particularly aware of his actions, the inadequacy of the clitoral stimulation – an important factor if she wishes to be aroused to orgasm.

Other situations can make this position an unsuitable choice. If a woman is suffering from a back condition, she may find that making love in this position will add to the strain. If her partner is much heavier than her, she may feel confined and burdened by the size difference.

A pregnant woman can feel anxious and uncomfortable about having any weight bearing down on her abdomen. Her breasts may feel particularly sensitive to pressure and, in the later stages of her pregnancy, this position may simply be impossible. In all of these cases, if the man is on top of his partner, he should take care not to put all his weight on her.

The man-on-top position puts the onus on the man to perform, and this may not suit him if he is tired or under stress. While he may desire physical intimacy with his partner, at a time like this it is usually preferable if the woman takes the more active role. Also, if the man is prone to premature ejaculation, he would do well to experiment with the woman-on-top positions which may slow him down and give him greater control over this process.

Intimacy in Intercourse

The man should always remain aware of his partner's sexual responses, and ensure that the shared intimacy which inspired the lovemaking is not suddenly abandoned in the heat of

Aiding Mobility

▲ *For a woman, mobility is more difficult when making love in the man-on-top position. She may find it helpful if a pillow is placed beneath her buttocks to tilt her pelvis. This will give her more freedom of hip movement and take the strain away from her lower back. By placing her feet firmly against the mattress, she can use her leg muscles to add leverage to her pelvic motions, to increase sensation for both of them, and to allow greater clitoral stimulation as it rubs against his pubic bone. To avoid pinning her down with his body, the man should support his own weight with his arms and hands, keeping the trunk of his body slightly lifted above her.*

arousal. Unfortunately, some men see penetration as a green light to go, and start thrusting away intent on an orgasm regardless of what is happening to their partners. In other scenarios, a man may be conscious of the woman's needs and start performing a series of mechanical manoeuvres aimed at giving her an orgasm so that he can go ahead and achieve his own. Neither type of behaviour is particularly desirable nor likely to please the woman, because intercourse is not a race or a gymnastic show, or a question of pushing the right buttons to gain an end result. It is all about two people meeting and merging, breathing

and moving together, feeling and responding, and abandoning themselves equally to the sheer physical and emotional pleasure of the moment.

Fortunately, recent research shows that most sexually active men, while still considering female sexuality to be something of a mystery, believe that their partner's satisfaction is as important as their own. For many men, giving sexual joy to their women is the best part of making love. According to the studies, the majority of men do believe that intimacy and affection during lovemaking are very important factors in a woman's sexual happiness.

Penetration with Care

◀ *Full penetration can create feelings of vulnerability as well as physical pleasure. These feelings need to be experienced and there is no need to rush ahead into immediate thrusting. It is important, too, that the man thrusts deeply only when his partner is physically and psychologically ready to receive him, or it may cause her discomfort. Initially, she can place her hands on his hips to help control his pelvic movements until she is ready.*

Sex with Sensitivity

▲ *It is important to stay in touch on an emotional level throughout intercourse. Slow down once in a while, and look deeply into each other's eyes. By allowing the intimacy you feel to be expressed, silently or with words, your lovemaking will become deeply satisfying. Women need to feel emotionally nourished as well as physically aroused during the sexual act. Men benefit too if they try to get in touch with their softer and more vulnerable feelings.*

Focusing Inwards

▶ *Some lovers like to keep their eyes open during lovemaking, while others prefer to keep their eyes closed. If your eyes are open, you can take pleasure in looking at your partner's body and watching his or her arousal and responses. Closing your eyes while making love takes you into a different dimension of sensual feeling because you are able to focus on and enjoy the exquisite bodily sensations arising within you. To savour both experiences, switch from one to the*

other, so that sometimes you have a total awareness of your partner, and at other times you have complete awareness of yourself.

Varying the Movements

When lovers are sexually compatible, their rhythm and movement seem to flow from one beat to another without orchestrated effort. This harmony arises when a couple have allowed sufficient time in foreplay for full sexual arousal, or because they are familiar and comfortable with each other's bodies and share a deep sense of mutual trust.

To experience a whole range of pleasurable sexual sensations when the man is on top, it is important to change the position and angle of your bodies occasionally, and to vary your pelvic movements. The man should take care not to thrust his penis in and out of the vagina with a monotonous regularity of rhythm and

Deeper Penetration

▲ *Deep penetration can be achieved from a position in which the woman arches her back slightly so that her vagina is raised and open. The man can help by lifting and supporting her pelvis, while pulling her slightly towards him. Many women find it very exciting to have the cheeks of the buttocks parted slightly while in this position, so the anus is exposed and gently stretched. Thrusting in this position creates intense vaginal sensations and by taking the weight of her pelvis with one hand he can use the fingers of his other hand to stimulate her clitoris at the same time.*

motion. This can make the whole experience very unsatisfying for his partner, not only because she may be unable to receive the clitoral stimulation she needs, but also because the

Varying Direction

◀ *Angles of thrusting should be changed throughout intercourse to produce a variety of sensations, and to stimulate different areas of the vagina. The man can use his hand to lift and tilt the woman's pelvis in one direction, so that his penis strokes along the side of her vaginal wall. Deep thrusting should only occur when the woman is fully aroused as her cervix and uterus will then have become elevated. He must also avoid thrusting too deeply into the side of her cervix.*

sex act itself can begin to seem automatic and boring. When this happens, and unfortunately it sometimes occurs in even the best sexual partnerships, the woman may start thinking about something else altogether. She may mentally vacate her body, beginning to wish the whole episode was over.

Pelvic motions can be wild, passionate and thrusting, or they may be deliciously subtle, depending on the intensity of sexual energy at any given moment of lovemaking. The man obviously has more freedom of movement in this position, but both partners should try to reach a synchronicity and fluidity in their motions to avoid the "bump and grind" effect. You can try moving

your hips from side to side to create a sexy wiggle, or circulate both pelvises simultaneously to produce some highly erotic sensations and to add a touch of variety to the more usual back-and-forth rocking motion.

If your movements do fall out of rhythm, don't hesitate to tell your partner you need to slow down for a while. Relax and breathe together and make eye contact so you regain harmony. You can remain like this for quite a long period of time, just moving your hips enough to ensure the penis receives sufficient stimulation to remain erect inside the vagina. Let the sexual feelings rise again, and focus on these inner sensations, letting them move you gradually into a new and easy flow of movement.

Enjoy the range of depth to which the penis can penetrate the vagina. Play teasingly between shallower and deeper thrusts. Shallow penetration can be very exciting to both sexes because it produces friction on the tip of the penis and stimulates the outer reaches of the vagina, both regions that are richly served with erotically charged nerve endings.

Deep penetration produces more powerful emotional responses, creating a profound sense of fulfilment and connection between the partners. So do add spice and vitality to your love life by enjoying and experimenting with varying thrusts, positions, pressures and angles to create maximum pleasure for you both. Let sex be adventurous and fun.

Watch and Enjoy
▲ *Watching the motions of the penis thrusting in and out of the woman's vagina can be highly erotic for both partners. By lifting his body a little way from hers, they are able to enjoy this visual stimulation. To make it more arousing, vary the speed and depth of the penile thrusts. For the man, having his woman watch his actions can make him feel very potent.*

Angled Approach
▲ *In this position, the man shifts his weight to one side, using one arm for support, and inserts his penis into the vagina from a slight sideways angle. This allows the woman to use more of her body and she can caress his thigh with her leg and foot, while he, in turn, strokes them. Men also enjoy being touched and stroked during intercourse, especially on the chest and nipples.*

Caress Her Body
◄ *Whole body sensuality should not finish just because intercourse has begun. This is especially important to a woman because every part of her body is sensitive to erotic stimulation, not just her genitals. While making love, you should continue to kiss, lick and caress her body and not just concentrate on thrusting movements. When she is aroused, the sensation of your lips and tongue on her breasts and nipples can drive her wild with excitement. She may also enjoy having her buttocks held, squeezed and stroked.*

The Woman's Satisfaction

Even though the woman assumes a more passive role in lovemaking when her partner takes the on-top position, it is important that she receives the right kind of stimulation to achieve sexual satisfaction. What constitutes satisfaction will be different for each woman. For many it will mean being able to reach their full orgasmic potential, while for some it may be the need to feel as equally involved as their partners. Others would say that emotional and physical intimacy is the most important aspect of lovemaking, whether or not they reach orgasm.

Sexual performance is as much subject to mood and change as any other function in life. It can be ecstatic, passionate and mutually orgasmic, or it may be comfortable and cosy – more like a cuddle. Most couples do take a realistic view of their sex lives, and do not expect to "feel the earth move" on every occasion. However, when a man is in the more dominant on-top position, he needs to exercise a certain amount of conscious control over his movements and arousal level. He may need to slow down from time to time, so the duration of lovemaking and the involvement of his partner provide fulfilment for them both.

How long it should last is a matter for the couple concerned, but the answer will probably lie in whether each person feels sexually and emotionally fulfilled during and after a session of lovemaking.

Side and Rear Entry

◀ This is an exciting lovemaking position, and one which adds to the woman's pleasure because of the pressure of his body against the back of her thigh and vulva. The man enters his partner partly from the side and partly from the rear of her body, so that her leg is drawn up and wrapped around his waist. He will need to support his weight with both hands.

Pulling Close

◀ While beneath her man, a woman may want to become more involved in the action. One way is for her to wrap her legs around the man's back, pulling him close in to her. This will bring their genitals in very close contact, creating a pleasurable friction on the clitoris, especially when the pelvic motions are circular or rocking from side to side. It is not a position that can be prolonged, however, as the man's movements are somewhat restricted, and it may become tiring for the woman.

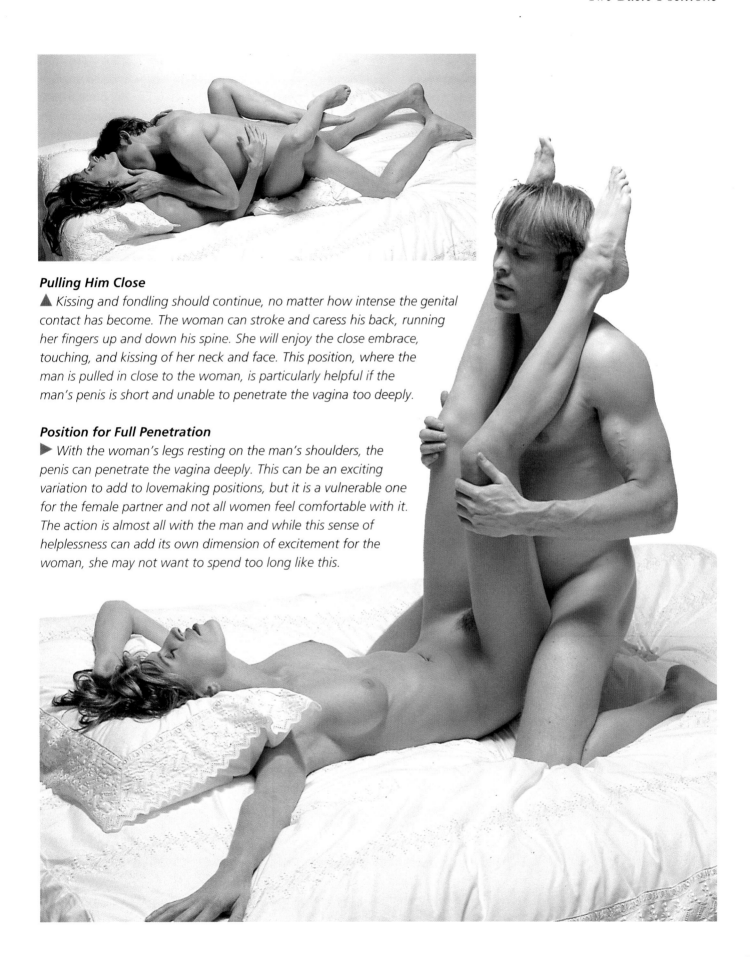

Pulling Him Close

▲ *Kissing and fondling should continue, no matter how intense the genital contact has become. The woman can stroke and caress his back, running her fingers up and down his spine. She will enjoy the close embrace, touching, and kissing of her neck and face. This position, where the man is pulled in close to the woman, is particularly helpful if the man's penis is short and unable to penetrate the vagina too deeply.*

Position for Full Penetration

▶ *With the woman's legs resting on the man's shoulders, the penis can penetrate the vagina deeply. This can be an exciting variation to add to lovemaking positions, but it is a vulnerable one for the female partner and not all women feel comfortable with it. The action is almost all with the man and while this sense of helplessness can add its own dimension of excitement for the woman, she may not want to spend too long like this.*

Unlike past decades, few women today would put up with a sexual encounter that only lasted a few minutes. On the other hand, anxiety about performance can lead some men to become too controlled, and that can also cause discomfort if the thrusting becomes prolonged and mechanical and out of tune with a woman's wishes.

Greater sexual awareness and openness have changed some basic patterns of male sexual behaviour. Only three decades ago, the famous American sex researcher Alfred Kinsey stated that, according to his studies, the majority of men interviewed considered it perfectly normal to ejaculate within the first two minutes of intercourse. Nowadays, most men are much better informed about a woman's sexual responses and her orgasmic capacity and it is quite standard for a man to ask his partner how he can give her the most pleasure.

What is more important is that both people continue to explore their potential for pleasure, allowing themselves to be more spontaneous yet constantly sensitive to each other's feelings, sensations and responses.

While the man remains on top of the women, he should ensure that she is able to adjust her movements to increase her pleasure and that both her clitoris and vagina are receiving stimulation. This can be achieved by allowing continuing contact between his pubic bone and her clitoris, or he can add gentle pressure to her vulva with his hand, or stroke her clitoris sensitively with his fingers.

Lifting One Leg

▼ *A more comfortable variation of the legs-raised position is for the man to lift one of his partner's legs over his shoulder. He is then able to thrust and move his body more easily, while also increasing the pressure on her thigh and vulva. The woman needs to be supple enough to stay relaxed, and as deep penetration is also possible, the position should only be adopted when she is fully aroused.*

Increasing Pressure

◄ *Here the woman's legs are between the man's as he squeezes her thighs with his. Although she has very little movement in this position, the extra pressure on her vulva is very arousing, while his penis fits tightly into her vagina. To increase stimulation, she can wiggle around a little, or contract her pelvic floor and vaginal muscles to exert extra pressure on his penis.*

Opening Wide
▼ If the woman's legs are straight and spread out wide, then her clitoris is in a good position to receive strong stimulation from the man's thrusting movements. He will need to support his own weight with his arms as he rocks his pelvis back and forth. A teasing side-to-side motion will rub and stimulate her whole vulva for even greater arousal.

Holding Tight
▼ Although this position does not allow the woman much pelvic movement, she can reach out to hold him tightly around the neck and shoulders and draw him closer to her. Some women like to scratch their partner's back as they become excited – he will enjoy this too, if it is not too rough.

Close Body Contact
▼ While the man is in the more active and dominating position when he is on top of his partner, she can exert her power too by pulling him towards her and enfolding him in her arms so that he surrenders to her embrace. Throughout their lovemaking, there should always be moments of close, intimate and passionate body-to-body contact.

Men's Sexual Attitudes

Simon, 57, divorced, father of three, a teacher: What turns you on most about a woman? *"The eyes and the voice."* What do you enjoy most about lovemaking? *"The sense of merging with another person."* When do you experience your most powerful orgasms? *"When I'm not too tired. It depends on how close and secure I feel with my partner."*

Dean, aged 23, a student, single: What turns you on most about a woman? *"Beauty and a feeling of warmth between me and the woman I'm attracted to."* What do you enjoy most about lovemaking? *"The closeness."* When do you experience your most powerful orgasms? *"When I'm in love. If it's a one-night stand it's more like a release."*

Terry, 42, a postal worker, divorced: What turns you on the most about a woman? *"The eyes, the smell, the breasts, her femininity."* What do you enjoy most about lovemaking? *"The closeness; the bonding, expressing our love."* When do you experience your most powerful orgasms? *"In a good relationship, sex is just more intense; or if I haven't had sex for a while. It's also a special mood, all openness, it is not something that can be planned."*

Paul, 30, a decorator, single: What turns you on most about a woman? *"Everything, and all kinds of women!"* What do you enjoy most about lovemaking? *"The intimacy, the closeness, giving and receiving pleasure."* When do you experience your most powerful orgasms? *"With my current girlfriend."*

Expressing Our Sexuality

The bedroom, of all places, should never be a battleground for power. So the question of who takes the dominant and submissive positions, or the active and passive sexual roles, should be a matter for lovers to decide after they have conducted a shared and joyful exploration into what feels natural, pleasurable, satisfying and sexually creative to them both. These days, most couples like to swap sexual positions and roles because it allows them to experience all the nuances of their sexual nature, which will have both feminine and masculine qualities, regardless of gender. This is how it should be because men and women today are breaking away from gender conditioning in every other aspect of their lives too.

Men do not always want to be "macho", and sometimes need to express the more sensitive side of their nature, while women are no longer content to be typecast purely in the "gentler sex" role. Since our sexuality is a profound expression of who we are, there should be enough scope within any sexual relationship for it to reflect the whole diversity of our inner selves.

Over the last three decades, women have enjoyed more sexual freedom than ever before. This may partly be due to the availability of efficient contraception, which has reduced their anxieties about unwanted pregnancy, and liberated them from the constraints of their biology to enjoy sex for reasons of pure intimacy and pleasure. In addition, women now know that they have an equal, if not greater orgasmic capacity than their male partners. Gone are the days when a sexually ecstatic woman was considered to be an aberration of her sex.

Women want and expect to have a satisfying sex life, and to take charge of their bodies in order to do so.

While it is largely true that for a woman the emotional, sensual and nurturing aspects of a relationship remain integral to her sexual happiness, she may also desire to reach the heights of sheer physical pleasure during lovemaking for which her body is uniquely designed.

The Woman-on-Top Position

A woman is able to express her innate sensuality and eroticism to a greater degree in the woman-on-top sexual positions than when the man

A Teasing Squeeze

▼ *When the woman is making love to her partner from the on-top position, she can lean towards him for full sensual skin-to-skin contact, lowering her body to cover his. She can kiss and stroke him, while at the same time, moving her pelvis from side to side or back and forth to rub her vulva against his pubic bone. If his thighs are between her legs, she can squeeze them gently between her own to create an extra teasing pressure.*

Relaxing Change of Role

◀ *If the man is lying beneath the woman, he no longer has to worry about his weight on her body or about maintaining a sexual performance. It can be a relief to a man to be able to surrender himself into the more passive role, and totally relax while he receives her tender and nourishing caresses. She can kiss him gently all over his face, and tenderly stroke his head, while rotating her pelvis to maintain genital stimulation at the same time so that his whole body begins to melt into hers.*

takes the active role. She has more freedom of movement, is less burdened by weight, and can gain the maximum stimulation for orgasmic excitation.

Most of the positions illustrated in this section not only allow a woman to enjoy the pleasure of taking her lover's penis inside her vagina, but also the choice of movements whereby her vulva and clitoris receive adequate friction too. Deep penetra-

tion is possible with many of these positions, particularly when she is squatting over her man, yet at the same time, she is better able to control the depth according to what feels comfortable.

For the man, having a partner on top and in charge of the movements can come as a great relief, especially if he is fatigued or would like some respite from the role of main performer. Not only is it erotically

and visually arousing for him to watch his woman express her sexuality so powerfully, he can enjoy relaxing into the more passive side of his own sexual nature.

Couples can use the woman-on-top position for the whole duration of a lovemaking episode, or incorporate it into any number of other exciting sexual manoeuvres. A change of positions should be made gracefully, slowing down the pace of

Sensual Stimulation

▶ *Many women enjoy the possibility of extending sensual play into lovemaking, and this position allows them to continue giving erotic stimulation to different parts of the man's body. Even while they are making love, she can kiss and lick her way down his body, turning him on to even greater heights of arousal. Flicking her tongue across his nipples and then blowing gently on them with her warm breath will drive him wild. If she is only moving her pelvis slightly at this point, she can contract her vaginal muscles around his penis to exert an extremely pleasurable pressure on it, as well as increasing her own genital sensations.*

action if necessary so that both partners can adjust their limbs and posture to become comfortable. When the rhythm and motion of lovemaking is harmonious and fluid, a couple can constantly change positions without interrupting their intercourse. Sometimes, however, it may be necessary for the man to withdraw his penis from the vagina for some moments in order to avoid clumsy movements.

The woman-on-top position requires some caution from the woman as she lowers herself onto her lover's penis. Sudden, abrupt or speedy movements from her before he has found a comfortable fit can injure him by bending his penis at an acute angle. She needs to remain aware of his comfort too if she is abandoning herself to uninhibited movement.

Controlling Penetration

▲ *While the woman is moving up and down on the man's penis, she is able to control the depth of its penetration into her vagina. She can tantalizingly raise herself upwards so that the tip of the penis is gripped by the lower end of her vagina only, though she should take care that it does not slip out. Then she can make subtle up and down movements, to intensify stimulation to these mutually nerve-packed genital zones. Or she can lower herself so that the penis satisfyingly fills her whole vagina. Even more pleasure is generated if she plays between the deeper and more shallow levels of penetration, constantly surprising him with her changes of motion. If, at this point, he lifts up to lick, kiss or suck her nipples, he can take her to the edge of orgasmic ecstasy.*

Pelvic Gyrations

◀ *Intense genital stimulation can be achieved once the woman lifts her body away from her partner and begins to gyrate her pelvis in varying motions to gain maximum vaginal and clitoral stimulation. While the contact between the lovers' bodies becomes less intimate, the arousal grows stronger as they both let go into their own waves of pleasure and movement. She can sway her body from side to side so that his erect penis strokes every part of her vaginal wall, and she can rub her vulva against his pubic bone for extra pressure on her clitoris. While the man's movements are more restricted in this position, he can wiggle his pelvis to increase the effect, or use his feet to lever his lower body up and down to add some deep thrusting motions. He should also use his hands to stroke and caress her.*

Clitoral Stimulation

Many women complain that men either ignore the clitoris, concentrating too much on vaginal thrusting, or they zone in too much on the clitoris, to the exclusion of the rest of the body. This looks like a no-win situation for the man. Happily, there is a way he can give her the clitoral stimulation she needs, and without her feeling she is being tuned up like a car before a motor race.

It is important for the woman to continue receiving clitoral stimulation throughout intercourse and during orgasm. This can be achieved by positions, which either partner can take, that give the woman freedom of movement and allow her vulva to press against the man's pubic bone. During penetrative sex, the man or the woman can also press on, or sensually stimulate, her clitoris manually. Stroking of the vaginal lips and over the mons pubis will also stimulate the clitoris, and may be more arousing and enjoyable than pressure placed directly onto it. Remember, though, that the clitoris is a delicate organ with a high density of sensitive nerves, so frantic rubbing or excessive pressure can be irritating and even painful.

While a woman may desire and need clitoral stimulation to reach the peak of sexual arousal, she may not want to receive it to the exclusion of loving, tender touches and kisses bestowed on the rest of her body. This also applies to her breasts, which when stroked, kissed and licked during intercourse can take her into sexual bliss, yet she does not want them to be the sole centre of attention while the rest of her is ignored. Every part of a woman's body is erogenous, and she can be greatly turned on by the emotional depth of the lovemaking too.

Boosting the Sexual Charge

▼ To keep a sustained and arousing pressure on her clitoris, the woman can raise her back and push her vulva towards the man's pelvic bone, leaning into it without motion for several moments. She can heighten her pleasure by tightening her buttocks and thigh muscles, thereby constricting her vaginal muscles in order to hug the penis, and this will increase the sexual charge in her genitals. Creating this kind of voluntary tension in the muscles of the genital area can bring some women to orgasm.

Arousing Caresses

◀ As the man lies back in this position, he can use his hands to stroke and caress his partner's whole body. He can also increase her arousal by stroking her vulva or rubbing her clitoris while she moves on top of him. At the same time, she is able to reach back with her hands to gently fondle his scrotum, which will certainly add to his pleasure.

Freedom of Expression

◀ A woman has a tremendous capacity for experiencing ecstatic sexual joy, and in this position, where she rides her man, she is free to move and express herself fully without inhibition or restriction of movement. She is able to raise and lower herself on the penis, bringing intense pleasure to the man, and enabling him to penetrate her deeply. She can also grind her vulva against his pubic bone to provide extra stimulation to her clitoris. As she abandons herself to her rapture, the man can touch her breasts and nipples.

Most women would probably say that they want all the tender, erotic touching and caressing of sensual play to continue after penetration, plus the right amount of clitoral stimulation – and they want their lovemaking to be exciting, yet relaxed and spontaneous too.

They do not want to feel that they are being programmed for an orgasm by excessive mechanical stimulation, or that their total sensuality is being neglected.

Ecstatic Moments

When a woman feels confident enough to take the more active sexual role, she can really let go into her orgasmic sexual energy. Suddenly her whole body is free, and she can move, turn and sway so that the waves of pleasure can rush through every part of her. If she has a partner who relishes her ecstatic expression, the experience can be intensely erotic for them both.

If she is truly uninhibited, she may even shout and scream, moan, or even cry and laugh in turns, and all of this can be very exciting to a man who is not afraid to see powerful female sexual energy unleashed. Or she may want to move in a very soft and sensual way, stroking and kissing her man, teasing him with playful and arousing movements, and touching his heart deeply with her gentle and nurturing femininity.

Taking Charge

One of the advantages for the woman when she assumes the on-top position is that she can take control of the movements to satisfy her needs in all the previously mentioned ways. Also, when a man is in the passive role, he is likely to be more attentive to her whole body, reaching out to touch and caress her because he is able to relinquish the tension of being the main performer. Yet at the same time, a woman needs to carry the same awareness that she expects from her man when he is the dominant sexual partner. Just like a woman, a man does not want to feel that his body is being used purely for sexual gratification, as if it is somehow separate from his whole person.

If both want to enjoy a prolonged session of lovemaking, she needs to be in tune with his sexual responses, so that the stimulation he is receiving does not propel him too quickly to his orgasm threshold. For a man, there is a certain point of no return, when he no longer has control over the process of ejaculation. The woman should remain alert to his signals, slowing down the pace of her movements, or even staying still, until the excitement level has subsided sufficiently to allow sexual activity to continue.

However, men who are prone to premature or early ejaculation can benefit from having their partner take the top position since it is likely to create less intense stimulation to the penis and can slow down the ejaculatory process.

Sensate Exercise

As the woman rides her man, she can begin to move slowly up and down on his penis, lowering herself so it penetrates deep into her vagina, and then raising herself so she is barely containing its tip. Closing her eyes, she should then try to merge herself entirely into each sensation, letting

Slow the Pace

▼ *Even at the height of ecstasy, it is wonderful to slow down the pace of action to simply feel the sensations which are arising like pulsing waves in the body. The woman can brace her back, clasping the man's legs behind her and then breathe deeply together with her lover. In this position, the penis will be exerting its pressure onto the front wall of her vagina to add increased stimulation to her G-spot.*

Vary the Movements

▲ *Lowering herself back gently, the woman can arch and extend the whole trunk of her body as she leans against the support of her partner's raised thighs, and takes her own weight into her arms. With the pressure of his penis against the front wall of her vagina, she can rock back and forth with tiny movements to stimulate this highly erogenous zone. She is now exposing her vulva to her lover, and he can lovingly caress this intimate area, and her thighs.*

Opening Up to the Pleasure

▲ *If she is supple enough she can lean right back into this almost yogic posture where her head rests on the mattress by her lover's feet, and her arms are spread-eagled so that the front of her body is completely open and extended. This will enable her to breathe very deeply so her whole body becomes infused with vitality. She is now in a perfect position for her lover to touch and caress her belly and thighs, before stroking and rubbing her clitoris and labia to give her immense delight and possibly bring her to orgasm.*

Moments of Merging

◀ *Between the waves of high energy activity and rapturous movement, it is always wonderful to rest awhile in a position that brings you both back to a sense of merging and melting with each other. The man will be happy to enfold his partner again in his arms, drawing the softness of her body close to his. These are the precious moments of stillness and silence in lovemaking, where both people can breathe together in harmony, connecting deeply through their love and intimacy for each other.*

herself imagine what each subtle change of depth and movement must feel like for her partner. She can also ask him to describe those feelings to her. Gradually, those sensations will transfer themselves into her sexual consciousness.

If the woman becomes extremely sensitive to her man, she may actually begin to feel what he is experiencing, as if the sensations his penis are receiving are also occurring within her own body. It is an experiment certainly worth trying, for it can lead to a deepening of mutual sexual joy and understanding.

Feeling Confident

There are some women who simply do not feel comfortable about taking the sexual initiative or adopting the superior position while making love. There can be all kinds of reasons for this and no one should feel forced into doing something which makes them feel ill at ease.

If it is simply embarrassment, it is worth gathering the confidence to give it a try, and almost certainly the male partner will love the new variation and the chance to lie back and enjoy. If, however, the man insists on always taking the dominant sexual role, this may be a symptom of a deeper problem within the relationship. No woman should allow herself to feel sexually repressed, and if she feels that she is, the couple may benefit from talking the issues over carefully, or seeking advice from a relationship counsellor.

A woman may be reluctant to assume the on-top position because of a sense of low self-esteem regarding her body. Perhaps she is shy to expose it so boldly to her partner, or maybe she feels overweight and too

New Angles of Pleasure

▼ *In this position, the woman squats or kneels with her back to her partner. Although there is less intimacy, because they are not able to see each other's faces, it can be an exciting variation to add to the sexual repertoire. The woman should lower herself carefully onto the penis so that it enters her vagina at a comfortable angle. Penetration can be very deep with any of the woman-on-top squatting positions, so care should be taken to avoid thrusting movements which may cause the penis to jar the cervix. To maintain the squatting position, the woman will need to be quite supple in her hips and legs; kneeling astride the partner may be easier for her. The advantage of this position is that the woman is free to stimulate her own clitoris, while the man surrenders to the pleasurable sensations of her movements.*

heavy to climb on top of her man. Most women make critical judgements about their bodies, but more often than not these views are not shared by their partners.

Feeling good about your body is more to do with your self-regard than your actual weight. You can be big and beautiful or thin and beautiful, if you are truly in touch with your inner beauty. However, if your concerns about your body image are actually interfering with your sexual relationship, and stopping you from expressing yourself to your full potential, then it is worth doing something about it.

A balanced diet, containing lots of fruit, vegetables and grains will give you vitality and energy and help you to stabilize your weight. Exercise will strengthen your muscles, giving you extra power for some of the more exciting sexual manoeuvres. Toning up your abdomen, buttocks and thighs will not only make you feel good, but add to your agility and suppleness and ability to accomplish an exciting range of sexual positions. Working on your pelvic floor exercises will benefit your vaginal muscle control to the delight of you and your man, and may increase the intensity of your orgasm.

Sensuously Slow Motions

◀ *If the man is sitting up when the woman kneels or squats with her back to him, then much greater physical contact and intimacy can ensue. Her back and buttocks will be moving against and stroking the front of his body, and he will be able to kiss and caress her. Intimate contact on the back of her body will be especially pleasant for her as this area is largely neglected during more traditional sexual postures. He can also reach around to stroke her breasts, belly and thighs. Using her feet and legs for leverage in her movements up and down on the penis, she may particularly enjoy savouring the sensual feeling and the slow motions of this position. In addition, she can continue to stimulate her own clitoris, or lovingly stroke her partner's scrotum.*

Visual Variations

▶ *While many women may be shy of exposing their buttocks and thighs so prominently to their partners, both sexes can find this variation of the woman-on-top position with her back towards the man a very exciting part of their love play. A man, in particular may be very visually stimulated by looking at his partner's buttocks, especially if she is kneeling and leaning forward so it is on display. Gentle stimulation on her anal area with his fingers can also increase her sexual arousal, though for hygiene reasons the fingers should not then be transferred to her vagina until the hands are washed. The woman's movements can become quite active in this position, as she lifts and lowers herself on the penis, or she can tantalizingly raise herself so the lower end of her vagina clasps just the tip of the man's penis, to make small but deliciously sensual and erotically exciting motions.*

Heightened Bodily Contact

▶ *If the woman is light and supple enough, she can follow on from the previous position, to lean her body back to lie flat against her partner's trunk. This will bring them both back into a very intimate contact as the length of her upper body sinks into the front of his. In this position, the couple should take time to relax deeply and breathe together, allowing a sense of physical and emotional merging. The pressure of his penis inside her vagina will rest against its front wall, supplying an intense stimulation to her G-spot area. While there is little movement in this position, the woman can tighten her vaginal muscles around the penis to exert pleasurable contractions onto it. The open and exposed position of the woman's body means that both of them can touch and caress her breasts and vulva at the same time.*

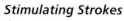

Stimulating Strokes

▲ *When the woman has lowered the back of her body against her partner's chest and belly, as in the previously described position, she can also easily masturbate herself to reach a peak of arousal or orgasm while the man strokes and palpates her breasts and nipples. This can be tremendously exciting for the man as he feels the waves of pleasure running through her body vibrate against his skin, and as she surrenders to her involuntary contractions against the safe support of his body.*

Sitting Positions

Sitting positions allow the man and the woman to feel equally involved in their lovemaking, and can add a completely different emotional and physical dimension to their sexual life. The position itself does not allow for a great deal of movement, and is more often used in between other manoeuvres, or when the couple needs to find a more restful connection during intercourse. Yet it can create a very profound feeling of intimacy and bonding between both people, allowing them to have close eye and body contact. Holding each other, and breathing together, can be emotionally fulfilling. It can also transform the excitement and passion of lovemaking into something transcendental: a shared experience with a more meditative quality of deep merging and union of mind, body and spirit.

Women's Sexual Attitudes

Vanessa, 27, graphic artist and single. What turns you on most about a man? *"His humour, his eyes, his sensuality."* What do you enjoy most about lovemaking? *"The tenderness and intimacy, lots of cuddling and kissing."* When do you experience your strongest orgasms? *"When I trust my lover completely with my vulnerability."*

Renuka, 31, a personal assistant and married. What turns you on most about a man? *"I was attracted to my husband because he was good looking and kind."* What do you enjoy most about lovemaking? *"When he takes control and is powerful and strong. It makes me feel very feminine."* When do you experience your strongest orgasms? *"When we are relaxed and I am not worrying about the children."*

Deidre, 42, psychologist and divorced. What turns you on most about a man? *"His charisma, his looks, and his self-confidence."* What do you enjoy most about lovemaking? *"I enjoy mostly everything, especially if we can laugh and have fun."* When do you experience your strongest orgasms? *"When I am in love."*

Carolyn, 22, married with one baby. What turns you on most about a man? *"Physically, I would have to say his height, his build and his buttocks. Emotionally, I would pick his ability to communicate and love me."* What do you enjoy most about lovemaking? *"When it is slow and gentle yet very erotic."* When do you experience your strongest orgasms? *"When we are making love at the same rhythm and pace, and when we feel especially close with each other."*

Freda, 35, artist and divorced. What turns you on most about a man? *"Everything, I love them all."* What do you enjoy most about lovemaking? *"When it is hot, passionate and lusty."* When do you experience your strongest orgasms? *"When I feel free enough to scream and shout and generally let go."*

Intimate Exchange

◀ *The closeness of the bodies, and the feeling of freedom and ease in the back and spine, can make the sitting position in lovemaking one of great intimacy and pleasure. It is a sexual posture which can feel erotically different from most others, and is best used in moments of deep emotional and sensual exchange. Neither partner is playing a dominant role, as both people are assuming a vertical posture. The woman kneels or squats astride her partner's thighs, and therefore, penetration can become very deep.*

Synchronized Sexuality

◀ *While making love in the sitting position, more movement can be attained if the couple separate their bodies, leaning back and supporting their own weight on their arms and hands. The woman can use the strength in her leg muscles to lever herself up and down on the shaft of the penis, and the man can thrust into her. Movements should synchronize, or be made by one or the other partner. The more separated position of the bodies also enables the man to stimulate the woman's clitoris with his fingers.*

Resolving Harmoniously

▶ *The intimacy and equality of the sitting positions make them some of the most satisfying and pleasurable in the repertoire. Such harmonious lovemaking can draw the man and woman into a deep sense of joyful union, which can be beautifully resolved and reinforced by sinking back gently into each other's arms and lying quietly together in blissful repose.*

Orgasm

Orgasm is the culmination of lovemaking – the sweet release of powerful sensations which are discharged when sexual arousal has reached its peak. For both the man and the woman, it can be a most exquisite and joyful physical experience. Orgasm need not be just a genital affair – a pleasurable release of pent-up sexual tension from the pelvic region. It is possible for the whole body to surrender to the pulsating waves of orgasmic energy.

Orgasm is not just a physical process – it is a holistic experience. It can encompass the whole spectrum of what it means to be a human being – involving also our love, our emotions and our spiritual nature.

It would be wrong, however, to assume that every orgasm should leave you feeling as if "the earth shook". There will be many occasions when the moments of climax and ejaculation will feel more like tender seconds of release, or gentle vibrations in the sexual organs. For the orgasm will largely reflect your mood at the time, whether you are tired, or under stress, or in tune with your partner. Sometimes it can even be a real source of disappointment, a feeling of being a bit let down. Honesty, exploration and experimentation will help most couples to improve their orgasmic ability and to find a greater compatibility in their lovemaking.

Most of all, do not let orgasm become an obsession in your lovemaking. Setting it as the goal of intercourse can create tensions in body and mind, detracting from the joy of the moment and actually interfering with the orgasmic process. Orgasm can be the cherry on the cake, but the

A Melting Moment
▶ *Both the man and the woman can feel as if they are melting and merging and letting go into something that is greater than themselves. For some moments the individual ego is dissolved, and for this reason orgasm has often been described as a potentially transforming experience.*

cake itself is also delicious and should be enjoyed for its own sake!

Orgasmic Variety

It is not necessary to have penetrative sex in order to have an orgasm. It can be attained from self-masturbation, mutual masturbation, and oral sex. Sometimes, during intercourse, a couple may choose to switch to oral sex to complete the orgasmic experience. A man who is concerned that he might not sustain his erection, or that he might ejaculate too soon, may even perform cunnilingus so that his partner has an orgasm before he enters her. So orgasm is very versatile and can be adapted to the mood of the individual or the lovers concerned.

Seek New Heights

▲ *Become more sensual and relaxed with each other so your bodies begin to resonate together. Try different positions for making love to see which ones can bring you to greater heights of arousal.*

Self-Discovery

▲ *Quite often, self-masturbation is recommended as an exercise for people who are experiencing difficulty in obtaining an orgasm with a sexual partner. By bringing yourself to orgasm, you can learn exactly what kind of stimulation you enjoy and also become more relaxed with your own sexual organs and bodily responses.*

Varying Orgasm

▲ *There are times when a man may choose not to ejaculate into his partner's vagina. Maybe penetrative sex is unwise because of a current infection, or there is a risk of pregnancy, or perhaps the couple want to add a little variety to their repertoire. In such cases the man can reach his orgasm threshold and then ejaculate onto his partner's belly, or even between the warm soft mounds of her breasts. (It goes without saying that he should only do this with her consent.)*

The Body's Response in Orgasm

Studies conducted into human sexual behaviour by American researchers William Masters and Virginia Johnson in the 1950s revealed for the first time that men and women follow a very similar physiological pattern before, during, and after orgasm. They discovered that the sexual response of men and women is divided into four phases: the arousal or excitement phase, the plateau phase, orgasm or climax, and the resolution or recovery phase.

However, they also discovered that the sexes differ in many respects. For example, the plateau phase in males can be much shorter than in females, with the result that the man may ejaculate before the woman has had an orgasm, unless he makes an effort to prolong this phase. In contrast, the resolution phase can be much shorter in females compared with men, enabling many women to achieve several orgasms during a single lovemaking session.

In addition, Masters and Johnson showed that the woman's clitoris is as erotogenic as the man's penis, and its sustained stimulation during intercourse may be necessary if she is to achieve orgasm. They also noted other distinct parallels between the male and female physiological responses, such as the buildup of neuro-muscular tension, the increase in heart rate and blood pressure, the quickening of breathing, and, if it occurs, a reddening or flushing that can spread over the skin.

Male Physical Response

Orgasm is triggered in the man when the muscular tension in his body and nerve stimulation of the sex organs

The Pleasure Surge
▲ *During orgasm, both sexes experience rhythmic contractions in the sex organs and pelvic floor muscles, followed by a release of tension which creates a surge of pleasurable sensations spreading through the body.*

Spasms of Ecstasy
◄ *Some men seem to experience sexual contractions only in their genital area, while others feel them throughout the body. During these moments of orgasm, a man may shout or cry out, and his face may contort for a few ecstatic moments as a result of muscular spasms.*

has reached the orgasm peak in what has been termed "the point of no return". Just before ejaculation, rhythmic contractions of muscles around the prostate gland, the seminal vesicles, and the epididymides, push seminal fluids and sperm into the base of the urethra – the urethral bulb – where they mix together. At this stage, the man's testicles are fully elevated and the opening between his urethra and bladder closes.

At ejaculation, intense rhythmic contractions of the urethral bulb and spasms of the pelvic floor muscles pump the semen through the penis, where it spurts out at the tip. These ejaculatory contractions follow each other in rapid succession. Initially they can be very powerful, though they progressively decrease in strength. At the same time the man experiences the intensely pleasurable sensations of orgasm.

Extra Stimulation

▼ *If a man ejaculates prior to the woman's climax, and so loses his erection, she cannot reach orgasm unless additional stimulation is provided, either by him or by herself. This can be achieved by the man performing cunnilingus, or manual stimulation of her clitoris. Alternatively, he can kiss, stroke and lick her body and breasts, while she masturbates herself to orgasm.*

Female Physical Response

Women do not always have an orgasm, even though they may have attained a high level of arousal during the excitement and plateau stage, and there can be a number of reasons for this. Some women may not reach orgasm at all during love-making, or during a particular episode of sexual activity, but this does not necessarily detract from the pleasure they have experienced during the other stages of intercourse, and they may feel sexually fulfilled just the same. In addition, a woman can be more easily distracted by her thoughts or concerns at this stage, in which case

Losing Control
◀ *During this time, the woman loses voluntary control over her muscles, so her face may spasm, and even her fingers and toes can curl. Often in the moments of climax, a woman will cry out or scream, and even dig her fingernails into her partner's back.*

These involuntary contractions work as a pump to release the vaso-congested genital area, so if a woman has almost reached the point of climax, but orgasm is interrupted, for whatever reason, this pent-up feeling of tension in her genitals can make her feel physically very uncomfortable and emotionally let down. She must either wait for this physiological feeling to subside by itself, or for her partner to bring her to orgasm – by oral or manual stimulation if he has already ejaculated. Alternatively, she can masturbate herself to reach her climax.

Faking Orgasms

It is worth mentioning here that many women feel obliged to fake orgasms, leading their partner to mistakenly believe they have reached a climax. Sometimes a woman will do this to finish a lovemaking session because she is bored or tired and her partner's efforts to please her are putting her under an unnecessary pressure. Perhaps her arousal level has dipped, and her vaginal juices have dried, so the prolonged intercourse is making her sore. For whatever reason, a woman may then fake an orgasm to please her partner and to soothe his sexual ego.

Many women, for all sorts of reasons, find it very difficult to be truthful in these sensitive moments. In such situations, the faked orgasm

even the effort of trying to reach an orgasm can be counter-productive.

Most women do not reach orgasm through vaginal friction alone, and need more direct clitoral stimulation during intercourse, either by skilfully applied pressure from the man's pubic bone, by her own movements, or by additional oral or manual stimulation.

When the conditions are right for the woman to have an orgasm, she may begin to feel it as an intense sensation of warmth spreading from her clitoris throughout her body, and a throbbing sensation in her vagina and the muscles in her pelvic region.

When this tension reaches its peak, it gives way to powerful rhythmic contractions which can occur in the lower portion of the vagina, the uterus, and around the anus. For many women, these waves of sensation can pulsate through their whole body. The first contractions are the strongest, but they may be followed by a series of milder pulsations – rather like the aftershocks that often follow an earthquake.

is something akin to a "little white lie". Problems arise if faking an orgasm is a constant pattern of behaviour in a couple's sex life. In this case, it is better if the woman can reveal to her partner that she is unable to climax while making love. Together they can then explore all kinds of sensual ways of bringing her greater pleasure. Perhaps they need to spend more time on foreplay, so the woman is more fully aroused. Or they could experiment with different lovemaking positions so that she can receive the right kind of clitoral stimulation – the woman-on-top positions may help. The issues involved may be even deeper, possibly relating to a sexual anxiety, and it would be beneficial for the woman, and even her partner, to seek professional help from a sex counsellor.

Multiple Orgasms

As the resolution, or recovery, phase in females can be very short – just a few seconds in some cases – some women are capable of attaining multiple orgasms one after another during sex. This is not possible for men because the male recovery phase takes anything from several minutes to many hours. However, there are many women who feel satiated after reaching one orgasm and, like men, will temporarily lose interest in continuing intercourse, although their arousal may return sooner.

There has been a considerable amount of discussion in the media about a woman's multi-orgasmic capacity. In one way this is useful information, for it alerts both men and women to the fact that female sexuality is powerful and profound. It is worth bearing in mind that it has only been in the last 50 years that a

woman's orgasmic nature has been fully acknowledged by Western scientists and doctors.

However, the hype over multiple orgasms can cause problems by creating tensions for men and women. A man may feel he is a failure as a sexual performer if his partner fails to achieve a certain quota of orgasms, while the woman may believe there is something lacking in her for being unable to climax over and over again. Every loving couple can benefit from exploring their full

Prolonging the Plateau

▲ *If the man is able to prolong the plateau phase of lovemaking – delaying or abstaining from his own orgasm – the woman may be able to have one climax after another. This capacity for multiple orgasms differs from one woman to the next.*

sexual potential, but ultimately their orgasmic capacity should be measured in terms of quality rather than quantity, just like every other aspect of lovemaking.

The G-Spot

We now know that the clitoris is the most erotically sensitive part of a woman's body and that it plays a fundamental part in her orgasmic process. However, in recent years there has been much debate about the woman's G-spot, so called after its discovery by the German gynaecologist Ernst Gräfenberg. Pressure on the G-spot, which is a complex of nerve endings located on the front wall of the vagina, is said to induce a particularly intense form of vaginal orgasm. Gräfenberg's studies went even further, stating that when the G-spot is adequately stimulated the urethra ejaculates a clear fluid which has "no urinary character". This exciting discovery has been refuted by other doctors and scientists, who continue to believe that the fluid is indistinguishable from urine. Many doctors

Locating the G-spot

▶ *You can gently probe your own vagina, to see if your finger pressure can find the magic spot, or you can ask your partner to do it for you. The G-spot is said to be located on the front wall of the vagina 5–7.5cm/ 2–3in from the vaginal entrance .*

Stimulating the G-spot

▲ *The G-spot can be stimulated by lovemaking positions in which the man's penis rubs against the front wall of the vagina, provided he can maintain this action for some time. In the position shown here, the woman leans back to allow the penis to press firmly against her G-spot.*

also deny the existence of the woman's G-spot. However, there is evidence to suggest that, in some women at least, this orgasm-triggering nerve bundle really does exist. It is definitely worth exploring.

Simultaneous Orgasms

When a man and a woman have orgasms simultaneously it can be a peak experience in making love, but it is not absolutely necessary for a satisfying sexual life. Most couples can have an extremely happy sexual relationship without ever achieving simultaneous orgasms.

If the man should happen to ejaculate first, he can continue to stimulate his partner to reach her climax with oral or manual techniques. Alternatively, if the woman orgasms before the man, she is usually physically able to continue intercourse and can then devote herself to his pleasure. She may even climax again if she is multi-orgasmic.

Simultaneous orgasms can happen when the couple are in harmony with each other's arousal signals. They may intuitively know when to hold back and when to go forward, slowing down if one or the other is dangerously close to the orgasm threshold. Talking to each other while making love can add an exciting dimension of shared intimacy, so do not be shy to tell your partner you need to take it easy, or that you need more stimulation, or request that he or she "hold on a second". Say these things seductively; you do not want to make them sound like an order. After a while, these verbal signals will become part of your love-play.

Resolution

Resolution is the final phase of the sexual cycle of response, as defined by Masters and Johnson. Here, for

Enjoy the Intimacy

▼ *During the resolution phase after orgasm, a couple can lie together in each other's arms, simply enjoying their close physical presence and the intimacy of the moment, allowing themselves to relax deeply.*

both the man and the woman, the body now returns to its normal pre-arousal state. In a man, the immediate stage after ejaculation is termed the refractory period, and it is impossible for him to resume sexual activity at this time. The length of time the phase lasts varies greatly from one man to another, but in most cases it increases with age.

Most men feel depleted after orgasm and need a period of time to recover, often wanting to withdraw into themselves, or go to sleep. However, a post-orgasmic woman can often remain in a state of sexual excitement after climaxing and may want the lovemaking to continue. As explained, a woman is often capable of going on to achieve more orgasms.

The main difference between the sexes immediately after orgasm is that the man is more likely to require peace and quiet, while his partner needs intimacy to continue, if only in

the form of cuddling, touching, and talking. This fundamental difference in the male and female response in the moments immediately after making love can create real problems in a relationship. Quite clearly, both have needs which must be met.

If a man consistently "turns off" after orgasm, his partner is likely to construe his actions as a sign that he does not care about her. His behaviour may render the whole sexual experience null and void for her and she may feel bitterly rejected. For the man, his need to rest may be paramount, and in fearing that he cannot meet his partner's demands he may cut off from her even more.

If after-sex behaviour is disrupting the harmony of your love life, it is really worthwhile talking about the issue with each other. It is best to try to understand your partner's needs and point of view, rather than becoming angry or defensive.

Chapter 6

Adventurous Sex Techniques

As a couple achieve greater sexual harmony by becoming more in tune with their partner's bodies and sexual responses, they will want to push back the boundaries of sexual expression and explore new routes to erotic rapture. This is an age-old quest, and past masters of the sexual arts devoted lifetimes to discovering numerous postures and positions that offer men and women new experiences of sexual intensity and orgasmic joy. But other, much simpler forms of sexuality can also provide powerfully new erotic experiences, such as allowing your partner to share your innermost sexual fantasies, or even acting them out yourself. Finding ways to enhance the full range of the skin's exquisite sensitivity, or just yielding to the animal passion of the moment, can take you to different states of sexual bliss. Whichever route you choose, you will soon discover that the sensual body is an unbounded playground of sexual delights.

Adventurous Lovemaking

There is nothing new about adventurous sexual positions, despite the plethora of advice that is currently in vogue. Detailed texts and manuscripts on the best ways to achieve sexual happiness, and explicit descriptions of sexual positions and practices, have appeared in many ancient cultures, including India, China and the Middle East. Some of these texts dealt with the pursuit of sensual and erotic pleasure, others were medically informed scripts to help couples achieve sexual health and happiness, and some referred to sexo-yogic practices through which men and women could attain a higher spiritual state of consciousness.

The Kama Sutra of Vatsyayana, which was written in India in about the fourth century AD, is one of the most famous of the texts giving frank and exact advice on how to achieve sexual fulfilment. The first English version of *The Kama Sutra* was translated from Sanskrit by the great Victorian explorer Sir Richard Burton in 1883, and privately printed for The Kama Sastra Society of London and Benares. At that time, this organization was devoted to the acquisition and translation of important and historical texts dedicated to the subject of erotic love.

It was not until 1964, however, that the text was widely published in the West, when its forthright descriptions of the sexual behaviour of the Indian bourgeoisie of an earlier era caused a considerable stir among the public. In particular, its ample detail of a variety of erotic practices and sexual positions really excited the readers' imaginations. The publication of *The Kama Sutra* during the 1960s was one of the many events of that decade that heralded a more open attitude to sexuality.

The Kama Sutra does not, in fact, concern itself solely with sexual issues, but also extols the merits of perfecting a life filled with art, pleasure and recreational activities which would have been deemed appropriate to the wealthy and privileged classes of fourth-century India. It is based on the principle of kama, or desire,

The Standing Position

◄ *Among the many positions of intercourse suggested by* The Kama Sutra *is the one it calls the "supported congress". This is a standing position in which the lovers support themselves, either against each other, or propped up against a wall. If you choose to try the standing position, use it to add variation and adventure to your other lovemaking manoeuvres, rather than as the sole position for intercourse, because, while it is fun and sensual, it can also become awkward and tiring, especially for the man. The woman will need to be lighter than her partner if he is to pick her up and hold her securely. She can swing her legs up around his waist and clasp him around the shoulders and neck, while he supports her buttocks and back with his hands.*

which is the celebration of the physical senses and the longing for love. In a spiritual context, this can be perceived as the human yearning to be united with the Divine.

It is the section on sexual union, however, which has spanned the divide of culture and history to become meaningful and relevant to modern readers. *The Kama Sutra* does not shrink from an explicit discussion on sexuality, even though it embraces the social mores of its time, some of which may seem alien to the contemporary reader.

It talks candidly about every aspect of erotic behaviour, including how to touch and caress, the art of kissing, biting and scratching, varying sexual positions, themes of domination and submission, and oral and even anal sex. This is not a text book

Advanced Standing Position

▶ *To make the standing lovemaking position a little more acrobatic and adventurous, the woman can lower herself slowly down towards the floor, supporting her upper body with her hands against the ground, while her partner secures her lower back and waist with a firm and secure hold. He can then move her pelvis gently to and fro to create the thrusting sensations. This is an exciting and unusual sexual position but should only be attempted by those lovers who are supple and fit. It cannot be maintained for too long before either partner becomes tired. The man should then carefully assist the woman in raising herself upwards, taking care she does not strain her back, or, alternatively, he can slowly and gently sink down on his knees until it is possible to lay her whole back safely against the floor.*

for the inhibited, or for puritans, or those who are content with the missionary position for sex.

It encourages its readers to explore every aspect of their sexuality, from their bestial instincts to their more sensitive and tender expressions of sexual love. It impresses upon men the importance of satisfying a woman sexually, speaks of woman-on-top positions, and comments that the use of certain types of sexual behaviour should "...generate love, friendship, and respect in the hearts of women".

Exploring Variety

To describe lovemaking positions with the kind of practical detail that appears in this section of the book necessitates adopting a somewhat clinical approach to the subject, and this has the unfortunate tendency of

divorcing sexual activity from its wider context of affection, intimacy, tenderness and passion. By discussing movements, angles of penetration and the various techniques of arousal for either partner, it inevitably risks reducing the wonder of making love to that of a how-to guide perhaps more in keeping with a gymnastics or a keep-fit manual.

No one can tell two people what is the correct way for them to have intercourse – lovemaking is their own personal act of creativity and an expression of their emotional, psychological and physical make-up. How a couple want to make love, or what they require from a sexual relationship, depends on the needs of the individual or the relationship. Those needs can change from day to day, year to year or from one partnership to another. Telling someone how best to achieve an orgasm cannot possibly address the complex emotions which are also integral to every person's sexuality, or even touch on the shared vulnerability and love which is surely the essence of a truly fulfilling sexual relationship.

Yet in even the most loving partnerships, certain patterns can set in which make the sexual relationship repetitive and eventually boring. Exploration and variety can be as much an enhancement to a sexual relationship as any other aspect of a creative life. Then there are simple physical facts about sexuality that people may simply not know or fully understand because it is often difficult or embarrassing to talk about the nitty-gritty details of sexual performance.

So, for instance, a man could regard himself as an experienced lover, yet despite his Olympian efforts in bed, still fail to satisfy his partner sexually because the positions he favours do not provide the stimulation she needs to achieve an orgasm. The woman, herself, may not understand exactly why she has been unable to reach her peak of arousal, for she may be attracted to her partner and even enjoy those same positions for all the other emotional feelings they provoke.

Examples of this are the various positions shown here where the woman's legs are vertical and resting on the man's shoulders. This position can be exciting for them both, because the man feels powerful and potent, while the woman may enjoy the sensation of surrendering her body to his thrusts. Yet this position precludes the possibility of her receiving direct clitoral stimulation, and is unlikely to lead her to orgasm, so it is not an ideal one to continue for any length of time. Knowing about the subtle variations of position gives partners a greater range of choices and also more understanding of how to fulfil their own and each other's overall sexual and emotional needs.

Deep Penetration

Some of the more adventurous sexual positions often rely on the man being considerably more active than his female partner, and taking almost complete charge of the movements of intercourse. The positions shown on these pages all require the legs of the passive partner to be held upright or pushed back towards the body, and are mostly variations of the man-on-top position, although the last illustration shown here shows how to

Command the Action

▶ *When the woman's legs are raised and leaning against the man's shoulders, he can penetrate her deeply from his kneeling position. She has less movement than him, although her partner can lift and lower her buttocks with his hands. She receives no direct stimulation to her vulva from this position, but her partner can apply some arousing strokes to her clitoral area with his fingers. She may especially enjoy being able to lay back and relax while her partner takes command of the action.*

Total Surrender

▶ *For deep vaginal penetration, the woman can draw her legs right back into her body, and bend her knees to rest the heels of her feet against his shoulders. The man can then lean into her, pushing her legs even further back, while supporting his weight with his arms and thrusting his pelvis freely. Again, the woman is able to move very little in this position, but can enjoy surrendering to the thrusting sensations. For easier penetration into the vagina, he can raise her hips by placing a pillow beneath her buttocks.*

reverse the roles so that the man assumes the more passive and traditionally feminine posture of drawing back the legs.

When the woman takes this passive position, she needs to be supple in her joints and limbs to remain comfortable, and it is advisable for the man not to keep her in this pose for too long. It is best used as an interesting variant to other movements which allow the woman greater flexibility of motion. Also, because her vulva is not in direct contact with his body, the woman is unlikely to gain direct clitoral stimulation from this position and so it is unlikely to lead her to orgasm, which is another good reason for the man not to pursue it for too long.

However, he can stimulate her clitoris with his hand, and caress her body while using this more adventurous lovemaking position, but this should be done only in a loving and sensual way. Most women dislike the feeling of being fiddled with in a mechanical way, and prefer arousal to come from a natural, flowing sequence of movements.

The pleasures to be derived from these positions are that they add variety, they allow deep penetration, which can be very arousing to both partners, and the man is able to express his strength and potency and thrust his pelvis freely. The woman may enjoy the feelings of surrender and "helplessness" that can accompany these positions, and to gain the maximum pleasure from them, she should totally relax her body and yield herself completely to her partner's thrusts.

Position of Power

▲ *The woman's body becomes even more compact if she draws her knees towards her breasts and places the soles of her feet comfortably onto the man's chest. This position provides little clitoral stimulation as her vulva is lifted away from her partner and her movements are limited. However, she may find the powerful surge of her partner's thrusts very thrilling and be content to submit to a passive role. While the man can enjoy feelings of power and strength as he makes love to his partner like this, he needs to be careful not to penetrate her so deeply or vigorously that he is hurting her cervix. If, in this position, he stops thrusting for a while and leans his body back a little, he can apply an exciting pressure from his erect penis to the woman's G-spot.*

Role-Reversal

◀ *This position offers a fun and unusual opportunity for role-reversal. Here, the man lies on his back with his knees drawn up and his legs raised so that he is assuming a position viewed more typically as a female one. The woman lowers herself onto his penis carefully, making sure its angle is right and that she does not bend it awkwardly by moving too quickly. She squats, so the backs of her thighs rest against the backs of his, but she supports her weight on her feet, and uses her legs as leverage to move up and down, or she can wiggle her hips from side to side. Only a supple man will be able to maintain this position for long, but it will certainly help him to understand a woman's perspective of the submissive role.*

Restraint in Lovemaking

The themes of domination and submission frequently provide a strong element of pleasure and desire in many sexual relationships. The feeling of "being taken" by a lover can be deliciously arousing and emotionally fulfilling for either sex, although it is usually only one aspect of a more all-rounded sexual relationship, where the active and passive sexual roles are equally shared.

Many couples, however, would not wish to go as far as acting out restraint or bondage practices, but find other ways to express more naturally the fluctuating surges in their need to dominate or submit to their partners. The two illustrations shown here capture the moments when sexual arousal has reached a particular peak, and one partner takes on the more powerful role and temporarily restrains the movements of the passive partner by pinning his or her arms, hands and body while taking command of the sexual activity.

Usually, this is initiated by the body language of the more submissive partner, who splays out the limbs in a position of surrender. Both men and women can enjoy either role, depending on which one of them is taking the on-top or beneath position at the time.

Sexual Surrender

▶ While a woman may like to play an active and equal role in lovemaking, she may also love those moments when her partner takes charge and she can surrender to his masculine power. When her arms have stretched out above her head, he can bind her hands together with one of his own. With the other hand, he can hold her buttocks, or raise one hip towards his body, so he can alter the angle of his thrusts. This allows his penis to also stroke along the sides of the vaginal walls to stimulate them.

Domination and Submission

◀ As the passion rises during lovemaking, a woman may stretch her arms out behind her head, and spread her legs so that she assumes a posture of supine submission. The man can then hold her hands down with his own, and bring his body close on top of hers, so his position is more one of domination. This element of restraint in lovemaking can be very arousing to both partners at certain moments. When the woman's legs are opened out and straight, her vulva is in contact with her partner's pubic bone, and though she can make little movement of her own, she will receive strong clitoral stimulation which may precipitate an orgasm for her.

Rear-Entry Lovemaking

Rear-entry lovemaking means the man inserts his penis into the woman's vagina from a position behind his partner's body. It is more commonly known as the "doggie position", so-called because this is the basic sexual position that is common to most animals, including dogs. Some women find the rather

Rear-Entry Sex

▲ *If the woman kneels on the floor and lays the upper half of her body across the bed, she can position herself comfortably for rear-entry sex, especially if she pads her chest with a cushion. The man then kneels behind her, so the floor gives him some solid support for his movements. If the woman enjoys making love in the "doggie position", she may be aroused by the slightly dominating aspect of her partner and by her own more submissive stance. Although they are not face to face, the man can be very intimate with her body, and can stroke her hair, back, and buttocks easily. He can also lift her away from the bed slightly to fondle her breasts, caress her belly, or to stimulate her vulva and clitoris with his fingers while making his thrusting movements.*

Armchair Sex

◄ *An armchair lends itself very well to rear-entry lovemaking, if the furniture is deep enough to take both partners onto its seat. She can lean her body against the padded support of the back of the chair and avoid any feeling of collapsing forward under the pressure of his thrusts. The man can then kneel behind her and, as she leans forward, enter her vagina from the rear position. He can use his hands to stroke and caress her erogenous zones, or to pull her hips closer to him.*

bestial connotations of this posture to be demeaning, and do not enjoy making love with their backs turned to their partners, or to have their buttocks so exposed. Other women find rear-entry intercourse very exciting, and enjoy the rather primitive nature of its stance, and the feeling of surrender that it engenders.

Rear-entry lovemaking can be enjoyed as a variation to other posi-

tions, and it is potentially very sexually satisfying to both partners because it allows for deep vaginal penetration. This position has been recommended by some fertility specialists for couples who are trying to conceive a baby because it assists the sperm to pool near the mouth of the cervix. It can also be a comfortable position for a pregnant woman to adopt, although the man must

take care not to penetrate her too deeply or vigorously in this situation.

A pregnant woman, or any woman, can make herself more comfortable in this position by kneeling, head-down, on the bed with her back to the man, and padding her belly and chest with pillows.

A bonus for the man is that it provides an ample view of the woman's buttocks, and this can be a powerfully arousing visual stimulus for him. For some women, however, the idea of revealing their buttocks so prominently may cause anxiety, especially if they are concerned about their weight or body image.

However, the buttocks are a highly erogenous zone in both sexes, and respond erotically to stroking, squeezing, patting, and even stronger forms of manual stimulation. In this position the woman receives no direct clitoral stimulation, but this can be rectified by the man caressing her vulva while he thrusts, or by her own self-stimulating strokes. If she is thus pleasured, both partners can reach an orgasm in this position.

Seat of Pleasure
▲ *This is another creative way of enjoying rear-entry sex in the comfort of the armchair. The woman starts by kneeling astride her partner's lap but with her back turned to him, and then carefully guides his penis into her vagina. Once the penis is fully erect, she can then lean forward slowly and support herself by placing her hands on the floor. The man's movements are limited, but he can lift her hips up and down with his hands to create more friction, and the woman can also wiggle sexily from side to side to increase the arousal for them both.*

A Fun Variation
▲ *Anatomically, it is obviously not possible for the "doggie position" to be reversed for penetrative sex. The couple, however, can enjoy other thrilling sexual sensations by having the man take the usual female position for rear-entry sex. First of all, he can be aroused by assuming the more submissive stance, while experiencing the sensual feel of his partner's breasts and belly moving against his back. He can wiggle his hips to rub himself against the edge of the bed, while the woman can use her hands to squeeze and pat his buttocks, or stroke and fondle his testicles or the erotically sensitive tip of his penis.*

Active Sitting Positions

The sitting position for lovemaking is popular for its particular ability to enhance a meditative sexual mood. It can be used while the couple remain on the bed, or chairs or the edge of the bed can be utilized to make it more comfortable for posture and movements. The following examples show the many diverse ways to adapt this particularly sensual and relaxed form of making love.

Slow and Sensual
◀ *When making love on a chair, the vertical posture of both partners enables them to relax deeply and bond emotionally and physically. They can embrace each other closely so their bodies are in intimate contact. This position is not chosen for vigorous movement, but more for slow, sensual and tender sex. As the man holds his partner tight to his body, he can lovingly kiss her neck.*

Bodies in Harmony
◀ *Making love like this can become very still and meditative, and the couple can sometimes just hold each other closely, harmonizing their breathing and even allowing their bodies to rock and sway gently together, but without excitement. During these quieter moments of lovemaking, if the man's penis becomes softer, the woman can tighten her thighs or her vaginal muscles to create just enough pressure and friction to keep it erect. Intimacy here is much more important than excitement.*

Varying the Action
▲ *The woman is the more active partner in this chair-sitting position. She can brace herself against her partner as she hugs him, while rocking her pelvis back and forth. Her motions will arouse and stimulate both of them. He can also place his hands on her hips to raise her up and down to vary the movements.*

New Angle of Arousal
▲ *If she is supple and confident enough in her body, the woman can slowly lean backwards so that her hands reach to the floor behind her while she is secured by her partner's hold. The angle of her pelvis will enable the erect penis inside her to put sustained pressure on the front wall of her vagina and G-spot, which can be very arousing. The openness and exposure of her body and genitals will be sexually exhilarating to them both. If she allows herself to relax into this position and to breathe deeply, the effort will be worthwhile.*

Erotic Charge
▲ *The bow-shape of the woman's body as she leans back against the support of her partner's thighs while kneeling astride him in an armchair, will, like the previous position, open and expand her lungs, diaphragm and abdomen so that she can breathe very deeply indeed. This will help her whole body to become charged with vibrant sexual energy. She can also wiggle her hips so that her vulva rubs arousingly against her partner's body. The man can lean forwards to kiss and lick her belly, which will increase the intensity of her sensations.*

Taking It Further

The sitting posture of lovemaking can be one of a whole variety of positions which a couple adopt during a period of coitus to express the wide range of shifting emotional and physical sensations that sweeps through them. By using the edge of the bed for a sexual sitting position, the couple can become more active and passionate than in other sitting situations which are more conducive to meditative lovemaking. Here, the man can balance himself with his feet and hands while the woman is astride his lap, enabling her to move more freely without fear of toppling them both over.

Wild Abandon

▼ *Perching on the edge of the bed while making love in the sitting position will enable the man to place his feet firmly on the floor so that the couple have better support and balance if their movements become more abandoned. The woman can grip the man's shoulders firmly, and while leaning her body away from her partner, can gyrate her pelvis vigorously back and forth to create strong sensations of friction.*

Synchronized Motion

▼ *Pressing one hand against the mattress for additional support, the man can clasp his partner close to him with his other hand, while rocking his hips back and forth. He should co-ordinate his thrusts to move simultaneously with the woman's motions, which are made by her levering herself up and down from flexed knees. When the woman lets go into her sexual energy, she may also begin to toss her head and neck from side to side.*

Easing Down

▲ This position follows on naturally and easily from when the woman is sitting astride her partner's lap if they are making love in the sitting position on the bed. She can slowly relax back onto the bed, using her partner's grip to ease herself down gracefully, even while his penis is still erect inside her. Then, with some careful manoeuvring, she can bring the leg that was lying across his thigh to rest beneath it. From this comfortable position she can move her hips from side to side and receive strong clitoral stimulation.

Change of Pace

◄ If the man lies back on the bed after his partner has done so (see illustration above), the couple's position falls into a cross-shape, and they can engage in a very relaxed form of lovemaking which will, at the same time, keep them both in a high state of arousal. By moving their hips around, they will receive adequate friction to keep them both stimulated, but they will be able to rest at the same time. When they are ready to change positions again, the man sits up and then pulls his partner upwards and they can continue with other movements.

Close to the Edge

▲ If the woman lies on her back, with her buttocks just at the edge of the bed, and the man kneels on the floor in front of her, he can then raise her legs up onto his shoulders so that he can easily insert his penis into her vagina, which in this position will be at the same height. Penetration can be deep and very pleasurable, but he should additionally stimulate her clitoral area with his fingers and caress her body if he makes love to her from this position for long.

Increasing the Stimulation

◄ If the woman lowers her legs and slides her body a little further down over the edge of the bed, the man's thrusting movements are more likely to add a stimulating friction to her vulva, which will increase her sexual arousal. He can also lower his body over hers so that he can kiss her lips and breasts too.

Over the Edge

Sooner or later, if the lovemaking is sufficiently wild and abandoned, the couple will work their way all around the bed. It usually takes some time before two people become so attuned to each other's bodily responses that these movements are compatible and graceful, and do not cause them to interrupt the flow of their intercourse. Winding and unwinding the limbs, rolling over, changing the postures, swapping active and passive roles and positions, all require skilful and nimble movements if they are to be executed with ease and fluidity. However, once a couple are comfortable with each other, they can let themselves go into passionate activity which can take them from one side of the bed to the other, and even over the edge.

Locked in Congress

▲ *Here, the woman is below the man, with her head just slightly off the edge of the mattress. She can hold the man very close to her body while she wraps her feet around his buttocks and locks him into her. This will inhibit his movement a little but the pressure of her feet will add extra pleasurable sensations, and they can just wriggle and rotate their hips for a while to create a whole variety of different stimulating motions.*

Exhilarating Sex

▲ *The man or woman can end up in a position in which the head is completely off the mattress and is resting against the floor. This can cause an exhilarating rush of blood to the head, but should not be maintained for too long or the pressure can build up too strongly, especially if the person is approaching an orgasm. There is something very liberating, though, about being this abandoned in your lovemaking that you almost topple out of bed.*

Masturbating Each Other

Mutual masturbation enhances the sensuality of foreplay by increasing arousal for either partner prior to penetration and intercourse, and it is a sure way to get the love juices flowing. It may also be enjoyed as a complete and totally fulfilling sexual act in itself through which lovers can attain orgasm even without penetrative sex. It is a delightful way to initiate a second round of lovemaking when both people are sufficiently rested from the first bout, and it can be used to lovingly assist a partner to complete sexual satisfaction if the other person has climaxed first or is unable to continue lovemaking.

One of the most important skills in the art of lovemaking is to learn how to masturbate your partner properly. To do it well is to know which touches bring maximum pleasure and to share in your lover's delight. Mastering the skills of masturbation will make you a special and much-appreciated lover.

Many couples, particularly the young, use masturbation as a way of enjoying each other's bodies before committing themselves to a full sexual relationship. It provides a safe means of exploring and becoming familiar with each other's sexual responses as well as enjoying sexual satisfaction without the implications and responsibilities involved in full penetrative intercourse.

Some people find masturbation acceptable but would only allow intercourse within the context of a committed relationship or marriage. Others may wisely consider the consequences of pregnancy or sexually transmitted diseases and prefer to abstain from a full sexual relationship, using masturbation as an alternative until these issues have been safely resolved.

Yet mutual masturbation should remain an integral part of any couple's range of lovemaking techniques, for it continues to provide an erotic enhancement throughout a sexual relationship. Arousing and satisfying your partner by skilful masturbation without asking for

Quick-Release Sex

▼ *Mutual masturbation can provide fast erotic arousal whether it is part of a whole lovemaking session or a separate episode from intercourse. By masturbating each other to orgasm, both of you can receive a satisfying release of sexual tension. Mutual masturbation while still partly clothed can be particularly exciting because it can recall memories of early sexual experimentation, and also because the friction of material against the genitals can be an additional form of stimulation.*

anything in return, except the joy gained from his or her pleasure, can be a very erotic experience.

If your libido is at a low ebb, perhaps as a result of tiredness or stress and you are not in the mood for making love, while your partner is, masturbating your lover can be a perfect way to answer both of your needs. If you have a back injury which makes movement difficult, or you are heavily pregnant, then again mutual masturbation can provide an extremely sensual alternative to full sexual intercourse.

In addition to masturbating each other, either of you can indulge in the pleasure of self-masturbation with the other partner closely involved in the process. This can be a very erotic experience, as you watch your partner self-pleasure his or her body next to yours. You participate with touches and caresses to increase the arousal and you can even join in the sighs, moans and changing patterns of breath as if the sensations are being transferred into your body too.

You can take it in turns to masturbate each other, or you may do it simultaneously while standing, kneeling or lying next to your partner so that your bodies begin to vibrate together with the mounting tension of your sexual excitement.

Many lovers feel that the orgasms they experience through masturbation provide a quite different sensation than those resulting from

Caresses and Fantasies

◄ *You can masturbate yourself to orgasm while your partner holds you close to his body, and touches and caresses your breasts and kisses your face and neck. You can let your own sexual fantasies run free in your mind, or he can even whisper his sexual fantasies to you while you are turning yourself on. Again, this type of masturbation can become even more enticing if you are wearing a silky textured item of clothing, like a camisole, which will rub sensuously against your nipples and skin.*

Mutual Pleasuring

▼ *You can masturbate each other at the same time. If you are attuned to each other's responses, it may even be possible to reach a simultaneous orgasm, or if not, take it in turns to satisfy one another sexually. Or you may only want to take the arousal level so far with your masturbatory motions before progressing towards other forms of lovemaking. Lie close to each other to have skin-to-skin contact, but position yourselves comfortably so that you can easily touch and stroke each other's genitals.*

intercourse. The masturbatory orgasm is sometimes described as being more physically intense than an intercourse orgasm, probably because it ensues from a sustained and specific stimulation applied to the most erotically sensitive areas of the genitals, and possibly because if you are on the receiving end, you can lie back and surrender yourself totally and quite selfishly into its powerful sensations.

For some women, careful and loving masturbation combined with oral stimulation are the only way in which they can achieve orgasmic satisfaction while making love. It may not, however, bring the same deeply

nourishing sense of emotional bonding and fulfilment which is more likely to occur when a couple climax during the act of penetrative sex. Sexuality, however, is multi-dimensional – a kaleidoscope of physical and emotional experiences – and mutual masturbation is there to be enjoyed as one of its many exquisite hues.

The Right Touch

Most people perfect their masturbation skills on themselves. So it makes sense that the person who can best show you how to apply just the right erotic touch in masturbation is your partner. Only he or she knows the rhythm and pace of the strokes which can be guaranteed to take them to the heights of arousal and on towards a mind-blowing orgasm.

However, that does not exclude the other partner being able to add something entirely new and extremely exciting of their own invention to this type of sexual arousal – so stay open to the possibility of experiencing some hitherto unknown peaks of pleasure.

Self-Pleasuring

▲ *Mutual masturbation can be enjoyed when both of you simultaneously pleasure yourselves. One way to do this is to lie comfortably next to each other in a top-to-tail position. Continue tactile contact with each other by resting a hand or arm over the other's body then focus totally into giving yourself pleasure, doing all the things that bring you sexual joy, but at the same time feeling the warmth of your partner close by. Don't be afraid to make sounds, or breathe deeply, because your ecstatic noises will increase your partner's arousal too.*

Men and women, for obvious reasons, masturbate themselves in quite different ways. Generally, a man will focus his attention almost entirely on his penis, though he may possibly include some self-arousing caresses to his scrotum, or finger-pressure on his anus. He is also likely to simulate the action of intercourse by creating the same type of pumping friction on the shaft of his penis, only this time by hand. He almost certainly prefers to use a firm grip of the hand, and may apply increasingly vigorous strokes until the moment of ejaculation.

A woman's way of masturbating herself is likely to be more sensual and slow, and involve more of her body, for she may caress her breasts and rub her nipples, and stroke her belly and thighs as if she is making love to herself. She is unlikely to concentrate her manual stimulation solely on her clitoris, but will move her fingers all around it and over her vaginal lips, separating them carefully to stroke over their folds and occasionally inserting the tips of her fingers to stroke around the lower part of her vagina. She may also rub and vibrate the pubic bone area above her clitoris, and tug gently on her pubic hair to stimulate the highly erotogenic nerve endings at the base of the hair follicles.

A woman is likely to start her self-masturbation in a slow, gentle and languid manner, varying the motions of her strokes, and building up speed and pressure only as she approaches her climax. She is more likely to lavish her attentions on her vulva, and less inclined to try to recreate the actions of intercourse, though some women insert a dildo or sex toy into the vagina during self-masturbation to increase the stimulation.

Observing Each Other

Knowing about the different methods employed by men and women during self-pleasuring will help you and your partner to become more sensitive to each other's sexual needs. If you can overcome your shyness, you can watch each other masturbate. If you are observing your partner masturbate, notice everything he or she is doing, which parts of the hands are used, what motions are employed and how the strokes vary at different stages of arousal. Watch your lover's

facial expressions and listen to the changing patterns of breath and the sounds he makes, for these will all give you cues to your partner's physical response and arousal patterns during masturbation.

If you are masturbating yourself, tell your partner exactly what you are doing and why a certain stroke or pressure is giving you pleasure. Describe the sensations as well as you can so your partner can begin to absorb all the nuances of those physical feelings into his or her own sexual consciousness. Then, when he or she touches your genitals in a certain way, the physical pleasure you are receiving can also be transmitted to, and consequently experienced by, your partner.

Note, especially, what your partner does as he or she approaches orgasm. Does the friction and stimu-

lation speed up, and does the pressure of palm and fingers increase? What happens on the point of ejaculation and orgasm, and immediately afterwards? In all of these things, your partner is your perfect teacher, but see below for more guidance on masturbation techniques specific to either sex.

Make It Like Music

Mutual masturbation, like oral sex, is a way of getting right down to your partner's genitals. Learn to love them completely so your touches convey your reverence, awe and pleasure for these most intimate parts of your lover's body. Become as familiar with them as you would with any other part of the body. Use your hands and fingers to play on and stroke over your partner's genitals as you would if you were making beautiful music

Study Her Style

▲ The best way to learn how she likes to be touched and stimulated in order to attain an orgasm through masturbation is to watch her do it to herself. She can show you exactly what she enjoys, because she has explored the best means of arousal for herself during self-masturbation. Witness carefully how she uses her hand and fingers, what pressure and movements she applies, and what kind of stimulation she gives to her pubic area, her labia and to her clitoris. See how her strokes change from slow to fast, and notice their rhythm and pace.

Watch Her Responses

▲ Look also at how her whole body responds to her self-stimulation. Watch how her facial expressions change as she registers the waves of pleasure rising within her. Notice too how she also caresses other parts of her body, not just her genitals, and particularly the way she fondles her breasts and her nipples. You can touch her lightly, but don't interfere with her process right now, because it is important for you to ascertain her full capacity for self-pleasuring and to learn from it so you too can give her equal joy.

on a classical instrument. Learn to perfect your rhythm and pace, recognize when to be subtle and when to go for the "grande finale".

Masturbating the Male Partner

If you are going to engage yourself fully and wholeheartedly into masturbating your male partner you will want to be comfortable yourself. You can lie beside him, sit or kneel between his legs, or straddle across his body that so you are facing his genitals. Remember that most men prefer the feeling of a firm grip on the shaft of the penis, so it makes sense to use your strongest and most agile hand. You can, however, swap the action over to the other hand if you are going in for a longer bout of masturbation.

You can hold the base of the penis with your more passive hand to keep it steady, and then clasp your active hand around the top end, settling it just below the coronal ridge. (If your partner is uncircumcised, draw the foreskin gently backwards to expose the head of the penis, but do not overstimulate the tip itself as it may

Follow Her Rhythm

◀ *Lay your hand gently over hers as she continues to touch, rub and vibrate her fingers against her vulva and clitoris. This is the best way for you to gauge for yourself the manner in which she sexually arouses herself. Try to imagine that your hand is hers, but let hers lead yours in movement and rhythm. Notice how she not only stimulates the clitoris directly, but also strokes her fingers over its surrounding areas and caresses her labia and vagina.*

Share His Fantasies

▼ *Now it is his turn to tell you exactly how he enjoys to be stimulated during masturbation. Listen and learn carefully from him because he knows best what turns him on. Lay your hand over his to find out how he begins to arouse himself, what strokes he may like to receive on his scrotum, and other parts of his body. If your relationship is open enough, he may like to describe to you the sexual fantasies he uses while masturbating and which help him to achieve an orgasm.*

be overly sensitive – unless of course, your partner insists otherwise.)

You can circle the penis with your thumb and index finger to form a ring around it, using this part of your hand as the main tool of stimulation. Alternatively, you can stroke your clasped hand up and down the shaft of the penis from its base to just above the ridge of the glans.

The focal point of stimulation is the erogenously sensitive coronal ridge and the frenulum on the underside, but all-over stroking of the shaft is also pleasurable. You can also roll his penis between your hands, against your thigh and belly, or very erotically between your breasts, although you may need to complete with hand movements to actually bring him to orgasm.

You can start off slowly and sensually, increasing pressure and speed as your strokes progress. Follow what your partner has shown you, varying between short and long, slow and rapid strokes. Build up a rhythm and pace that suits your partner and is in tune with his responses, increasing the tempo as his arousal heightens.

If you both want to prolong the moment of his orgasm, you can slow down teasingly and temporarily just before the ejaculatory process begins, and then start the action all over again. If you do this several times, he may feel as if he is going to burst with increasing sensation and his orgasm, when you allow it to happen, is likely to be very intense.

Learn to recognize the signs that your partner is about to climax so you can speed up your strokes, but stop or slow down once he has started to ejaculate. Continued stimulation at this point may not be welcome as the tip of the penis becomes extremely sensitive and further rubbing can even be painful.

His pleasure may be increased during masturbation if you also caress his thighs and belly, stroke and gently palpate his testicles, apply finger pressure onto his perineum, or press or stroke around his anus. Try it and check out his responses.

Masturbating The Female Partner

Start by stroking, gently rotating and vibrating the flat of one hand over the whole of her vulva, applying some pressure from its heel onto her

Use Firm Pressure

▲ *A mistake that women often make when masturbating their partner is to use only light pressure because they are afraid of hurting him. Most men, however, prefer a firm strong grip on the penis, and fairly vigorous strokes. He may have particular preferences on how he likes the pace of masturbation to progress; whether he likes to start off slowly and then speed up, or enjoys to tease himself towards an orgasm by taking the heat off just before the ejaculatory process begins and then resume his strokes. He can also show you exactly where the most erogenously sensitive parts of his penis are and which areas respond most to your touch. By clasping your hand over his while he masturbates, you can learn exactly what brings him the most pleasure.*

pubic bone. You should aim to get her love juices to flow, so remember to kiss and caress her whole body, giving loving attention, especially, to her breasts.

Do not zone in right away on her clitoris, and then rub away madly. If you do, you will irritate her, and make this delicate organ feel bruised and sore. Also, remember that she needs to be well lubricated when you are stimulating her clitoral area. Use your finger to gently spread some of her vaginal juices around and over her clitoris. You can also use a little saliva or a drop of KY jelly as a lubricant, but most exciting would be to moisten her with your tongue.

Softly but deftly explore her vulva with your fingers, parting its lips

gently and stroking the tip of a finger all around them, and then rub your finger back and forth just above the clitoris. Your middle finger, pointing downwards, is the one long enough to easily stroke over her clitoris, while its tip can gently massage inside her vagina.

Give to her the pleasure she is able to create for herself, applying your strokes with the motions, pressures, and rhythms you have seen her use. Let her guide you with her pelvic movements, and her sighs of delight. Build up your pressure slowly and remember, if she climaxes, to sustain it for the duration of her orgasmic contractions. If the rhythm is wrong or pressure is reduced during these precious moments, you can interrupt the full intensity of her orgasm.

Sharing Sexual Fantasies

Sexual fantasies are common to many people and provide a rich resource of aphrodisiac material which contributes towards their heightened sexual arousal, either during masturbation or intercourse. These fantasies can be extremely diverse, even bizarre by real-life standards, but very erotically imaginative. Whether the content of someone's sexual fantasy is lurid or mild, it is deeply personal to that individual's sexual psyche and private world of erotic imagery.

Some people have a consistent theme to their fantasies, other people change the material, adding new detail, new scenarios and different characters to their fertile sexual imagery. Studies show, however, that there are certain common patterns of imagination prevalent in people's fantasies, such as themes of domination, submission, being forced into sex against their will, making love to a stranger, an ex-lover or a favourite film star, or being watched while having intercourse.

Sex researchers believe that for many people fantasies are formed in substance from their earliest associations with sexual feelings, while others are constantly updating their erotic imagery to reflect the changing circumstances of their lives. Fantasies based on primal experiences can explain why, for some people, themes such as spanking, or other punishment from an authority figure can feature so strongly.

In another circumstance, a fantasy involving forced sexual compliance, such as a rape scene, may be just a creative way of permitting intense feelings of sexual arousal without having the burden of guilt. In the imagination, that person has no control over what is happening and therefore carries no responsibility for the ensuing erotic feelings.

It is important to realize, however, that fantasies involving forced sex, however descriptive on an imaginative level, will bear little relation to an individual's real-life behaviour or desires, and so do not necessarily

indicate that a person has masochistic tendencies. The fantasizer is always in control of events within the fantasy, because he or she is the creator of those images and can carefully manipulate them to bring about the desired result: that of increased sexual response and orgasm. This scenario is totally different from a real-life event, during which a person would have absolutely no control over an incident involving aggressive behaviour resulting in forced sex, and from which they would derive no sexual pleasure at all.

Many people love their sexual fantasy world, using these mental

images to enhance and enrich their sex lives and sexual responses. Their fantasies seem to have a life of their own, emerging and existing within a vivid arena of sexual imagination. Some people, however, may feel guilt and anxiety associated with them, fearing that the erotic and extra-ordinary content of their mentally created eroticism reflects a deep inner psychological disturbance. This anxiety may be compounded when the fantasies contain material which is strongly in contrast to their normal moral values and sexual behaviour.

Members of both sexes may have sexual fantasies, although some

A View to a Thrill

▼ *Making love in the doggie position in front of a mirror can give you both a good view of your sexual activity, including the excitement of watching your expressions while becoming aroused, and being able to witness your movements. As the man, you are also able to see your partner's breasts in the mirror as you fondle them from this rear position.*

Images of Passion

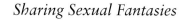 *Watching each other masturbate is another highly erotic way to use the mirror. You can sit beside your partner, stroking her and touching her body and breasts, while being able to see exactly how she likes to arouse herself. The mirror will provide a very clear view of her vulva and the way she stimulates her clitoris.*

people do not have them at all, and cannot see any value in this mental erotic resource. Such couples may regard fantasy as a mental distraction which will prevent a truly spontaneous interaction between the lovers – a flight into cerebral sex rather than an ecstatic surrender to the physical sensations of the body.

Most sex experts agree that sexual fantasizing is normal behaviour, and can be an important and useful way for people to explore their capacity for sexual arousal and response, either during masturbation or lovemaking. Sex therapy can help, however, if sexual fantasizing has become disturbing to an individual, or is having a serious adverse effect on a sexual relationship.

A sex counsellor or therapist will talk over the issues with the person concerned, helping the client to change the undesirable and habitual patterning of his or her erotic thoughts, or enabling them to accept and integrate it into the context of a loving and fulfilling sexual relationship.

Sharing Sexual Fantasies

Many people who enjoy using sexual fantasy to induce sexual arousal or orgasm would never consider revealing the content of these mental images to anyone else, not even a partner. For them, the fantasies must

and do stay within the realm of privacy. They may feel that once a fantasy has been verbalized or shared it loses much of its power and impact.

Other couples discuss their fantasies with each other, and even describe them openly during lovemaking to increase mutual sexual excitement. Some people even feel safe enough within their relationship to act out their fantasies with each other.

Not every person is able to understand or tolerate the erotic imagery that may be part of a partner's sexual consciousness. You need to know and trust your partner's ability to handle this information before revealing your fantasies, or discretion may be a wiser course of action. Your partner may be less than thrilled to know that during lovemaking you have been fantasizing about having sex with your favourite film star or a stranger.

If fantasy is not part of your partner's sexual agenda, then he or she may have no comprehension of your need for it and may even regard it as a personal rejection. In that case, it may be better just to enjoy your fantasies as your own private creation.

This section explores some of the sexual fantasies which can be shared and played out between couples. Some of them are mild and teasing and generally involve a playful

content which would probably be viewed as unthreatening and fun by both partners. Other fantasy games, such as domination and bondage, or even cross-dressing, would need to be revealed or acted on only when a relationship is strong enough to withstand their impact.

No one should ever try to impose a private sexual fantasy on another person, or coerce them into acting it out against their will. However, as a loving couple, if you can enjoy sharing each other's fantasy world in a context of trust and mutual exploration, then your erotic imagination can add a new and exciting dimension to your love-life.

Mirror Fantasies

Some people like to use mirrors when they make love because the thrill of watching themselves in different sexual positions increases the excitement of intercourse. It adds a voyeuristic element to their lovemaking because they can actually see themselves making love, as well as watching their partner's body from a different vantage point.

When a mirror is strategically placed, the couple can see the more erotic and intimate parts of the body in action, such as the vulva, the scrotum, and particularly the buttocks and anus, and they can even witness the process of penetration and thrusting. It can seem as if you are watching yourself and your lover acting the part in a blue-movie, which is an added turn-on to those couples who enjoy watching pornographic films together.

Another fantasy that can arise through the use of a mirror is a sense that other people are copulating alongside you while you are making love. This can provide a safer and less emotionally damaging way of acting out a group orgy sexual fantasy rather than actually doing it for real.

Some couples are fairly blatant about their mirror fantasies, and have one permanently fixed to the bedroom ceiling to provide them with a bird's eye view of their love-making activities. You may not want to go as far as this, and perhaps the use of a mirror during sex is just an occasional fantasy. In that case, a transportable mirror which is easily moved to any part of your bedroom or home to provide a good reflecting angle is the answer.

Strip-Tease Fantasy

It has been said, in a tongue-in-cheek way of course, that inside every woman there is a stripper trying to get out. Not all women are going to agree with that, but it is true that, even among the most reserved, the idea of doing a strip-tease can hold a certain allure. It may even provide material for a sexual fantasy.

There can be something very exciting about the idea of performing an exotic strip-tease dance. If you are confident and extrovert enough, you could have a lot of fun displaying your body to the man you love in such a bold and tantalizing way – and it can be very rewarding to have him adore your every revealing move.

If you do a strip-tease then you must be the one who is in charge of your sexual exhibitionism, and during it your partner is in your control and at your command. He can watch and relish the sight of you, but he must not touch you unless you so desire. The tease is the main point of the exercise so you are allowed to

Build the Suspense
▲ *One of the more fun ways of acting out your strip-tease is to perform for your partner when he is least suspecting it. Or you can set a date for it to build up his eager anticipation. Put on some of your prettiest lingerie, but make sure you have a few layers on top so you can take your time peeling them off, so keeping him in suspense. White underwear is a particularly good choice – the combination of snow-white innocence and your sexy routine will add extra appeal and excitement. Also, wear pretty stockings which you can roll sexily down your legs, or you can add a suspender belt to the strip-tease kit.*

arouse and play with him, showing yourself off little by little, promising hints of your naked body, but you alone must decide when and how to take off your clothes, and how much he can touch you.

Perform your exotic dance for your own pleasure as well as his. You are celebrating your own eroticism,

Shimmy and Shake
▼ *Once you have got his interest, begin your strip routine. To the sound of raunchy music, start to move and sway in front of him. Motion is important in strip-tease, because the sight of your swaying body will be arousing and it should be executed as a dance and a performance. Tease your petticoat straps on and off of your shoulders. Roll down one strap to allow the petticoat to slip slightly off one side of your body. Then haughtily replace it, while you let the other strap fall teasingly off your other shoulder. Keep moving to show him the back and front of your body, and toss your hair with each seductive turn. Then shimmy the petticoat straps down your arms to expose your bra and cleavage.*

and what is more, you are enjoying showing it off.

One of the more fascinating aspects of performing strip-tease is that it allows you to counteract an aspect of your gender conditioning. While women are often portrayed as objects of desire, society also expects them to behave in a demure and chaste manner. Stripping for your lover helps you to challenge that restraint, and you can flaunt your body in such as way that you are making a statement about your own sexuality.

If it is your fantasy to do a strip-tease, then pluck up the courage to do it for your lover. It could be one of his fantasies too, but he may have been too shy to ask you to do it. Visual arousal is an important part of male sexuality, and he is sure to enjoy the invitation to become your captive audience. Devise your own dance routine, and if you need to build up some confidence, practise your steps in front of a mirror when you are alone. The illustrations and further suggestions shown here should provide you with some inspiring ideas on how to turn your strip-tease into an art.

The Art of Strip-Tease

Good strip-tease should be an art, a dance and a performance, so it is worth preparing properly to do it. If you have practised a few routines on your own, you should, by now, have built up your confidence. The two most important props for your show are the right music and sexy underwear. You might like to use additional accoutrements like a feather boa or silk scarves which you can stroke and trail all over your skin, and which you can use to reveal a glimpse of your body.

Seductive Sex Kitten

▼ *Allow the silky petticoat to slide slowly down your body so that you begin to reveal more and more naked skin. Gradually expose your chest and belly but for now do not let the petticoat fall any lower than your hips. The main idea is to keep him in suspense. Pose and move in such a way that you accentuate your curves. In a playful game like this, you can adopt the classic "sex-kitten" postures of movie starlets in the 1950s. Flexing your knee to balance one leg on the ball of your foot will define its shapely contours, and tilt your pelvis back seductively. In strip-tease, you are totally in control of the situation, as you send out inviting come-hither looks. At this stage, though, the man should look but not touch. The whole purpose is to tease him.*

The music you choose should be sexy, or slow and sensual, depending on your dance routine. Or select songs which hold romantic memories for you and your partner. Whatever music you pick, it should have just the right rhythm to put you into an arousing and playful mood.

Concealing and Revealing

▼ *Very slowly let your petticoat slide over your hips and down your legs to reveal your buttocks. You can tantalize him further by letting it slip a little and then re-adjusting it several times before you are ready for full exposure. Sway your hips seductively from side to side, and then rotate to the beat of the music so that the whole of your pelvis is in constant motion. Then turn a little to the side, so that he can see the profile of your body, and enjoy its undulating contours. Panties that are saucy and skimpy will show your buttocks off to their best advantage. For most men, the sight of a woman's bottom is very visually stimulating. When you are ready, turn your back to him so he can enjoy seeing it in full-view, then bend over to allow him a closer look.*

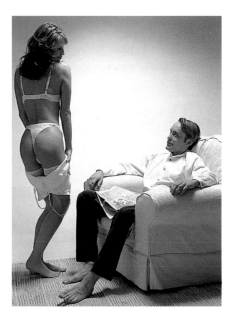

If you want to make strip-tease a regular part of your fantasy play to enjoy with your lover, it is worth investing in several sets of lingerie. Select different colours and styles, and save them for these occasions as well as for your most romantic nights. You need a bra and panties of matching colours and soft fabrics. Silk and lace items always look wonderful. You might like to wear a suspender belt, or choose stockings which cling to your legs. You then need a sexy petticoat, or a slinky dress, so that you are fully covered when you first appear. The fun of strip-tease comes from peeling off the layers piece by piece. You can go for the vamp look, dressed all in black, and even wear high-heeled shoes. Red is exotic and brazen, while white is pure and innocent.

The correct actions during the strip-tease are very important if you are to create the right alluring effect. They should be slow and sexy but slightly exaggerated. Your aim is to pose and move your body as erotically as possible. Lots of pelvic gyrations will excite him and you.

However, you should let your dance be an expression of your own inner sexuality. Do what feels good to you and what turns you on. Find that sex queen part in yourself and act it out to the full.

While you tease your partner and peel away your clothes, stroke and caress your own body as if you are making love to yourself. You can run your hands sensuously over your breasts, along your inner thighs, and in between your legs.

Although the aim of the strip-tease is to excite and tantalize your partner, it should be done for your pleasure too. Love your body and have fun showing it off, and let your liberated eroticism turn you on too. Enjoy the thrill of your sexual power.

Involve Your Partner

▲ Now let your petticoat slip to the floor, and begin to remove your stockings. Like everything else in strip-tease this should be done slowly with a constant "Will I? Won't I?" tease. You can roll your stockings down your legs – one at a time – either by yourself, or involve your partner in the action. Before, he had simply been a spectator, but now he gets a chance to touch. However, you must stay in control, and allow him to touch you only to help you undress – part of the fun of strip-tease is that he knows you have the upper hand.

Peel to Appeal

▲ Everything about your movements should be seductive, sensual and erotic, but it needs to be graceful too. So when it comes to taking your stockings off completely, you should enlist your partner's help. Otherwise, you may be struggling in this position, unless you put one foot on the chair or sit on the floor. One way is to give him your leg to hold and have him peel the stocking right off your foot. At the same time, you can sexily stroke over your own leg, thigh and buttocks. Self-caressing is an alluring aspect of strip-tease.

Teasing Touches

▲ The show goes on – and you can now get down to the nitty-gritty of your strip-tease. When you are just wearing your panties and bra, take lots of time to remove them. Move and dance around his chair, coming in close enough so he can give you a fleeting touch, and then moving slightly out of his reach. Start to turn up the heat in your act, by rolling your panties down just enough to give him a little peek. Stand close enough that he can begin to touch and caress you, and even let him tug at your panties with his teeth.

Unsnap the Strap

◀ You can enlist his help to undo your bra fastener, especially if undoing it yourself would prove too awkward. Perch saucily on his lap with your back to him and stay in your performance mode, gyrating your pelvis subtly on his knee. If you have long hair, sweep it sexily away from your shoulders and back to expose more bare flesh to him, and if he wants to, let him plant little kisses on your skin. It is too soon to let the bra slip off, so once he has undone it, cup it to your breasts with your hands. The point of the exercise is to keep him wanting more.

Caress Your Breasts

▶ Let the rounded swell of your breasts begin to show, but don't expose your nipples yet. Turn to face your partner, and incline towards him so your breasts come close to his body. Gently palpate your breasts with your hands as if caressing them, and let the bra material stroke across their skin. Don't let your partner touch your breasts yet – at this point you are using visual stimulation to arouse him – but you can move your leg closer to him so he can stroke your thighs. Gradually let your bra slide down from your breasts, to expose the edge of your nipples.

Panty Time

▲ Now comes the really sexy part, as you start to peel off your panties. Keep the movement going in your body as you turn from side to side and back and forth, sometimes leaning your hips or buttocks within reach of his touch. Begin to edge your panties very slowly downwards. Turn around sometimes to give him a little glimpse of your pubic hair, but change angles constantly so he gets an all-round view of this very erotic part of your body.

Move in Close

▲ Still holding on to your panties, languidly roll them over the curve of your buttocks so they rest on the top of your thighs. At this point, your whole body is almost entirely naked. Make the most of these last tantalizing moments of your strip-tease, but moving very close to your partner and dancing erotically in front of him. Let different parts of your body brush and rub against him, and then allow him to reach out and caress you a little more.

Fun Finale

▲ Find an easy way to roll your panties down your legs so you remove them completely from your body. If necessary, you can rest one foot on the chair for easy manoeuvring. Then use your panties as part of your dance. Stroke them softly over your skin, between your legs, against your partner's face, and hook them around his neck to pull him playfully towards you. The strip-tease is over, what you do next with all that smouldering sexual excitement is up to you.

Feeding Frenzy

A fun fantasy to share with your partner is to prepare a sumptuous banquet of delicious desserts, only instead of laying the food on a table, you spread it on each other's bodies – and then have a wonderful time nibbling and licking it off. You can gather around you all kinds of delicious ripe fruits – tropical mangoes are an exotic choice. Or you may

Cream Stream

▼ *When she is lying down, pour the cream or sauces, or rub the juicy fruits on her body. If you are pouring a liquid cream, let it trickle out slowly so she feels its cool sensations running down over her skin. (If you are worried about making a mess, cover your mattress with a washable sheet.)*

Fruity Fiesta

▲ *Start off your bacchanalian feast with a fruit cocktail for the hors d'oeuvres. Feed each other juicy pieces of exotic fruits to excite your taste buds and make your mouths water. Be sure, though, to spice up your snack with plenty of kisses and cuddles.*

Taste Sensations

▶ *Begin to lick the cream from her body. Slow, languid licks of your tongue, and then some darting motions, will thrill her skin and delight her. Spend extra time on the most sensitive areas, such as her belly. Run your warm tongue around and around her navel and tell her that she tastes delicious.*

want to go for the smoother tastes of icecream, honey, chocolate sauce, cream, and yogurt.

This is a sensual and hedonistic feast in every way, so make sure you pick the most mouth-watering foods you can find. If you want to make the event simpler, go for one type, such as cream, which has a soft consistency and can be easily poured over the skin.

Just Desserts

Gerry, 32 years, a masseur and keep-fit trainer: "My girlfriend, Nicole, and I made love one time covered from head to foot with fruit pulp and cream. It was a totally spontaneous event, though we were at home and just in our underwear at the time. It started out as a joke, her flicking a bit of the food at me, and then me retaliating. One thing led to another and we ended up smearing our dessert all over each other's bodies and then licking it off each other. The whole thing just got more sensual and erotic by the moment. We were slithering all over each other in the end. I can definitely recommend it. It was yummy!"

The idea is to let your tongue travel slowly around your partner's body so that you lick off the food in such a slow, sensual and titillating way that you drive your partner into a frenzy of arousal. Linger awhile over the more erogenous zones of her body, teasingly nibble around the breasts and nipples, or seductively run the tip of your tongue over her belly, or along the inside of her thighs. Sup on the succulent juices and creams, telling your partner that she is "good enough to eat" whenever you reach certain pleasure spots on her body. Let yourselves luxuriate in an epicurean orgy of sensual taste and skin pleasure. No need to hurry over this feast and, at this banquet, seconds and dessert are definitely in order!

Feast on Her Breasts

▼ *Pour drops of the cream onto her breasts and take as long as you like to savour its taste. Work your tongue slowly around the circumference of her breast, before adding a little more cream to her nipple. Suck and lick her nipple teasingly, relishing in the erotic feast.*

Dressing-Up Fantasies

While most of us present a particular personality to the outside world, with which we predominantly identify ourselves, within us all there are many other character traits which weave together to create the rich tapestry of our human psyches. At best, the varying shades of our personalities can mingle with each other and become integrated, each part having an opportunity to express itself at an appropriate time.

Occasionally, though, certain aspects of our internal world become suppressed or denied, perhaps because of moral conditioning, fear of judgement from others, or through self-censure. Sometimes it is just a lack of opportunity that forces us to resign some of our more colourful internal personality traits to the back shelf. This is particularly true in regard to our sexual consciousness, and one of the reasons that fantasy can often be so helpful is that it enables us to access those more obscure parts of ourselves.

In a close and loving relationship, where two people trust each other and are willing to share each other's fantasies without condemnation, there is a tremendous opportunity to play-act roles which allow them to express and have fun with some of their sexual identities. One way to do this is by dressing up, thereby allowing your hidden sexual fantasies to emerge in full regalia.

You can even dress up to be theatrical, turning your bedroom into a fantasy land where you act out heroes and heroines from the movies, the stage, literature – or even those from your imagination. You can turn yourselves into Heathcliff and Cathy, or Romeo and Juliet for the night. Or

Dressing the Part

▲ Look for the kind of outrageous outfit or underwear you would never normally wear. It should be pure show biz or downright sexy. If you want to be a James Bond girl or an Amazon Queen, leather, latex, rubber or chain mail will give you the tough, sexually assertive look to help you play out your fantasy role.

perhaps one or the other of you has a favourite film star – so why not be Humphrey Bogart, or Marilyn Monroe, or whoever else you admire, and play-act the part for the night for your favourite audience? Or, if you trust each other, dress up to manifest your sexual secrets and fantasies. Raid your wardrobe, or scour the sales for items of clothing which will help you to fulfil your complete sexual personality.

The Temptress

So you have a respectable job, your life is well-organized, you may be a mother and have a secure long-term relationship. Or you have strong feelings about sexual equality, support the feminist movement, and hate to see women portrayed as sexual objects. There is, however, a part of you (it may be a very small part!) that has an on-going fantasy about being a scarlet woman, a femme-fatale, a bordello queen, or a temptress.

If you give yourself permission to allow that side of your nature to come out once in a while, it does not mean to say that your whole value system and way of life is about to change. Dressing up and play-acting your sex queen or brazen woman fantasy in the safety of your bedroom

Lavish Your Attention

▲ *You have succeeded in winning over the man and now he is putty in your hands. Wrap him up in your feather boa and pull him close to the warmth of your skin and into the soft curves of your body. Now that you have him in your arms, you are going to lavish attention on him. How about planting kisses from those full red lips of yours all over his face.*

An Offer He Can't Refuse

▶ *Pose yourself to look alluring, and make the most of your feminine curves. For extra effect, drape your feather boa around your body. Learn to pant seductively. Let everything you do signal a hint of promise and pleasure. Then pat the bed beside you expectantly and invite him to join you.*
How can he refuse?

and together with your partner will just be an exciting and fun way to express a certain side of yourself. You may feel enriched by it too, because an important aspect of who you are can claim its place in your life.

Cross-Dressing

Nobody knows for sure how many men enjoy cross-dressing or even fantasize about it. The subject is still taboo in our society, although transvestite issues are now being discussed more openly. However, research shows that a considerable number of men do cross-dress and become sexually aroused by wearing, or thinking about wearing, women's clothes, and especially women's underwear.

The reason why this is one of the most secret fantasies of all is that many men, who clearly identify themselves as heterosexuals and who only want to make love to female partners, are afraid of the ridicule and condemnation that cross-dressing invariably causes. Studies conducted on men who cross-dress, show that over 75 per cent of them are married and have children. Their sexual orientation is towards the

Fantasy Femme Fatale
▼ *Is there a temptress or a femme fatale inside you waiting to express herself? Do you have a fantasy about being a Mata Hari, a high-class courtesan, or an expensive mistress? Enjoy playing your role. Go for the glamour look, and keep it totally feminine. Choose passionate red, lace, and feathers, and lots of make-up. Go all out to seduce your man.*

opposite sex, and they clearly identify their gender as male.

There are various reasons why a man may fantasize about cross-dressing. It may be due to curiosity and the desire to discover how it feels to "be like a woman"; soft, feminine or exotic underwear may appeal to him, or he may even need to wear female underwear or other clothing to become sexually aroused. In the

Enjoying His Fantasy
◀ *Not all women are disturbed by a man's cross-dressing fantasy. She can be happy to join in, selecting items of her clothing for him to wear, or taking him out on a shopping trip to choose his female underwear. In fact, her role of dressing him up may be an acted-out fantasy for her too.*

latter case, this can be termed as a transvestite fetish, as the man is reliant on these objects to become sexually fulfilled.

Having fantasies, or wearing female clothing, is not a problem in itself, unless the man feels confused or unhappy about his sexual identity, is plagued with guilt about it, or his female partner feels distressed, offended and threatened by his transvestite tendencies. (Some sex counsellors specialize in cross-dressing, transvestite, or transsexual issues and are able to help the individuals concerned to talk through any problems that may result.)

Many wives and girlfriends, who discover their partners are cross-dressers, find it almost impossible to accept or understand their behaviour.

Coming to Terms With Cross-Dressing

Melanie, 42 years, has been married to Tom, also 42, for 14 years:

"We had been married for about nine years before I discovered that Tom liked to wear women's underwear. I found out because I walked into the bedroom one afternoon and found him wearing a pair of my best knickers – a black, silky pair that I kept for special occasions. I don't know who looked more shocked – Tom, for being found out, or me.

"We had a terrible scene about it, during which he confessed that he often fantasized about wearing women's clothing, and that he did sometimes dress up as a woman, whenever he was alone in the house. I went a bit hysterical, and I said some awful things to him, accusing him of all kinds of perverted behaviour. He said he had always felt guilty about this trait, and he was obviously very distressed about me knowing about it.

"On my side, I felt he had turned into a stranger in a second, that he was no longer the man I knew, and I even wondered if he was actually a real man at all. Our relationship went through a very rocky patch, but somehow we managed to keep talking it through because the bottom line was that we really loved each other, and we had a good relationship. We were lucky because we met some people who knew a great deal more about cross-dressing than us and we were able to get advice from them.

"Slowly, Tom felt less guilty, and I came to accept this side of his sexuality. I became less suspicious and judgmental about the whole thing. In the end we even started to use his cross-dressing as an occasional 'extra' in our sexual relationship. When he feels the need, and I am ready for it, I dress and make him up. We don't discuss this with our friends, but it has become our special secret and we even make it fun."

Tom's response:

"All I want to add to what Melanie has said is that none of this ever had anything to do with how I felt about her because I have always really loved her. At the end of the day, it was a relief that she knew. I am very lucky to have someone like Melanie who could eventually accept and understand this part of me."

They may fear that their partners have homosexual tendencies, are effeminate, or they may regard the behaviour as a perversion. Some female partners, though, are happy to comply with this aspect of the man's personality, and even enjoy dressing him up, putting make-up on him, or choosing his specialized items of clothing. It is their secret, and it becomes part of their sexual agenda – an important feature of their relationship, even if it is something that is hidden from others.

Perhaps your dressing-up fantasies might include cross-dressing. This could be a response to the man's real desire to sometimes wear women's clothing, or it might just be a one-off game to act out the opposite-sex gender role. If this is acceptable to both people involved, and you feel your relationship is strong enough to withstand the implications, cross-dressing can become a shared fantasy game involving you both.

Feminine Role-Play

◀ *He may just want to wear women's panties or stockings, but he might also want to dress up completely as a female and play-act the role of a woman for a while.*

Getting Turned On

Some people are very turned on by the idea of skin teasing, where they are stroked all over the body with the lightest of touches and using all kinds of textures which can result in an almost unbearable intensity. At the other extreme, so long as both partners are willing, lovers can find it stimulating to act out fantasies that involve bondage and domination.

Skin Teasing

It is not a fantasy for the ticklish, but if the idea of a session of skin excitation appeals to either of you, then gather around you all kinds of sensual materials so that you can enjoy a variety of tactile sensations. Find out from each other if either of you has a particular tactile fetish – perhaps you love the feeling of feathers, or of soft, luxurious silk on your skin, or even the firmer texture of leather or rubber being stroked against the surface of your body.

Even more exciting is to use different materials and different touches, perhaps even blowing or licking the body all over, or trailing your fingers very lightly over the most sensitive parts of the skin. Erotic touches on

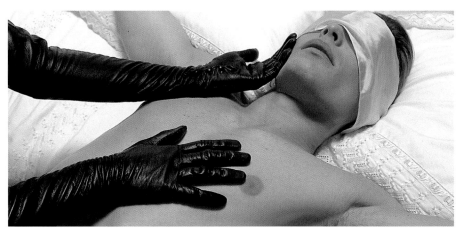

Feel of Leather

▲ If your partner is turned on by the idea of black leather, find a pair of erotic-looking soft leather gloves to wear and begin to stroke very lightly but slowly over his whole body. Blindfold him loosely with a silk scarf so he doesn't know where your touches will go, or exactly what you are planning to do, and this will add to his excitement. Stroke all over his face so he can take in the smell of the leather, and then draw one hand after the other lightly on the surface of his skin down over his body to the tips of his toes.

Caress of Silk

▲ The soft caress of a silky scarf will create a contrasting skin sensation compared to the feel of leather. Its light sensual texture will barely put any pressure on the skin at all. This will heighten the nerve sensation, drawing your partner's feeling senses out to the very surface of his body. Silk can produce a wonderful sense of luxurious caress, particularly when trailed over areas of highly sensitive skin. Velvet or chiffon are also texturally sensual materials.

Featherlight Touches

▲ The ruffling of downy feathers against the skin will tickle and tease it pleasantly. Feathers are even softer than silk, so light they can fly away. For the tantalizing effect of many feathers stroking the skin, loosely bunch up an ostrich feathered boa, and rub it back and forth gently across his chest. Then you can loosen it and trail its length all over his body, asking your partner to turn over at some point, so it can caress the back of his body.

Plumes of Pleasure

▼ *Lots of people fantasize about having their skin teased lovingly by peacock feathers. The rich colours and beautiful designs in the peacock's plumage give them a very exotic appearance. Then the fan-shaped top of the feather and its delicate quill make it a perfect tool for exciting the skin if it is stroked very lightly all over the body. Give your partner a feathery thrill, running the peacock feather over the surface of her skin with almost imperceptible pressure. It will make her whole body tingle and shiver with pleasure.*

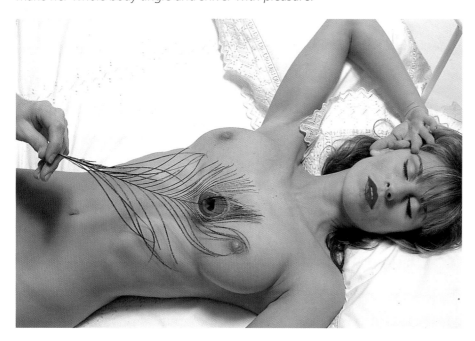

the skin involve brushing its surface, with almost no pressure, so they enliven the skin's most peripheral sensory nerves. All the hair follicles that cover the skin are packed with nerve endings that are stimulated by these erotic caresses. Sometimes your whole body is left tingling and quivering to the point that you are tempted to beg your partner to stop. Yet the pleasure is in being taken right to the height of skin sensation.

There are several ways to enjoy this fantasy game. You might want to try all the different kinds of skin stimulation in one session, so that you experience a whole variety of touches and textures. You can enjoy the caress of any material including leather, silk, satin, chiffon and feathers. Or you might make it a totally

feathery event, tantalizing the skin with delicate caresses from a whole variety of exotic plumes. Perhaps you prefer to be excited by the warmth of your partner's touch. Your skin can

be stroked all over with the light brush of fingertips, the sensual moistness of the tongue, or the caressing breeze of the breath.

If you are being skin teased, try to relax as much as you can into the intensity of your skin responses. While the touch is exquisitely light, your sensory nerves will be in a state of high excitation. If you tense up it will become too ticklish, but if you surrender to the tantalizing touches, it can become an extremely pleasurable sensation.

Ticklish Delight

▼ *Barely any weight at all, a single boa feather feels like a breeze whispering over the skin – watch the goose bumps come and go! Sweep this lovely, delicate feather over all her erogenous pleasure zones. Run it around her nipples, under her arms, along the side of her neck, and over her belly, groin and thighs. When she turns over, skim the feather over the soles of her feet and on the very sensitive spot at the back of the knees, and then circulate it over her buttocks. See how she squirms with this ticklish delight.*

Tongue Teasing

▼ *Bathe the whole body with the warm, moist sensations of your tongue, flicking it and licking lightly over the surface of the skin. This is a very erotic form of skin teasing, inciting his sensual and sexual feelings to fever pitch. Languidly roll your tongue around and around the surface of his lips and the rims of his ears. Then dart it back and forth over his nipples and further down, circle it around his navel. Let your tongue travel down lightly over his genitals, but try not to over-excite him here. Continue running your tongue over the whole of his body, to keep him on the sensory edge.*

Sensual Breath

▼ *When the skin has been moistened by the tongue, blow gently over the wet areas. The warmth of your breath against the damp of the skin is particularly sensual. Brush his whole body with sweeps of your breath, sometimes caressing his skin like a gentle breeze, and sometimes blowing a little stronger in circular motions so it seems as if you are creating a mini-whirlwind on the surface of his body. Breathe on his nipples for a special effect.*

Tracing Her Contours

▲ *She can lie back and surrender to the gentle touch of your fingers running softly over her face. There should be no pressure at all in your hands, just a feathery motion that will awaken the most peripheral of her skin's sensory nerves. Let the feeling in your fingers be tender and loving, and move them flowing down over her face, tracing the contours of her features. Run your fingertips delicately over the edge of her eyelashes and over her lips. Try to see how light you can make the touch.*

Stroke Play

Patsy, aged 33: "When we were little, my sister and I used to spend hours tickling each other and I loved that very light touch on my skin. I had special places where it felt particularly pleasurable, like my back, my underarms, and most especially my feet.

"In all of my relationships since becoming an adult, I have always wanted a boyfriend to touch and tease me in that way. I just want to lie there, and be lightly stroked all over – the more subtle it is, the more exciting I find it. It is not always sexual, but it is immensely physically pleasurable.

"Now, finally, I have a boyfriend who loves it too, so we spend quite a bit of our physical time just teasing, tickling and stroking each other's skin with all kinds of things. We always take it in turns, so one of us can just give in to enjoying the pleasure of all those lovely skin sensations. To me it feels like luxury and my dream come true. Sometimes I enjoy it as much as making love."

Linger Lovingly

▶ *Use the back of your fingers, your fingertips, and even the edge of your nails to heighten her skin senses. Linger sensually over the most sensitive places where the skin is particularly soft and defenceless to tease and excite it. Stroke over her belly and along the sides of her ribcage and then slide your fingers along the inside of her thighs with these teasing and pleasing touches which bring the warmth of your skin to the surface of her body.*

Dominance and Bondage

Domination and bondage are common themes in sexual fantasies. Images of being tied up, spanked, or even "forced" (albeit erotically) into having sex are typical fantasies which can run through some people's minds while having intercourse. More often than not, these day-dreams remain in the mind as a private fantasy and are never actually acted out in reality.

A lot of people would never even discuss these fantasies with their partners, either because they feel too shy, or just because they want to keep them in their own private world. However, for many, the fantasy of being the dominant or submissive partner in a sexual scenario, or being restrained while being slowly teased into an orgasm, is an imaginative way to become erotically aroused.

Some couples even like to play out their sexual fantasies together in the bedroom, switching between the dominant and submissive roles from time to time, or settling into a particular routine depending on which excites them most. Bondage, discipline, or dressing up in leather and

other fetishist gear may be a big turn-on for some people but abhorrent to others. The major rule of these sex games is that both partners are happy and willing to give them a go. No one should ever pressure his or her partner into this kind of fantasy sex play, nor should anyone submit to it just to please a demanding partner. However, if you both enjoy a little rough play in your sex life, and the idea of taking your eroticism right to the edge excites you, then there is no reason at all why you should not add these saucy alternatives to your sexual repertoire.

Rules of the Game

Some people fear that their tough love sex play could mean that they are bordering on sado-masochism. There is no need to worry unless you are actually hurting your partner or you feel you are receiving real pain and abuse. What we are discussing here is pretending to use domination and force and playing with these concepts because you find them sexually arousing and enriching to your sex life. So where do you draw the line?

First of all, these fantasy games must always be by mutual consent.

Then make some rules and stick by them. Only act out domination and submission games when you are in a relationship you trust, and you know your partner well enough to be sure he or she would never hurt you, or ever force you into something you do not want to do. If spanking the buttocks is part of your play, then only take it so far as you find it fun and exciting.

Don't cause real pain, cause bruises or break the skin. You can pretend you are humiliating your partner, but you should know the boundaries between play and offence. Don't say things you may regret later or which will emotionally scar your partner. Talk over exactly what kind of fantasy behaviour turns you on, what your limits are, and what you do and do not want to happen, and then stick within these guidelines.

Make sure you have a signal or code word which you both recognize as the sign to stop the game immediately. The moment one or the other of you says this word or gives the sign, you must stop!

If being tied to the bed post while your partner makes slow, tantalizing love to you, or gives you orgasmic oral sex (research shows that restraint is probably the most popular fantasy) interests you and you plan to act it out, then make sure he or she does not tie the knots too tight, and that they can be undone immediately if you request it, or whenever necessary.

You can restrain the wrists and ankles, but you must never tie anything around the neck, and covering the mouth can also be dangerous. If your partner is restrained, do not leave him or her alone – even for a short time. You need to be conscious and present during the whole time your partner is tied up.

Some people may fantasize about restraint, and even desire to act it

Master and Slave

▼ *Some men can be very aroused by playing a submissive role in a sex game, especially as a release of tension if they otherwise hold powerful positions. Some couples enjoy a "master and slave" game, where the woman plays a dominating role and disciplines her partner. If you are acting this out as the dominator, dress up to look sexy but stern and severe. Thigh-length black leather boots will put you in the mood for the part. Assert your dominance over your partner, threatening to discipline him if he does not follow your every wish and whim.*

out, but are simply too afraid to be tied up. Respect that anxiety and just pretend he or she is tied up. One way is for that person to grip the head-board so the arms are spread-eagled, and the legs are splayed out wide in the posture of restraint.

Getting the Gear

Fetishist tools may be in order for these games, and you can get these from a good sex shop. Black outfits

---

Playing Power Games

Jonathan, aged 33, a salesman has lived with his girlfriend, Anja, for five years. "It was Anja who first suggested that we should introduce some domination and submission games into our sex life. She said that in her last relationship, her boyfriend would sometimes tie her arms and legs to the bed posts, and then make love to her, and that she found it to be incredibly sexually arousing. I was more than happy to give it a go because I had always wanted to do something like this myself, but my last girlfriend would have never agreed to it. Now, once in a while, we take it in turns to be tied up. Sometimes I do it to her, and she just goes wild, especially if I am giving her oral sex. She says that this kind of sex game gives her the most intense orgasms. It's the same for me, because there is something incredibly erotic about having to absolutely surrender and be helpless while she is making love to me. She does everything very slowly, and takes me almost to the point of an orgasm, then cools it down, and then starts again. In the end, I feel like I am going to explode – and I usually do."

Clara, aged 27, a landscape designer, has shared a home with her fiancé for two years. "Jack and I enjoy all kinds of sex games, and we are pretty hot on the ones with domination themes. He is the dominator, and I get turned on by the submissive role. We do all kinds of things, and I am sure people who know us would be quite shocked about what we get up to on some weekends because we look so normal. I trust him completely because I know he loves me and he would never do anything that would actually hurt me. I have my code word, and if I say it, he always stops. We also make love in all the more normal ways too because we don't want this to be our only sexual theme. The interesting thing is that it is only in our sexual relationship that Jack's domination fantasy comes out. In every other aspect of our relationship, we are absolutely on equal terms."

Kirsty, aged 26, a teacher, has been married for two years. "This kind of sex play is definitely not for me. I don't even have fantasies about it, though I know that some of my girlfriends do. I can't relate to it at all. For me, making love is all about just that – it's a way of expressing all our loving and tender feelings for each other. I just want to be me in bed and there's no room for fantasy. I think it would make us feel as if we were having sex with a stranger."

Demand His Obedience
◀ Stay haughty and proud as he grovels at your feet. Let him adore you from his lowly position. He must touch, kiss or caress you in any way you command, but you must appear to be above feeling excited by his attentions. Complain and make him do more. The fun is in acting as if you have total control and can demand complete obedience from him.

Assert Your Sexuality
▶ If you think he has been "bad" or is showing too much will of his own, you can rough him around a little. Or you can display your assertive sexuality, pulling him to your body and holding his body tight to yours. You can even make love to him, but you must stay in charge.

are a popular choice for bondage and domination games. Boots, corsets, armbands, and elbow-length gloves in leather, latex or rubber are the normal gear that turn people on. Men are more visually stimulated than their partners by these outfits, but women can enjoy dressing up to arouse their men. (Some women might find the whole idea chauvinistic and absurd!)

Soft ropes, silk scarves or strips of cotton material can all be used for restraint, but make sure that nothing you use will burn or chafe the skin. If you want to use more serious-looking equipment, there are sexy handcuffs available which both of you can undo, if necessary. Don't use real handcuffs which are too threatening and may be difficult to release.

Helpless to Resist
▲ Restraint, or being softly tied to the bed post, and having your lover slowly, tantalizingly and deliberately turn you on while you pretend to be helpless can be extremely arousing. The added thrill is the restriction on movement which can take your excitement right to its peak. He should pay attention to every part of your body. If he licks and kisses your breasts and nipples while you are tied like this, you may feel as if you are going to explode with erotic sensation. He should deliberately do everything slowly, taking his time to keep you dangling at this almost excruciating pitch of excitement.

Begging for More
▲ Slow, erotic oral sex while being restrained can be an amazing sexual experience. Again, he should take his time, doing everything in a teasing and super-sensual way. If he is sensitive to your responses, he will know just when to slow down to delay your moment of orgasm, so that you beg him to go ahead.

Good Vibrations
▲ Another variation to add to your fantasy play, is for him to use a vibrator to bring you to orgasm. After kissing and stroking every part of your body, and waiting till you have reached a peak of arousal, he can use a sex toy and vibrate it against your vulva. At the same time, you can let the fantasies in your mind run riot.

Spontaneous Sex

Spontaneous sex refers to the proverbial "quickie". It is the stuff of best-selling airport novels, full of erotic heaving, panting and writhing bodies, bodice-ripping sex scenes and exotic or, at least, unusual locations. It is not slow and sensual, or particularly intimate, but it is hot and passionate and deliciously primitive. When spontaneous sex happens it is the meeting of the "wild" man and the "wild" woman – there are no formalities to play out and clothes are cast aside along with inhibitions.

Does spontaneous sex have any place in a loving and intimate sexual relationship? Yes, it certainly does, if the two people concerned are equally eager for the action. It is sexual appetite at its most voracious, a hunger immediately satisfied by two consenting partners.

Spontaneous sex can be extremely exciting and exhilarating, affirming a mutual physical attraction and enlivening any sexual relationship with its raw and untamed content. It can happen anywhere, and when least expected, because by its nature it does not run to a schedule.

The one thing you must guarantee, though, is complete privacy, with absolutely no one else in sight, because neither the law, nor your family, nor your neighbours will applaud you if you are caught in the act.

Spontaneous sex rarely happens in the bedroom, it is much more likely to occur in the kitchen, the living room, the bathroom, or on the stairs. It may be even more licentious – forbidden moments in the office basement, on a bed of

Change of Mood
▲ *Sexual arousal can happen when you least expect it. You may be planning simply to relax with your partner after a tiring day at work and watch a little television before going to bed to sleep. The two of you snuggle up for a cosy but quiet evening, then suddenly the mood changes, and your bodies become electrified just from their closeness to each other.*

Desire Takes Over
▶ *A sense of urgency rises. You don't even feel you have time to go to the bedroom. Most of your clothes are hastily removed, either by yourself or your partner. Now you can make better use of that comfortable old settee. As the woman, you can climb astride your partner's lap and mount him immediately.*

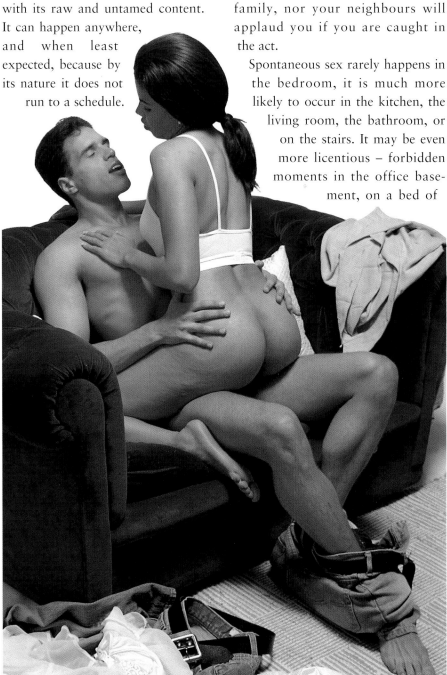

Sexual Heat is On

◀ *Both of you can let go into a passionate session of lovemaking, using the settee to its best advantage. The back of the chair is a good place to sit if your partner wants to perform cunnilingus on you. The heat of the moment will increase the arousal and excitement for both of you and you can let go into waves of pleasure.*

Primal Passion

▼ *Making love in the doggie position, with the male partner entering the vagina from behind, will add to the primal intensity of your spontaneous sexual happening. You can lean your weight onto the back of the settee, and while he is thrusting, he can also stimulate your clitoris with his fingers.*

soft grass, against an inviting tree, or on a windswept beach at night.

The wonderful thing about this kind of sex is that it can recapture the excitement and spontaneity of your early days of romance, when your sex hormones were rampant and the two of you could hardly wait a second longer to make love. A "quickie" is the pep pill which can put the zest back into your sexual relationship.

Standing Up

Standing up is a classic but awkward position for the "quickie" way of having intercourse. It usually implies fast and furious sex, with no preliminaries, but it is hot and impetuous and therefore probably very exciting. If you do it standing up, it is best to have something to lean on, such as a wall or a tree, and it definitely works better if the partners are a similar height and weight. The main problem is that the penis can easily slip out of the vagina, and the vertical position makes it difficult for deep thrusting. However, the impulsiveness of the situation usually indicates that the man is so aroused he is likely to ejaculate very quickly.

Standing Sex
◀ *You can't wait to make it to the bedroom so, pressed against the wall, you make love to each other in the standing position. Your partner will be able to penetrate you deeper if he elevates you slightly, and you curl one leg around him. He must take care not to push you too hard against the wall while he is thrusting.*

This is not an uncommon position for young lovers to take when first exploring their sexuality, perhaps because they cannot take their partner home and so have to resort to more furtive methods of sexual contact. It may also be a natural follow-on from a heavy-petting session. However, in these situations, penetration does not necessarily take place, but the female may close her thighs around the penis, allowing it to rub against her genitals. In this way, both people can gain a quick release from their sexual excitement and tension.

Passion and Lust
Passion is the spice of life – it's sexuality in Technicolor. It fascinates and frightens us a bit, because under its spell we temporarily lose our minds, while our emotions and bodies take over. Lust is a sign of a healthy libido racing along in top gear, and life would be pretty boring if we never encountered it at all.

The main thing about sexual passion is the intensity and the speed with which it can come and go. While in the throes of a passionate love affair, all other areas of life pale by comparison. What else would drive politicians, amongst others, to risk their careers, marriages and reputations which they have spent years meticulously building up?

Passion is the source of inspiration for a thousand songs and poems – the story line for most of the successful movies. It seems as if we need to have passion in our lives, even if we are not the ones actually experiencing it.

Passion and lust inevitably burn themselves out, but in a stable relationship they can leave in their place the warm glow of intimacy and companionship. Sexual love can grow instead, and a physical relationship can become more harmonious and compatible, integrating itself within the context of everything else that is meaningful in life.

Yet even within the most contented relationships there is often a secret yearning for the flame of passion to be lit again. We miss the excitement, and the thrill of the unpredictable and uncontrollable experience

Business Suitors

▶ *Full spontaneous sex may be out of the question, especially if you are in a business situation, but if you and your partner meet up somewhere at work, you may not be able to resist a surreptitious petting session behind closed doors. There is something especially exciting about this kind of erotic encounter because it will be in strict contrast to your professional persona.*

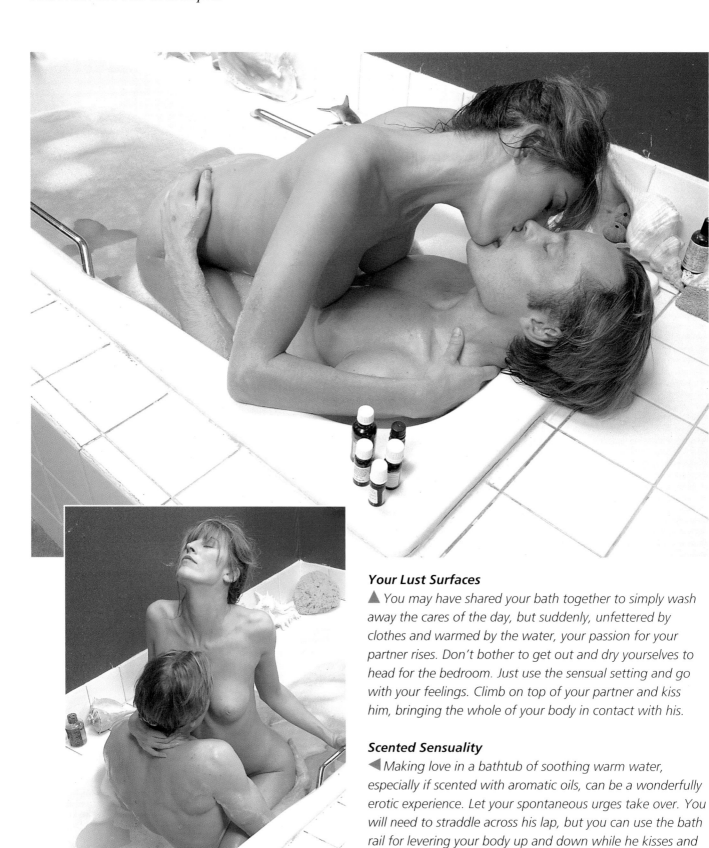

Your Lust Surfaces

▲ You may have shared your bath together to simply wash away the cares of the day, but suddenly, unfettered by clothes and warmed by the water, your passion for your partner rises. Don't bother to get out and dry yourselves to head for the bedroom. Just use the sensual setting and go with your feelings. Climb on top of your partner and kiss him, bringing the whole of your body in contact with his.

Scented Sensuality

◄ Making love in a bathtub of soothing warm water, especially if scented with aromatic oils, can be a wonderfully erotic experience. Let your spontaneous urges take over. You will need to straddle across his lap, but you can use the bath rail for levering your body up and down while he kisses and caresses you all over.

of overwhelming physical and emotional sensation. Most of us would become exhausted if we lived in a state of passion all the time. However, it is a lucky relationship which can retain its elements, for if a couple can relive those moments of passion and lust and magical chemistry which drew them together in the first place, the mantle of complacency and boredom which can descend on any relationship would have difficulty taking hold.

So spontaneous, wild and lustful sex has a therapeutic place within a relationship. When the mood takes you, you can be creative with it. Let go into it, and allow your erotic fantasies to come true immediately. Don't worry about the time of the day, or what part of the house you are in – let your mutual passion surface unbridled, and use whatever props you have around you, such as the chairs, stairs or bathtub to their best advantage.

Arousal on the Boil
▲ You can even go for the bodice-ripping "take me-I'm yours" scenario if the urge takes over. Neither of you should hold back; let lust command you. The kitchen table will do, even if you don't have time to clear it. Don't even wait to take your clothes off. You might not be able to wear that dress again, but you can hang it in the wardrobe as a glorious memento!

Torrid Table-top Sex
◀ This could be an extremely lustful episode of spontaneous lovemaking. You have torn off each other's clothes and she is laying face down across the table. You can enter her from the rear position, and make love to her passionately, but take care not to press her too hard against the surface of the table.

Chapter 7

Overcoming Difficulties

In any relationship there may be times when the flames of passion begin to dim, or even to burn out completely. The reasons for this are many and various, but often come down to the simple fact that it is sometimes difficult to maintain erotic intensity when your libido has to compete against the pressures of work and family life, or the many minor domestic disputes that can act as a barrier to sexual expression. Sometimes the problems are more deeply entrenched, and the couple would benefit from seeking advice from an understanding and qualified sex counsellor to try to resolve the underlying issues. However, a loving and supporting couple can also help each other through sexual difficulties with simple, sensual exercises which they can do on their own. It is at times like these that a couple will need to re-discover the innately sensitive and nurturing side of their sexual selves and to find a new way to realize their orgasmic potential.

Overcoming Difficulties

Lack of sexual interest shown by one or both partners is the most common form of sexual problem occurring within a relationship. There may be a number of factors that block the sexual response. Sometimes stress at work or in the home can cause fatigue or anxiety and consequently a diminished libido. If there is anger or other negative feelings between the partners, and a lack of clear communication skills, then the sexual relationship is ultimately bound to suffer.

Sadly, in many relationships, once the first flush of passion and excitement has subsided, lovemaking can become perfunctory, focused mainly on penetration and thrusting, and regarded more as a relief from sexual tension than a sensual, nurturing and fulfilling encounter. In these circumstances, either partner may withdraw from the sexual arena, and this can lead to a buildup of frustration within the relationship.

Sensate focus exercises are the backbone of psychosexual therapy, enabling couples to overcome their sexual difficulties and regain, or even discover, a more sensual and intimate side of their physical relationship. They work by helping the couple to change their focus away from penetrative sex, performance and sexual obligation. While a couple are working through these exercises, they make a commitment to ban all intercourse until the very last stage.

The point of sensate focus is to help people break old habits and patterns of sexual behaviour which have proved unsatisfying. The pressure is taken away from the need to initiate or respond to sexual overtures, giving the couple an opportunity to relax with each other's bodies and to recreate their sexual relationship in an entirely new way.

Sensate focus exercises, originally devised by sex researchers, William Masters and Virginia Johnson, are based on encouraging couples to discover the joy and pleasure of sensual touching for its own sake,

and not for an end result. This is a very important factor which may be missing from a sexual partnership. Sex is often directed towards penetration and thrusting and can become a way of using another person's body for self-gratification.

In their haste to reach a climax, many individuals may not actually experience their own sensual pleasure and may completely miss their partner's sensual responses. If the sexual relationship falls into this mode over a long period of time, it is hardly

The Effect of Stress

▲ *Sometimes a man can go through a temporary period of impotence due to factors such as stress or anxiety, but with the understanding and loving support of his partner, he should eventually recover his enthusiasm and ability to achieve an erection.*

surprising if one or other partner becomes disillusioned or resentful and eventually withdraws from physical contact.

The human body has an enormous capacity for sensual joy and pleasure, especially that experienced through the medium of touch, but this fundamental sense is often suppressed within us from an early stage of life. Young children are frequently told "not to touch" either their own bodies or the objects around them, thus inhibiting the development of their sensory perceptions. Touch, in western cultures, is generally associated with sexuality once we have reached adolescence. We forget how to communicate and feel through touch, how to enjoy its nurturing qualities and, by doing so, cut ourselves off from a vast dimension of tactile sensory awareness.

If you and your partner are experiencing serious or long-term problems within your relationship, or your communication has begun to break down so that conflict ensues whenever sexual or emotional issues are discussed, you would probably benefit from seeking professional help from a qualified psychosexual therapist. The therapist will be trained to deal with a whole range of sexual disorders or dysfunctions, including premature ejaculation, loss of desire, erectile dysfunction, inability to achieve orgasm, fear of penetration, or intercourse avoidance.

He or she will also help you to improve your communication skills, so that you are able to relate to each other and negotiate solutions on difficult issues. It is very difficult for any couple who are experiencing relationship or sexual difficulties, to gain a clear perspective of the situation for themselves, simply because they are too emotionally involved in the issues. A psychotherapist or sex counsellor will act as a mediator, providing practical advice, and helping you reach your own understanding of the problems.

When a couple work through the sensate focus exercises with a therapist, the professional will be able to help them resolve physical and emotional conflicts which may arise between them at any stage of the process. What follows here is a programme of sensate focus exercises, adapted from the therapeutic model, but designed for couples to work with by themselves. They are based on Masters and Johnson's sensate focus self-help programme. You can use them to enhance your relationship, especially if you feel you are able to work on your sexual problems with your partner without professional intervention.

The success of these exercises depends upon a genuine commitment that you and your partner will make to follow the rules of each stage of the process, and your mutual dedication in setting aside a regular time to carry them out.

Choose a specific time during the week when you can both give your full attention to the exercises and decide which partner should initiate the session. Try to choose a time when you both feel generally relaxed and agreeable towards each other. Allocate 40 to 60 minutes per session, and ensure that you have

Explore Her Face
▲ *Carefully, you should explore the angles and contours of her face, feeling the difference between the firmness of the bones and the softness of the skin and muscles. The whole point of this touching experiment is for you to increase your sensory awareness and your sensitivity of touch.*

complete privacy, picking a time when there will be no interruptions from the children, or visitors, and remembering to take the phone off the hook.

You need a warm room as you will both be naked, and a comfortable mattress or base to lie on. If possible, choose a room in the house other than a bedroom – somewhere where you are not reminded of the charged issues of your sexual relationship. You are trying to create something new between you, moving away from past patterns, expectations and memories.

Stage One: Non-Sexual Touch

During the first weeks of your sensate focus exercises, you must refrain from sexual intercourse. This is the period when you will, instead, explore your sensual receptivity to

one another's bodies, and develop your tactile communication. You will take turns to touch each other, as if you are discovering and exploring the human body for the first time. The person who is touching must remember that he or she is not aiming to arouse the partner, but is simply dedicated to developing his or her own sensory awareness.

You can touch anywhere on your partner's body except the genitals or other erogenous areas, such as the woman's breasts. You should allow yourself to feel through your hands and fingers all the different sensations of touch, texture and temperature of the skin. Vary how you apply your tactile contact, using your palms, fingertips, or even the backs of your hands.

You should experiment using one hand at a time, or stroking with both hands, and keep taking note of the different sensations as they occur. The passive partner has only to lie there and focus on the sensation of being touched.

Do not try to reciprocate touch, or go into any sexual fantasy. Both of you should try to avoid analysing the situation or making judgements, such as "this feels good" or "am I doing it right". All you have to do is focus your whole attention on the physical sensations you are experiencing, whether it is through touching or being touched.

Agree beforehand that if the passive partner is uncomfortable about the type of touch he or she is receiving, they can say so and the session can stop, to be resumed at another time. Each partner should spend up to 15 or 20 minutes giving and receiving touch before swapping roles. Do not go on for so long that you become bored or tired. When the exercise is over, you can share with each other what each of you has experienced.

Stage Two: Adding Lotion

You can continue to touch in the same way as before, but now, if you want, you can add oil or lotion. This is still a touching exercise, not a massage. The aim is to experience

Vary the Contact

▶ Take it in turns to become the first active partner in each session. Touch and explore every nuance of his body as before, only this time use a lotion or other lubricant for a different quality of contact. Let your hands touch his skin with varying degrees of pressure, and mould over the rounded curves of the body, such as the buttocks, hips and waist.

Experiment with Touch

▼ Take the time to touch and feel your partner's body in a way you have never done before. You are not trying to please him or turn him on; this experiment is purely for your own sensation. Run your fingers around his nipple, and along the soft skin at the side of the ribcage, feeling the difference between bone and skin. Explore his body with your touch, feeling each and every part, except for the genital area. Move his joints, wiggling his fingers and toes. Notice the skin's temperature changes and its rougher and smoother parts.

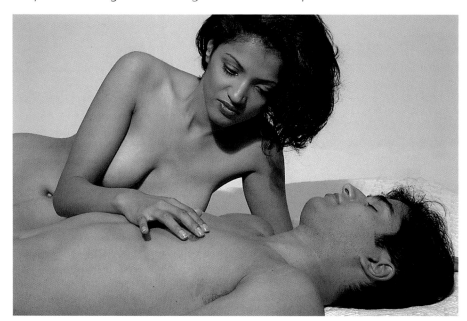

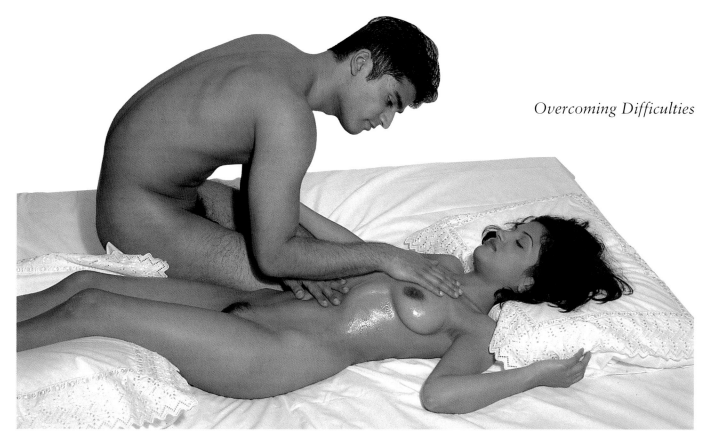

Let Your Hands Flow

▲ *Try to continue to touch in a sensual but non-sexual way when it is your turn to spread lotion over your partner. Feel the fluid quality of your hands as they slide over her skin and around the curves of her body. Use your fingers, thumbs, and the heels of your hands to make varying levels of pressure in your strokes. Stop moving occasionally, letting one hand rest on the heart and the other over the belly. See if you can feel her heartbeat under your hands, and sense the movement of breath in her body.*

yet another dimension and aspect of touch, which may become more smooth and sensual, more flowing and soft with the addition of lubricant. Remember, the purpose of these exercises, at this juncture, is not about pleasing the other person but about discovering new tactile responses for yourself. Stroke, knead and press the flesh, each time becoming aware of the different sensations of movement and touch, especially now that you have added the oil or body lotion.

Stage Three: Touching the Genitals

Once you both feel ready, you can progress to the stage of these exercises where you are allowed to include the genitals and breasts into your programme of exploratory touch. However, your tactile contact should not be intended to create sexual arousal, although this may happen inadvertently. Do not zone onto the erogenous areas immediately but start with all-over-body touch as before, with or without lotion.

There is still no goal in mind except to experience fully the present moment of tactile awareness. If you find yourself becoming too excited, then move on to another area of the body, as you

Keep Touches Innocent

◄ *Even though you can now make tactile contact with her more sexual areas, such as her genitals and breasts, you should be stroking and caressing her erogenous zones in the same manner as you have been touching the other parts of her body – with a sense of wonder and innocence. This sitting position can be adopted during this stage when the man is the active partner.*

Let Yourself be Guided

▲ She can lay her hand over yours and, through her touch, give you a gentle direction of where to go, how firm or soft your pressure should be, when to move your hand to another place and when to return. See if you can pick up her signals through the receptivity of your skin. In this way, you are becoming more deeply attuned to her physical messages. You can also reverse the position of your hands, so that your hand lies on top of hers.

Simultaneous Sensations

▲ Once you begin the mutual touching exercise, you must be very careful not to turn the episode into a session of foreplay or full lovemaking. Lie comfortably close to each other so that you can simultaneously touch and explore each other's bodies with the sensual awareness that you have steadily been developing through this programme. Focus all your attention on the sensations that you are experiencing of touching each other and of being touched.

did in the first stage of this exercise. If you are the male active partner, you can use a sitting position during this phase, so your partner's back is leaning against you. Prop yourself against some pillows and reach comfortably around to touch the front of her body. Also, become aware of the feel of her back as it nestles against your skin. As the woman during the active phase, you can kneel between your partner's legs to gain easier access to his genital area.

Once you are touching the genitals, the passive partner can also guide you by laying his or her hand over yours, and giving you silent cues as to how he or she likes to be touched there. Move your hands with synchronicity, and try to remain receptive to the passive partner's subtle directions. You can even swap the position of your hands, so that at some point, your hand overlays the hand of the receptive partner. Follow their movements, gauging how your

partner likes to stroke himself or herself and what variations of pressure he or she may like to apply.

Your intention is not to arouse each other to orgasm, as your focus is still on gaining a greater sense of tactile awareness. Do not concentrate only on the genitals, but continue to touch other parts of the body as before. You should not kiss at this stage, or pursue any activity which may lead to intercourse. If, however, either partner does become orgasmic while being genitally stroked, you can continue your manual touching, with just your own hands, or your combined hands, to allow orgasm to happen.

Stage Four: Touching Each Other

Mutual touching is now the new phase in your sensate focus programme. Here you begin again with your sensory awareness exercises, but this time you are touching each other simultaneously. There is

still a ban on kissing and sexual intercourse, but you can now use your tongue to explore one another's bodies, although not with the purpose of arousal. Now you must simultaneously focus your attention on touch and on the sensation of being touched. Explore each other's bodies with different types of strokes, using fingertips or palms, just as you have done in the previous exercises.

Stage Five: Making Love

Begin this stage of the programme with your whole-body touch, including sensual touching of the genital regions. However, during this phase, you can now move onto the first steps of resuming sexual intercourse. The man should lie on his back and, as the woman, you should climb on top of him so that you are kneeling across his hips.

Carry your sensual awareness with you, and begin by just letting your genitals make contact. Absorb these

Gentle Penetration

▲ *When you are ready, take your partner's penis and very carefully slide it just inside your vagina so that only its head nestles within you. Both of you should now fully experience this sensation and refrain from thrusting movements or deeper penetration. Try also to feel what your partner is experiencing. When you are ready, you can allow the penis to penetrate a little further into your vagina and then, once again, stop and concentrate on how this feels.*

sensations into yourself. Then, as the woman, take your partner's penis and gently guide its head into your vagina. Avoid any thrusting or deep penetration. Explore the different feelings which arise with each motion that you make. Gradually, you can deepen the depth of penetration and begin to move very slowly and gently, continuously focusing on your immediate physical experience, while having a greater awareness than ever before of the sensations your partner is experiencing.

You are now ready to resume your full sexual relationship, but with a completely heightened sensual awareness. This does not mean you cannot have passionate and wild sex again, but every once in while, go back to the exercises to enrich your intrinsic feeling senses.

Overcoming Erection Failure

A failure to get an erection or to maintain one during sexual activity happens to most men at some time in their lives. This may be the result of stress and tiredness, sexual boredom, lack of attraction to a partner, or ill health. This is usually temporary, and the man's arousal response will improve by itself, or when circumstances and events change for the better.

Erection failure, which is also called impotence, can have psychological or physiological causes – or a combination of the two. Erection failure often has an organic basis, so if the condition is a persistent problem it should be investigated by the man's doctor, or a medical expert who specializes in sexual dysfunction. Possible physiological causes include diabetes, neurological and vascular disorders, a side-effect of certain medications, abnormal hormone levels, or alcohol- and other drug-related problems.

For many men, though, it is the fear of impotence and anxiety over performance that most often lead to consistent erection failure. A man may be putting himself under a lot of pressure to achieve super-stud status

every time he makes love. Sometimes, a bad sexual experience, perhaps compounded by the unsympathetic comments of a sexual partner, has increased his anxiety about how well he is going to perform. This worry may then become a self-fulfilling prophecy in all future sexual relationships. If the man does not have a secure relationship, and so is constantly involved in new sexual situations, his fears about his performance in bed may become so extreme that the tension makes it virtually impossible to get an erection, or to keep one once he has started penetrative sex.

Alternatively, if a man has been orientated solely towards thrusting, penetrative sexual intercourse, driven along by high levels of excitement, and his relationship then becomes more companionable, he may be unable to achieve or sustain arousal in this new climate of intimacy.

When a man is struggling with the emotional and physical factors of erection failure, for whatever reasons, the best thing he can do is to take the pressure off the situation. Temporary abstinence from sex will give him the time he needs to unlink the connection between anxiety and performance. If he has a sympathetic partner, who is willing to assist him at this time, they can benefit from the sensate focus exercises described previously.

They should work through the programme step by step, not reaching the last stage until the man has been able to relax totally into sensual touching and receiving touch for its own sake, rather than to achieve a climax. Once the woman has started to touch his genitals, she should avoid focusing on them too closely. If an erection occurs it should not become central to the sensory experience of whole-body touching.

When the man begins to relax into his whole-body sensuality, the woman can stimulate him to an erection, either manually or orally, but should then allow the erection to subside while she concentrates on other areas of his body. When his penis has become softer, she can again stimulate him to an erection. At this stage, she should not try to bring him to an orgasm.

In this way, the man begins to realize that he can have an erection, lose it, and then regain it at a later time. The couple should practise this phase of the exercises for about three weeks, or for however long it takes for the man to accept the fluctuations of his erections without anxiety.

As the couple progress through the mutual touching and genital-to-genital contact stages of the sensate focus exercises, the man should continue to involve himself totally with touching and caressing the woman's body, and avoid focusing on whether or not he has an erection. The woman can help by continuing to touch and stroke his

body and genitals without expecting something to happen. When the couple are able to reach the sensual lovemaking stage, the woman should begin by taking her partner's penis slowly into her vagina as described. If the penis becomes soft at any stage, both partners should simply continue with their sensual touching, allowing the erection to return later, or not as the case may be.

Gradually, with patience and loving support, the man may be able to break the cycle of anxiety which has inhibited his responses. By becoming less focused on his penis, and more involved in the pleasures of sensual contact with his partner, he will be able to relax and gain a new confidence in his sensuality and sexuality.

A single man who has anxieties about his performance should try to avoid casual sexual encounters which may confirm his insecurity. It is better to develop a secure and loving partnership where the sexual relationship has time to build slowly and where his sexual confidence is not immediately challenged.

Overcoming Premature Ejaculation

Premature ejaculation is fairly common in younger men who have not yet learned to control and extend the plateau phase of their sexual response, which occurs just before orgasm. In all men, there is a point when ejaculation is inevitable. However, some men ejaculate almost

Applying the Squeeze

◀ *Whenever you feel your partner is close to ejaculating, you can apply the squeeze technique so that his erection subsides slightly. Then you can begin to stimulate him again.*

immediately upon genital-to-genital stimulation, or even during the initial stages of physical contact. This is disappointing for both partners, but is particularly frustrating for the woman if she has no time to achieve orgasm herself.

A consistent pattern of premature ejaculation will cause anxiety because the man feels unable to control his bodily responses, and fears disappointing his partner. Such anxiety can lead to erection failure, or sex avoidance, especially if he is regularly criticized for "poor performance" in bed.

Fortunately, premature ejaculation can be successfully treated by sex therapy. Ideally this should involve both partners. If the couple have a good basis of communication, and are mutually willing to explore new sensual techniques to help change the man's habitual patterns of sexual response, they can benefit from the following self-help exercises using the "squeeze technique" (see opposite).

However, if there are other fundamental problems within the relationship, the couple are better advised to seek professional help to improve their communication, and resolve the emotional or sexual problems involved. In the self-help method, the couple must agree to abstain from intercourse during the period of time they are following the exercises until a certain stage of progress has been reached. However, the man can help his partner climax through oral or manual stimulation whenever she wants him to.

Having committed themselves to this programme, which should be practised at least three times a week, the couple begin with manual stimulation. The woman masturbates the man, applying the "squeeze" to the top of the penis whenever he begins to approach his orgasm threshold. Once the erection has subsided slightly, she stimulates him again by hand, repeating this procedure up to three times. He is then allowed to ejaculate. After several sessions, which ought to be no more than two days apart, the man should begin to feel more confident in his ability to delay ejaculation.

At this point the couple can progress to genital-to-genital contact. The woman sits astride her partner and uses her hand to move his penis around her vaginal lips and clitoris, while applying the squeeze technique as necessary. Once both partners feel confident that the man has achieved some control over his ejaculatory process in this more intimate situation, they can apply the squeeze technique to the first stages of intercourse. The woman should position herself astride her partner and then guide his penis into her vagina. They should both then remain still.

If the woman senses her partner is close to ejaculating, she must lift herself off of his penis and apply the squeeze technique. The couple can then repeat this procedure at least three times before allowing ejaculation to occur. If the man ejaculates prematurely, despite their efforts to delay it, neither partner should regard this as a disaster. Anxiety, expectation or criticism all work against the possibility of overcoming premature ejaculation. By patiently persevering with the exercises, and with the loving support of his partner, the man gradually builds up his confidence and ability to delay ejaculation.

If good progress is made after three or more sessions in the penetration phase described above, the woman can begin to move very gently while his penis is inside her. Again, as she becomes aware that her partner is reaching the point of no return, she should stop moving, lift up from his penis and apply the squeeze technique before resuming penetration and gentle movement.

The Squeeze Technique

The basic squeeze technique is useful in helping a couple tackle the problem of premature ejaculation. The squeeze is applied by the woman who simultaneously presses her thumb pad against the frenulum, just below the head of the penis, and the pad of her first finger just above the coronal ridge on the top of the glans, while her second finger rests parallel to the first on the shaft of the penis. Pressure must come directly from the pads of the fingers and thumb (avoid a grasping squeeze) and needs to be maintained firmly for at least four seconds. It should not be applied to the sides of the penis. The man can indicate how much pressure feels comfortable if his partner is unsure. This pressure should cause the erection to subside slightly and delay the ejaculation. The procedure is carried out at least three times in one session, always just prior to the ejaculation phase. The woman should learn to recognize the signals that indicate when her partner is close to this level of arousal, or he can let her know himself.

The couple should continue with these exercises until the man is able to sustain his erection for up to 15 minutes inside his partner before ejaculating. The more the couple engage in this phase of the exercise, the more likely it is that the old patterns of sexual response will dissolve. They should not worry if the man occasionally ejaculates too soon, but should persevere with continued good humour and optimism.

Once the partners are able to sustain a longer period of intercourse, and feel confident enough to increase thrusting and movement, they can start to apply a different form of squeeze which does not necessitate the woman dismounting from the penis. The pressure is now applied, by either the man or the woman, to the base of the penis, with the thumb pad pressing on the area just above the scrotum, and the first two fingers parallel, applying pressure on the opposite side of the penis. Again, the penis should not be squeezed at the sides.

Eventually, the couple can experiment with other lovemaking positions, using the squeeze technique when necessary, especially if the man resumes the on-top position, which is more likely to lead to premature ejaculation. The squeeze technique can also be incorporated into the sensate focus exercises and applied throughout each stage whenever necessary.

Many men may wish to prolong lovemaking without ejaculating before either they or their partners are ready. The sensate focus exercises will help them to relax more into sensual touching and leisurely intercourse and are bound to enrich their sexual relationship.

Learn to Relax
◀ *Once you are able to fully relax into your own body and sensual and erotic feelings of pleasure in touching and lovemaking, without worrying about performance or results, you may find that your orgasmic capacity increases.*

Overcoming Orgasmic Difficulties

There are many reasons why a woman may have difficulty in reaching an orgasm, but most of these can be overcome by creating a new and more sensual attitude towards her body, and by the willingness of her and her partner to explore more mutually satisfying forms of lovemaking.

For a woman who has difficulty in achieving an orgasm, or who has lost this capacity altogether, the following self-help suggestions may enable her to attain sexual fulfilment.

She should learn to enjoy self-pleasuring, not only through masturbation, but also by becoming more sensually aware of her whole body. Self-massage, stroking and caressing herself, applying aromatic moisturizing creams to her skin, and learning to love her own body, will help to boost her body image and self-esteem. If she is shy, or has negative feelings about her genitals, exploring herself, using a mirror and her fingers, will help her to accept these most intimate parts.

Once she has established a better body image, she will benefit from self-masturbation, allowing herself to stroke, caress and rub her vaginal lips and clitoral area to find out which pressures and motions that are most arousing. The more sensual she makes this experience, the more enhanced her responses are likely to be. She should dedicate time to regular self-pleasuring, letting her strokes involve her whole body, including her face, neck, breasts, belly, thighs, buttocks, mons and vulva.

To put herself in the right mood, she can bathe in an aromatic bath beforehand so that she feels totally relaxed both mentally and physically, and then moisturize her skin with lotion to leave it soft and glowing. She can then retire to a warm and private setting, perhaps lit by candles and with relaxing or sexy music playing in the background.

The woman can begin to let go into erotic fantasy, conjuring up whatever sexual pictures help to arouse her. Some women find it difficult to allow sexual fantasy, either because of guilt feelings, or because they do not have an adequate source of erotic mental images. Women who feel guilty about having erotic fantasies should read Nancy Friday's book *My Secret Garden*. Here, the author's careful research reveals the rich diversity of women's fantasies, some funny, some bizarre, some lurid, but all giving testimony to the fertile, erotic female mind. The woman can also use a vibrator to explore her sexual responses.

Sometimes, a woman may block her orgasmic reactions because she is reluctant to really let go, fearful of losing control over her body. Enacting out an orgasmic response to the full, breathing deeply, writhing on the bed, sighing and crying out will give her more confidence to abandon herself freely when she is orgasmic with a lover.

Self-stimulation techniques allow the woman to become familiar with her own unique sexual responses, so she can regard herself as orgasmic in her own right, rather than as a result of what someone else does to her. She can then use this greater understanding of her own physical and mental erotic responses in a sexual relationship.

When a woman is experiencing orgasmic dysfunction within her sexual relationship, both she and her partner will benefit from the sensate focus exercises. They can learn or rediscover how to touch each other's bodies in a sensual rather than immediately sexual way. They can also benefit from the non-demanding genital contact exercises, during which the woman shows her partner how she prefers to masturbate herself.

Leisurely foreplay, including kissing, caressing, manual clitoral stimulation and oral-genital contact, all enjoyed for the sheer sake of pleasure, rather than focused purely towards orgasm, will help the woman to feel cherished and become more fully aroused before penetration occurs.

The woman should not feel she has to have an orgasm to soothe her partner's sexual ego, or to prove herself to be sexually responsive. This demand can create a mental and physical tension which is likely to block her natural responses.

It is also important for the couple to resolve their relationship conflicts before making love, because hidden resentments, and other negative feelings may also affect the woman's ability to relax sexually. Choosing the right time to make love, when neither partner is tired or under stress, or when they are unlikely to be interrupted by their children, will enhance the sexual responses of both of them.

A woman who is unable to come to an orgasm by any means of stimulation – a condition known as anorgasmia – will benefit from the guidance of a qualified sex therapist if she wishes to become orgasmic.

Treating Vaginismus

For some women, penetrative sex can be an uncomfortable, or even painful experience. In rare cases, intercourse may be impossible because of involuntary contractions of the muscles surrounding the vagina – a condition known as vaginismus. Many sufferers may otherwise have completely normal sexual responses, and may easily attain orgasm through non-penetrative sex such as masturbation or oral-genital contact.

Vaginismus occurs most commonly in young women. However, a woman may suffer this disorder throughout her sexual life, and it can cause great distress to both her and her partner who may, in every other respect, enjoy a close relationship. The problem can be so serious that the woman is unable to insert a tampon, a pessary, or even her own finger into her vagina, and a pelvic examination is an impossibility without sedation.

If the woman has never been able to experience vaginal penetration, the condition is known as primary vaginismus. If she has had penetrative sex in the past, but has consequently developed these distressing symptoms, the condition is called secondary vaginismus.

Vaginismus can result from a number of complex causes. If it is primary, the problem may stem from early childhood or adolescent conditioning, possibly due to parental or religious influences, which have created negative feelings about sexuality in general, or her genitals in particular.

Other causes include trauma due to rape or childhood sexual abuse, a painful and insensitive gynaecological examination in adolescence, or an exaggerated fear of becoming pregnant or of contracting a sexually transmitted disease. Secondary vaginismus may occur as a result of a genital infection, a difficult childbirth, or other pathological causes which previously made intercourse painful and have consequently precipitated the involuntary muscular response. The woman may then become fearful of further pain on penetration.

Whatever the reasons for vaginismus, and sometimes they are complex and indefinable, a woman must first be examined by a sympathetic gynaecologist to discover whether there is an identifiable underlying cause, such as a physical abnormality or infection.

Vaginismus is almost always treatable once the woman, and her partner, if she has one, decide to seek professional advice and receive sex therapy. The complexity of the psychological issues involved in vaginismus, and the need to ascertain whether the condition is a primary or secondary one, makes it advisable that the woman's circumstances are assessed by a psychosexual counsellor. The therapist will then be able to guide the woman and her partner through the treatment strategy that is most appropriate to her.

Mutual Understanding
▲ *Through loving care, mutual support, and the changing of existing patterns through simple exercises and techniques, problems such as premature ejaculation and vaginismus can be understood, coped with, and hopefully overcome, especially with the aid of sympathetic counselling.*

Chapter 8
Enhancing Sex

When a relationship has become established into a routine pattern it is all too easy for a couple to take each other for granted. Like putting on a comfy pair of slippers, you know exactly what to expect from each other. But this is also fraught with pitfalls because once you begin to feel that you know your partner inside out you can miss the signs that indicate when things are not well in a relationship. To avoid this you need to develop your communication skills so that you can stay attuned to your partner's innermost thoughts and desires. But in addition you need to find new ways to enhance your sexual relationship, to adapt to the changes that age and ill-health can make, to experiment with new approaches to your sexuality and sensuality, such as learning how to massage each other lovingly, or by playing games and exercises. Also, you can seek to enhance the spiritual dimension of your sexual relationship, learning to make love in a new and meditative way.

Communication Skills

Communication and listening skills are essential keys to unlock the tensions and problems which inevitably occur in any ongoing relationship. They enable you to verbalize those issues that are important to you, and help you to express your most vulnerable and emotive feelings, without descending into a tirade of blame and criticism that will only serve to alienate your partner.

Learning to listen carefully to your partner's thoughts, values, opinions and feelings without the need to become defensive, or argumentative ensures that open and honest communication continues between you. If both of you determine to practise the communication and listening skills described in this section whenever problems arise, you may be able to respond more positively to difficult situations. In this way you can support, understand and accommodate each other's needs and differing opinions.

No relationship is without its stresses and strains. In the beginning, when you first fall in love, the pull of your mutual attraction can mask aspects of your individuality and ego and also blind you to the truth about your partner's personality. Only when your relationship settles down do your personal views, values, needs and temperaments begin to emerge in detail. If you marry, or form a long-term relationship, create a home together, raise children and pursue

demanding careers, inevitably these additional challenges will test your relationship in different ways. While you strive to make your relationship a secure and nurturing base from which you can both draw emotional and physical support, you must also constantly adapt and respond to life's ever-changing realities.

Everyone evolves in mind, body and spirit as they mature. No one can expect a partner to remain exactly the same as when they first met. Nor can you stop the process of change within your own life, and you may come to realize that the things which made you happy or content in earlier years may no longer bring you such fulfilment. As in any partnership, there will be a constant need for negotiation if you wish to navigate your relationship safely and successfully through the turbulent waters of life.

Areas of Conflict

There are countless situations in which the needs and boundaries of a relationship have to be carefully re-

examined and re-defined. Small issues can build up into a major area of conflict if you fail to communicate your needs, or listen to one another.

For example, you might feel neglected by your husband because he watches football at the weekends, leaving you feeling aggrieved and abandoned. Perhaps your partner has forgotten your birthday, or a wedding anniversary, and you take that as a sign that he no longer cares about you. Maybe you feel your girl-friend criticizes and harasses you, especially at those times when you feel most under stress. Or she resents your friends, and that makes you feel she is trying to change you.

Issues can be intensely personal, such as the way you make love, whether you are honest with one another, the degree of intimacy you share, and whether you care enough about each other. Domestic problems can arise over the housework, parental responsibilities, and especially over the finances.

In almost every area of a relationship, some rules and boundaries need to be made to help it function well. Two mature adults should be able to make agreements which incorporate their mutual needs. Even so, those rules will be subject to change and re-negotiation as time goes by.

The Need to Stay Cool
◀ *Avoid accusatory statements, harsh words and criticism. Be aware of body language – hardening your eyes and mouth or pointing your finger will make him defensive.*

Words You'll Regret
▲ Bombarding each other with personal insults, shouting or talking louder than the other person, or aggressive words and actions will alienate you from each other, ensuring neither of you has a chance to communicate or even be heard above the din. Words spoken in the heat of the moment are often greatly regretted once your tempers have had a chance to cool down.

Attacking the Ego
▲ Don't undermine your partner's self-esteem in order to accentuate your point of view. It will only make her angry or hurt. Overwhelmed by these feelings, she is totally incapable of hearing your side of the story. Her body language may demonstrate that she is virtually cutting off all her points of access to you, by covering her face, ears, eyes and mouth.

Signs of Stalemate
▲ The body language here clearly indicates that both partners are saying "back-off". If you have failed to communicate and listen carefully, then you are probably going to reach a stalemate situation where nothing more is going to be resolved. Things may carry on relatively normally for a while, but both of you have become even more entrenched in your own points of view. Sooner or later the attack will begin again.

Listen Without Judgement
▲ Instead of using verbal tactics, take it in turns to discuss your feelings and needs and state clearly what is bothering you about a certain situation. Take responsibility for how you feel, using "I" rather than the accusatory "You". Keep eye-contact and let your bodies be open and undefended towards each other, and remember to breathe deeply so you stay relaxed. Listen carefully to what your partner has to say to you, avoiding judgement or criticism.

Taking Responsibility
Words of war will never heal a relationship or help you and your partner to find a solution to troublesome issues. In good communication, you need to take responsibility for your own feelings instead of blaming your partner for your emotional state. Accusation will force him or her into the mode of protection and the need to block your words, either by retaliating with a damaging counter-attack or by withdrawing.

Comparing your partner negatively or with derision to someone else is demeaning to that person, and can only result in more anger or bad feelings. Insulting your partner's family, friends or beliefs can deeply hurt his or her feelings and cause lasting damage to a relationship.

Manipulation may work in your favour temporarily, but your partner will know he has been duped. If you threaten your partner, you may gain a tentative victory, but revenge is likely to be in store. Making your mate feel guilty about who he is will guarantee defensive behaviour, and criticism can only serve to lower your lover's self-esteem.

Stubbornness demonstrates an unwillingness to work on a solution and an entrenched point of view. If you placate your partner, you are dismissing her needs and avoiding the real nature of the issue, and withdrawal is the ultimate weapon of power because your absence leaves the other person feeling helpless.

What you say is one thing, and how you say it is another. Shouting and raising your voice "deafens" your partner, and continually repeating yourself, nagging, complaining or whining is guaranteed to make your partner react in a negative way.

Listening Well

How you listen to your partner complements your communication skills. You can hear the words, but still not listen to their content. You can make your own judgements about what your partner is saying, while failing to comprehend what she is really trying to get across.

Listening to someone with an armoured or defended attitude which says "Here we go again" indicates that you are unwilling to be receptive. Imagining that you know what

is best for your partner and your relationship means that you are unable to consider the other person's point of view. Thinking up a retaliatory statement while your partner is speaking to you renders you incapable of listening at all. Tuning-out is the aural version of physical withdrawal – you are not going to hear what your partner is saying if you have one eye on the television and the other on your newspaper.

All of the above are typical examples of relating patterns which any of us may employ when real communication breaks down. Instead, we may revert to our "parental voices" blaming and punishing. If we are on the receiving end of this critical tirade, the "child" within us is provoked and it is inevitable that the reaction that ensues will be petulant, hysterical, sullen, angry or argumentative.

Communication and Listening Exercise

Communication between two people who love each other should never become a power struggle, or a battle to win at all costs. It should be a

Repeat to Show You Hear

◀ *Reflect back to your partner what you think you have heard her say so she can correct any misunderstandings that may have occurred. The fact that you have absorbed her words and are able to feed them back to her so succinctly will restore her confidence in the relationship because she will feel you have listened carefully to her.*

Listen to the Other Side

◀ *Once you have expressed your needs and feelings and felt that your partner has fully understood them, allow him the chance to respond in a similar way. Now it is your turn to listen carefully to his point of view. If he doesn't think he is going to be criticized or judged, he may be able to reveal aspects of himself that he has previously felt unable to show. Focus carefully on what he has to say, nodding or smiling to show you have grasped its content. Even if you do not share his opinion, let him express it.*

Tackling the Issues

▼ *The communication exercise will enable both of you to move positively towards solving a tricky dilemma because you will have gained an understanding of each other's feelings and needs. This will provide you with the useful tools with which to tackle the issues involved, and hopefully find a suitable solution.*

mutual search to try to understand and support each other, respectful of the needs of both the individual and the relationship. It takes courage to talk about your feelings honestly and to take responsibility for them, and diligent awareness to locate the true source of your emotions and unhappiness. It needs respect and empathy to listen carefully to what your partner is saying without immediately feeling threatened, or needing to defend your corner.

If you are experiencing communication problems within your relationship, you can try the following exercise which allows you to explain your needs and opinions clearly, and to listen empathically to your partner's truth. At first the exercise may seem awkward and too formal but this is because it is a new way of sharing with each other.

When an important issue is at stake, or whenever you are feeling hurt about something within the relationship, make an appointment with each other specifically to sit and talk it over. Resolve to do this calmly and without recrimination, and try to enter this communication exercise with an open heart and mind. Relax your body and breathe deeply so you release pent-up tensions before you begin.

Sit opposite your partner so you can have eye-to-eye contact. You may find it more comfortable to have a table between you which you can consider as a neutral arena. Uncross your arms and legs so your body language is not defended, avoid using your eyes to intensify your words, or gritting your teeth, or tightening your jaw, and do not point your finger accusingly at your partner.

One partner takes five minutes to speak while the other's task is simply

Sharing the Workload

▲ *When both partners are working outside the home, household tasks need to be shared. How you negotiate that division of labour should take into consideration your needs and preferences, the time that either of you expect to put into the housework, and when any particular task should be done. There should be flexibility in the arrangement, so, for example, if your partner is working late, you may offer to cook the dinner – even if it isn't your turn.*

to listen. If you are the speaking partner, state clearly what your feelings are and what is bothering you. However, take responsibility for those feelings. Avoid phrases like: "You don't love or care about me any more. You are so selfish around the house and you never do your share of the chores. You make me feel like I'm the servant here."

Instead, phrase this in a different way, such as: "I realize that over the last weeks I have been getting very angry and snappy towards you. I am finding my work very stressful at the moment, so when I come home, I do not feel able to cope with the cooking

and housework alone. Recently, I have been doing most of the tasks in the evenings. What I would like is for us to draw up a new agreement on how we can share the jobs."

In this way, you have spelt out your needs clearly. You have identified your emotions and put them in a context. In addition, you have explained, without accusation, why you need extra support at this time, and you have offered a framework for a solution.

As the listening partner, you do not interrupt or defend yourself, and this is made easier by the fact that you are not being blamed for the situation. You can show your partner that you are listening to her empathically by leaning towards her as she speaks, or nodding your head to show you are assimilating her words.

At the end of the five minutes, sum up for her what you believe you have heard her say. In this way you reflect back to her the content of her communication, and by repeating it, you absorb the information better. Your feedback enables her to correct any misunderstandings you may have gained as to what she actually said and it assures her that you have been actively listening.

Swapping Roles

Now it is the listening partner's turn to speak. If you do not feel ridiculed or criticized, you have a better chance of communicating your own version of the situation. In the past you may have retorted with something like: "You never stop nagging. Sometimes your complaining makes me so sick that I want to walk out. Anyway, the house looks perfectly fine to me – the problem is that you are neurotic". This reply is a defensive attack which

manages to combine an accusation, a threat, a denial and an insult all in one delivery!

During this exercise, you have more chance to respond rather than to react in the manner above. You might tell her instead: "I've also had a lot of pressure at work recently, and when I come home, my immediate need is to take time to unwind. The difficulty between us seems to be that you like to get things done straight away while I prefer to do them later, or at the weekends. What usually happens is that you go straight ahead with the chores, and I usually skulk off feeling guilty. I am very willing to do my half of the work, but my main priority is that we make more time to relax and enjoy each other's company in the evenings."

If you are now the listening partner, you should summarize and reflect back what your partner has just told you and allow him to correct you if you have misheard any of the content of his communication. If you need more time to continue your reciprocal communication exercise, then you can use its structure again. If you were to use the above

Enjoy the Chores – Together

◀ *Household jobs do not have to be turned into chores, they can be a great opportunity for you to spend some time together, joking and chatting over the day's events. After dinner, rather than one partner being relegated to the kitchen while the other person goes to another room, why not share the washing-up tasks? That way, you can catch up on the gossip, and create extra time for relaxing together.*

example of the exercise, it would have enabled you to refrain from blame and criticism, while stating clearly your paramount needs.

You have established a framework in that you both agree that the housework needs to be done and the chores shared, but you now need to discuss how the jobs can be better divided and when is the best time to do them. You will need to negotiate a solution which encompasses the needs and wishes of both of you, but that will be far easier to do if neither of you feels angry or in the wrong.

Unless relationship issues are dealt with as they arise, their undercurrents are likely to affect other aspects of your lives. Sexual disharmony or reduced intimacy and affection can often be a reflection of other unresolved issues, rather than being directly related to sexual problems. Good communication and listening skills are as important to the health, harmony and growth of your relationship as is the happiness of your sex life.

Catharsis

Pent-up feelings of anger and frustration can become locked in your body's musculature, making you feel tense and irritable, and more inclined to provoke arguments in the home. Sometimes the cause of these feelings is not directly related to anything that has happened between you and your partner, but your charged emotions spill out and you react negatively to the slightest comment. Perhaps you are under stress at work, or you have been angered or disappointed by a certain event, or maybe there are issues in your relationship that you are too wound up about to discuss rationally.

One way of helping to discharge this emotion in a safe way, without hurting or blaming any one else, is by catharsis. By acting out and giving vent to your feelings when you are alone, you can release your intense emotions.

Beating the cushions is a method that is sometimes used in therapy sessions, enabling clients to express their anger in a non-harmful way. You can do this in the privacy of your home, too, though it would be better to wait until you are alone. You can shout and yell at the same time, if you can do so without disturbing the neighbours.

Let rip for up to ten minutes, giving yourself permission to discharge your rage into the cushions by beating your fists against them. By allowing yourself to feel and express your anger without judgement, it may transform itself into a wave of non-emotive energy which will leave you feeling full of vitality as your tension blocks are released.

Sometimes, sadness lies behind anger and you may get in touch with your more vulnerable feelings. If the anger turns into tears, then hug the pillow to your body, and allow yourself to cry until you feel a release from your pain. When you have experienced your catharsis, rest for at least five minutes, and breathe deeply so your whole body relaxes.

If this technique is suitable to you, then use it at times when you feel your body racked with emotion but are unable to express your feelings adequately in words. This way no one else gets hurt, and you may find it a great relief.

If you cannot imagine yourself undergoing catharsis, another good way to release pent-up frustration is through strenuous physical activity, such as running, brisk walking or dancing. Try to breathe deeply and move your body freely in order to discharge all your tensions and regain a sense of equilibrium.

Being Vulnerable

No matter how mature and responsible we have become as adults, a part of us remains child-like, retaining the vulnerable and playful elements of

Expressing the Anger

▲ Build a pile of cushions in front of you on a supportive base such as the mattress on your bed. Make fists and begin to pound the cushions. At first you may feel self-conscious and resistant to expressing your anger in this physical way. Get in touch with your emotions and allow them to gather momentum and express themselves through your body. Release the tension from your body.

Releasing the Tension

▲ If you feel able to shout and yell without disturbing other people, then do so and this will help you clear the emotional tension that has been "choking" you. You can even say all the nasty things you have been carrying in your mind and let them evaporate into thin air. This will help you to dispel your more negative thoughts so that later you can approach your problems more calmly.

The Inner Child

▼ Even as an adult there are times when you will need to be comforted and supported by your mate. A partner who is able to respond to your "inner child", and is not afraid of it, is secure in himself and in touch with his own sensitive side.

our nature. If you accept that part of yourself, and learn to love your "inner child", it will help make you a more balanced person and better able to respond to those aspects in your partner. The inner child is the part of your personality that is magical and inquisitive, but that also feels insecure and is easily hurt. It is the part of you that sometimes needs nourishment, comfort and reassurance.

In an adult relationship, there will be times when the "child" within one partner will meet the "parent" within the other. A balanced relationship is one in which these roles can be shared, so that you are able to respond to each other appropriately in times of need.

Long-Term Relationships

Your sexual relationship may improve with time as you and your partner become increasingly compatible on an emotional and physical level. As intimacy grows between you, and the relationship becomes stable, you may be better able to relax together in every way. In these circumstances, your sexual relationship can mature with age like a vintage wine.

Many women are only able to open up sexually once they feel emotionally secure, finally reaching their true orgasmic potential when they trust that they are truly loved. For some men, the early stages of a relationship can be fraught with tension, particularly the pressure to perform well in bed. They may be so nervous and excited in the early stages of a relationship that they engage in intercourse with undue haste and ejaculate prematurely. Only when they have relaxed into a sexual relationship can they allow the more sensual side of their nature to shine through in their lovemaking.

Time and familiarity will allow you and your partner to know each other's arousal responses, to tune in to your mutual sexual needs, and to feel increasingly comfortable with your own and each other's bodies. As sex is an expression of caring as well as desire, your lasting and loving relationship can, by its very nature, enrich your sexual exchange.

Knowing and trusting each other well gives you the opportunity to explore new avenues within your sexual preferences. The safety of the relationship may allow you to reveal and act out your sexual fantasies and this can add an extra erotic input into your conjugal activities.

Changing Patterns

If you are in a long-term relationship, your sexuality may pass through many phases, and it would be highly unusual if it never changed in content or style from your early days of

A Deepening Sexuality

▲ Intimacy, deepening companionship, and knowledge of each other's bodies and physical responses can enhance your sex life in a long-term relationship. As both of you relax deeply into your sexuality, it can become more expansive, creative and loving.

Spicing Up Your Love Life

▶ Confidence in the relationship, and trust with each other, may inspire you to reveal and experiment with some of your more playful sexual fantasies. This is also a good way to pep up your sex life when things have become dull and routine. A little kitchen erotica may convince him that there is more on the menu than just supper!

romance. For the reasons mentioned above, it can steadily improve, and it may enhance in quality if not in quantity. However, there may come a time when the frequency of your sexual activity declines after you have lived together for more than a few years.

Seeing each other every day, and concerning yourselves with the other important demands in your lives, you may no longer have the energy, wish, or need to make love with the same intensity as when you first met. Quite naturally, like any two people who begin to build a home together and improve on their careers, or decide to start a family, you may focus your attention on other matters of mutual and personal concern.

The passion which drew you together and ignited the flame of your love is unlikely to sustain itself with the same degree of desire throughout the duration of your long-term relationship. The familiarity which makes your partnership so comfortable and supportive can be the very thing which erases the excitement of the earlier days, when just the sight of each other would be sufficient to arouse you.

Seeing your lover every day, and sharing the hard times as well as the good, may create a supportive and nurturing relationship, but does not necessarily arouse the libido to the same extent as before.

Often, these changing patterns of sexual behaviour will settle into an easy and compatible rhythm which happily satisfies you both. There will be times when your sexual interest rises, and periods when it subsides, and this will largely be affected by outside pressures, such as stress, the needs of your children, the demands of your work, and the general accord between you both in other areas of your lives. ·

Differing Sexual Needs

Problems may occur in an established partnership, however, if you and your mate develop very different patterns of sexual need. One of you

A New Kind of Intimacy

▶ *It is perfectly normal for the frequency of sexual activity to subside after some years in an established relationship as passion gives way to closeness and intimacy of a different nature. This can be a mutually satisfying situation if there is no great disparity in your sexual needs. Just being together, relaxed and aware of each other, while quietly involved in your own activities, can be a very nourishing experience in itself.*

Lovers and Friends

▶ *One of the most wonderful aspects of a long-term relationship is that it can deepen your friendship with each other. Once you know that you can see each other as much as you like, the sexual pressure begins to subside and you can explore many different avenues of pleasure and leisure. You can learn new pursuits, pastimes and games to enjoy and just keeping each other company will be rewarding and relaxing.*

may lose interest in sex altogether, or be content with occasional sexual episodes. What one of you might regard as an adequate level of lovemaking might be vastly different from the other's expectations.

There is no rule that dictates how often a couple should make love. You may feel deprived if you are not having sex every day, whereas your partner may think that three times a week is a happy routine. The disparity could be even greater, with one of you believing that once a week is sufficient for your needs while the other is rarely interested in making love more than once a month.

One of you might even lose interest in sex altogether, especially when

you have been together for a number of years, or following illness, childbirth, the loss of a parent, or promotion to a more stressful job. The emerging differences in sexual needs can create a severe problem if you do not look at the issues, adapt to the changes, and reach a mutually satisfying arrangement that suits your varying levels of libido.

The one who is more deprived can feel aggrieved, and personally rejected. If you are in this position, you may begin to put pressure on your partner, berating the person you love, and you may feel demeaned by your unsatisfied sexual needs.

If you are the one who has lost interest in sex, you may resent your

partner's desires, and even begin to feel that he or she is making unreasonable demands on your time and intimacy. A situation like this, if it is allowed to develop unchecked, becomes a vicious cycle. One of you will become increasingly obsessed with the need for sex,

Rekindle the Flames of Passion

▼ *Make love in parts of the house other than the bedroom so that the change of setting inspires new and delightful ways of lovemaking. If you have one, light the fire in your living room hearth and abandon yourselves before its flames. By breaking old patterns of sexual behaviour, you can keep your relationship very alive.*

Dealing with Sexual Disparity

◀ *There are many reasons why you and your partner may have differing sexual needs. At various times, and for different reasons, a low libido can affect either one of you. If this continues, and is affecting the happiness of your relationship, you will need to explore the reasons and find some way to improve the situation.*

while the other may withdraw and become even less romantically inclined.

A couple may allow time to pass before realizing the extent of the problem or feeling sufficiently resolved to face up to its issues. This dilemma may be compounded by the difficulty of talking about sexual matters – a subject in which egos can so easily be bruised. Tact, diplomacy and negotiation, however, are needed to approach and address the subject. If you are facing this situation, you will need to develop your communication skills so that you can explore your varying sexual needs and

Seeking Spiritual Uplift

▶ *After a time, the passion and heat of sex may no longer enthral you. You may seek to change the quality of your lovemaking into something that is more sensual and increasingly spiritually and emotionally uplifting. If you are able to let go of the excitement of sex, and make love in a more meditative way, your intimacy and bonding will continue to flower.*

feelings. You may then discover the root cause of your differences and find new ways to resolve it.

Be Creative

One of the main causes for your sexual indifference may be that your love-life has become too routine. Flopping into bed after a busy day may not provide the ideal scene for an ardent encounter. Try to create new and exciting opportunities for lovemaking, away from the more predictable situations. Make love in the living room instead of the bedroom, or stay at a hotel for the weekend. The change of

Looking and Feeling Good

◀ *Familiarity in a relationship is no reason to lose interest in looking and feeling good about your body. The desire to remain attractive will continue to matter to your partner and will boost your own feelings of self-worth. When you plan a romantic evening in or out, first soak in a relaxing bath perfumed with aphrodisiac essential oils. Moisturize your skin so it is soft to the touch. Little efforts like this show you are not taking the relationship for granted.*

environment can make sex more adventurous and exciting.

Alter the timing of your sexual interludes, so you make love in the afternoon, morning or early evening before you get too tired. Bring a little spice and passion back into your love-life with the occasional "quickie" session of spontaneous sex to recapture the fervour of earlier years.

Sexual fantasies are an excellent aphrodisiac and you may like to explore together new and exciting variations of sexual behaviour. It is also possible that as your intimacy deepens in other aspects of your partnership, lusty sex is no longer appealing to you. In this case, why not try a different way of making love which is less orientated towards orgasm and performance and more focused on being meditative, sensual and calm.

When You Have Children

If the responsibility of childrearing has become the main focus of your relationship, seek a way to balance your love and caring so that your partner is equally included. It is easy to feel that, as parents, your sexual and emotional life must take second place to the needs of your children.

In the first months after the birth of a new baby, sheer exhaustion causes the libido to flag and this is a

normal and usually temporary state of affairs. But if you start to perceive your partner or yourself only in terms of "mother" or "father", your sexual relationship may begin to suffer.

However, the strength of your family rests on the supportive and loving bond which exists between you as adults and, if this remains the primary relationship, you and your children will greatly benefit.

Try to create some time when you can be alone together, away from domestic demands. This may be diffi-

cult, especially when the children are young, but resolve to make it possible. Look for a reliable baby-sitter and give yourselves an evening off once in a while to go to the cinema, the theatre, a restaurant or just for a walk.

If you have a loving extended family, then as the children get older perhaps a relative could take care of them for the occasional weekend while you and your partner go away for a break. Adjustments like this in your relationship will help to keep your romantic feelings alive and vibrant.

Bathing and Bonding

▼ *Whether or not you have an active sex life at the moment, find ways to keep the sensuality alive in your relationship. Soaking together in a bath of aromatic oils provides delicious skin-to-skin contact. Massage and stroke each other's bodies; this tactile stimulation will leave you feeling nourished and relaxed. Making the effort to create precious moments of closeness and intimacy, which the two of you alone can enjoy, will keep the sparkle in your relationship.*

Sex in Maturity

Sexuality is not the sole prerogative of the young and there is no reason why people in their mature years should not continue to enjoy a happy sex life. Indeed, there are aspects of ageing that may actually enhance a sexual relationship, and research shows that even very elderly people can retain a healthy libido. While certain changes do occur in the sexual responses and reproductive organs of men and women as they grow older, if people can accept and adapt to them both physically and psychologically, then age itself does not preclude the capacity to be sexually fulfilled.

If a woman is past the menopause and no longer concerned about issues of pregnancy or contraception, she may feel more free to enjoy sex. Studies show that many women actually become more orgasmic in the later years of their lives, compared to when they were younger. However, as a man gets older he will often need more time and extra stimulation before he is able to get an erection.

If his partner is able to respond positively to this natural process of change, she may enjoy taking a more active and creative role than ever before in initiating the love play between them.

As people age, particularly if couples have been in a relationship for many years, their sexuality often becomes less focused on the act of penetration alone and more open to other forms of sensual and tactile contact, such as hugging, kissing, and loving caresses.

Even if a couple no longer desire penetrative intercourse, or if it is no longer possible because of health reasons, they can still pleasure each other with alternative forms of erotic love, such as oral sex and masturbation. In ways such as these, the physical intimacy between partners can actually develop as they grow older together and embrace a whole new sensuality that may have been missing in their earlier days.

Overcoming Taboos

One of the main problems facing the older generation is society's attitude towards sex and ageing. It is as if sex is seen as the domain of the young and beautiful alone, and that there is something indecent or embarrassing in acknowledging that older people may also have sexual needs.

Age and Intimacy
The twilight years of a relationship may allow a couple to discover a new level of intimacy.

Many older people feel embarrassed about revealing their sexual needs, finding it easier to repress them, and resign themselves to the commonly held opinion that at their age they should be "beyond it". Unfortunately, this view may prevent a mature couple seeking the specialist help they may need to resolve their physical and psychological sexual concerns. Even in long-term relationships, partners may give up all forms of physical intimacy because they feel unable to surmount these problems.

Many members of the older generation may believe that certain practices, such as oral sex and masturbation, are harmful, disgusting or even perverted. It is unlikely that, at this point in their lives, their views are going to change. However, oral sex is an excellent addition to a couple's love life, when sexual functioning is otherwise impaired by the ageing process or arousal responses have begun to slow down. An older man may find that he is more easily aroused and can maintain his erection better if his partner is willing to perform fellatio on him or to apply manual stimulation, strokes and caresses to his penis and testicles.

In a woman's case, after the menopause, her vagina may undergo various physical changes, losing much of its lubrication and elasticity. This can cause her discomfort in penetrative intercourse and reduce her enjoyment of sex. These changes are not related to her libido, which can still function healthily, and ageing should not affect the responsiveness of her clitoris, which is her most erotically sensitive organ. Cunnilingus is an excellent option in lovemaking, and one way that her partner can continue to give her sexual satisfaction.

Prostate Problems

Many men, particularly in their later years, experience urinary problems due to the enlargement of the prostate gland, which can obstruct the flow of urine. This can be rectified by medication, surgery, or by other forms of therapy. Men are often reluctant to seek treatment when they first realize they are having difficulty urinating, usually out of embarrassment. However, it is important to seek medical advice at the earliest opportunity, because delay risks serious complications, such as bladder infections and kidney damage. Treatment should not necessarily affect a man's sexual functioning, although a possible side-effect of prostate surgery is retrograde ejaculation, in which semen is propelled backwards into the bladder, rather than being expelled from the body.

The risk of cancer of the prostate also increases with age. This is one of the most common forms of cancer found in men but it responds well to treatment if detected in the early stages. Symptoms, if any, may be the same as for an enlarged prostate, and so this is another reason why it is important to seek medical advice if you experience problems urinating. Treatment carries some risk of infertility and impotence.

Changing Sexual Health

Health issues are the most significant factor in causing diminished sexual response as we grow older. It is natural for some people, as they age, to become less interested in sex. However, a sudden loss of libido, in men or women, could be due to illness or other physiological factors, and this should always be checked out with a doctor. Certain medications can inhibit sexual response, as can medical conditions such as diabetes, cardio-vascular diseases, and prostate disorders. Some women experience a loss of sexual feeling after the menopause, but this is by no means inevitable, and many women actually feel more sexual at this time than they did before.

However, there are natural changes in sexual response and functioning which occur as part of the ageing process. In themselves these do not necessarily prevent men or women from continuing to enjoy a happy sex life, especially if they are able to adapt to these changes and have an understanding partner who is also willing to explore new ways of enhancing the sexual relationship.

A man's reproductive capacity can remain throughout his life, although a decline in testosterone levels in later years may decrease his sperm production. However, as some famous men, such as Clint Eastwood or Anthony Quinn, have demonstrated in recent years, age is no bar to becoming a father. As he gets older, a man may find that he is slower to become aroused, and that his erection is less firm. He may take longer to ejaculate when making love, and may ejaculate with less frequency than when he was younger. Also, the refractory, or recovery, phase between each ejaculation will increase, and it may take several hours or even days before he can be aroused again.

There may also be psychological reasons for a man's changing sexual

Enjoying Leisure Together

▶ *Many couples, in their later years, have the opportunity to spend more leisure time together, free from work pressures or the demands of childrearing. This gives them more chance to enjoy each other's company so that their bond of affection and intimacy can deepen.*

responses as he gets older. Many men equate their sense of virility and potency with their earning capacity and careers. When a man retires from work, he may feel that he is no longer useful and this can adversely affect his sexual performance. It is important for a man to maintain and develop absorbing or worthwhile interests and take up pursuits which will help him re-establish his self-esteem. Talking over these issues with an understanding partner, who can reassure him that he is still a real man in her regard, or discussing his problems with a counsellor, can help him to come to terms with his new role in life.

A woman will experience far more dramatic hormonal changes than a man as she ages. This change can herald a whole new phase in a woman's life, and can instil in her a range of emotions. She may feel that she is finally her own woman; many women consider the post-menopausal years to be the best time of their lives. This may also be tinged with a sense of loss that a certain aspect of her feminine role has gone for ever.

On average, the onset of the menopause occurs at around the age of 50 (although it can begin much earlier or later) and takes around two to five years to complete. During this time, there will be dramatic hormonal fluctuations

in the woman's body, and her oestrogen levels will steadily decline. Menstruation often becomes irregular, and there may be times when her periods are close together with a heavier than usual menstrual flow, and then more widely spaced, with only a very light showing of blood. Excessive bleeding or other menstrual problems should be investigated by a doctor to rule out possible disorders.

The menopause can affect women very differently, partly due to psychological factors such as whether they are mentally well prepared for the change, their attitude towards growing older and no longer being fertile, and the symptoms experienced during this process. Some women travel through this time without a backward glance, and suffer few of the more uncomfortable side-effects.

Many women, however, experience one or more unpleasant physical and psychological symptoms which can be directly related to the hormonal changes. These can include

hot flushes and night sweats, palpitations and anxiety attacks, loss of concentration, mood swings, lethargy, vaginal dryness and thinning of the vaginal tissues. In some women, the reduced oestrogen levels leads to osteoporosis, a thinning of the bones caused by calcium loss, leading to increased risk of fractures.

However, it is important that women realize the menopause in itself is not an illness but a natural part of the female life process. At the same time, no woman should hesitate in seeking medical advice if she is suffering from any of the debilitating symptoms described above.

Many doctors recommend that women take hormone replacement therapy (HRT) to safeguard their health during the menopause and even for a longer duration, while other medical experts disagree. The pros and cons of HRT are still being debated in the medical world. HRT will usually alleviate the physical side-effects of menopause, and is effective in reducing the risk of developing osteoporosis and heart disease.

Whether or not a woman chooses to take HRT, she should ensure that her lifestyle is balanced and healthy. A good nutritious diet, plenty of exercise, avoiding smoking and keeping alcohol intake to sensible levels will all enhance her state of well-being at this special time in her life.

As a woman ages, she may notice some change in her sexual organs and sexual responses. As oestrogen levels drop, it is possible that her vaginal secretions will decrease, and the vaginal lining will become thinner and so more vulnerable to tears and infection. To reduce friction and soreness during intercourse, she can use a lubricating jelly or obtain a locally applied oestrogen cream. She may also notice that, as she ages, her arousal responses are less intense, not because of a lack of desire, but because of physiological changes. There is no reason for her to become less orgasmic, although her climaxes may not seem as powerful as when she was younger.

For various medical reasons, a doctor may recommend that a woman undergoes a hysterectomy but it is advisable to seek a second medical opinion regarding the suitability of this operation in her circumstances. While a hysterectomy is more common once women have reached their forties and beyond, it may sometimes be necessary to carry out this procedure in a younger woman.

Once a woman has had a hysterectomy she is no longer able to have children, and if both ovaries are removed, she will become menopausal. In these circumstances, hormone replacement therapy is usually offered to the woman by her doctor. While a hysterectomy is a major surgical procedure, a healthy woman should recover well within six weeks of the operation if she is able to receive the adequate after-care and rest she needs.

A hysterectomy does not have to mean the end of a woman's sex life or capacity to enjoy sexual or orgasmic pleasure, although in some cases, women do report that the intensity of their orgasmic contractions reduces slightly. If a woman has to undergo a hysterectomy, it is important that she realizes the operation does not make her less feminine in any way.

Life Without Sex

For some people, sexual passion declines quite naturally after a certain age, and not only are they happy to accept this, they may even find it a relief. The freedom from being driven by sexual desires which had to be fulfilled can open up a whole new vista on life, allowing that person time to relax into other pleasures and pursuits. If this happens mutually within a partnership, the couple may find that their relationship changes to allow greater compatibility and growth in other areas of their lives.

If one partner loses the sex drive, while the other retains an active libido, they obviously need to talk about their incompatible desires and try to find a compromise. A couple who face this dilemma may also benefit from counselling to help them confront the changing nature of their relationship and enable them to acknowledge their own and each other's needs.

Sometimes the end of penetrative sex in a relationship can open up new horizons of loving sensual contact and deepening companionship through which both people can derive even greater emotional nourishment than before. For some people, to whom sex was more of a chore than a pleasure, the cessation of their sex lives can feel liberating.

There are circumstances, of course, when the loss of a sex life in the later years of life is not a matter of choice. Death, divorce, or separation may leave one partner alone, and often as we grow older, it becomes less possible or desirable to form new partnerships. Many people, from middle age to elderly years, face the prospect of spending the rest of their lives without a sexual companion. In a situation like this it is important to assess one's real needs and hopes, rather than abandon the idea of finding a new partner.

Some people take active measures, joining dating agencies or broadening their recreational activities to make new acquaintances, and achieve success in doing so. Others learn to accept their single status. Even so, it is still possible to keep the flame of sexual energy burning bright.

Dancing, having fun, sharing good times with friends, receiving a massage, cuddles and hugs from people who care, all help to keep sensual and sexual vitality alive. Masturbation is also a way to achieve release from sexual tension, but it can also be much more than that. Self-pleasuring can be a way of nurturing oneself, if time is taken to touch the whole body with care and love and it is done without haste, guilt or judgement.

Getting older, with or without a partner, does not mean that you can no longer enjoy the sensual and sexual pleasures of your body if you so desire. It is good and healthy for you to acknowledge and enjoy your sexuality, whatever your age.

A New Beginning?

◀ *Being alone need not be the same as being lonely. It is never too late to form a new relationship, perhaps as fulfilling as any you've known before.*

Touch & Sensual Massage

Introducing sensual massage as a regular event in a relationship is one of the most effective ways of enhancing physical and emotional communication. The loving and confident stroking of hands upon the skin, the way they mould into the body's curves, and the gentle palpation of muscles and tissues speak volumes in the silent language of touch about your innermost feelings for each other.

A sensual massage can help you and your partner unwind from the stresses of the day, creating a precious opportunity to relax and enjoy each other's company. A massage can be offered as a spontaneous gesture to ease a partner's pain or tension. You may want to give a soothing face massage, to relieve stress, anxiety or headache, or focus your strokes on the back, shoulders, and neck, to alleviate muscular aches and strains. You can pamper your partner by offering her a luxurious foot or hand massage.

The session may evolve into a truly sensuous affair, involving flowing caresses of the whole body from top to toe. A massage can include a variety of strokes, from soft, languid touches to firm, invigorating movements. The beauty of massage is that its motions are like notes of music or the steps of a dance, varied enough to enable you to always respond creatively to your partner's changing needs and moods.

It may become a prelude to a loving and sexual encounter so that the whole body is more ready and responsive to pleasure and erotic feelings. Sensual massage helps to build physical and emotional trust because one partner surrenders his or her body into the hands of the other, while the person giving the massage must learn to respect and tune in to its innate needs and responses.

Touch as a Healing Force

The most important healing element in any massage is the power of loving touch. Touch is known as the mother of the senses, being the first to develop in the human embryo and in all other species, and the one on which all the other senses are based. The tactile sense resides in the skin, that miraculous organ covering the entire body. By means of its countless nerve endings, which respond to a whole variety of pressures from pain to pleasure, the skin relays messages through the central nervous system to the brain, transmitting information about the external world beyond its

Loving Therapy

 *Massage is a loving and therapeutic process which relieves tension in body and mind, and so allows more freedom to enjoy spontaneous interaction. By taking turns to massage each other, both partners can learn to enjoy sharing the roles of giving and receiving pleasure.*

Emotional Nourishment

▶ *Massage is the perfect medium for close physical contact at times when the libido of one or both partners is low, or there is a sexual dysfunction or physical condition that is inhibiting or preventing full sexual intercourse. By remaining in touch with one another's bodies, the essential emotional nourishment which ensues from physical intimacy can continue, thus avoiding a build-up of frustration, need and feelings of isolation. The strokes can release muscular tension from those areas of the body closely associated with sexual response, helping your partner to feel more alive and receptive to her sexual feelings.*

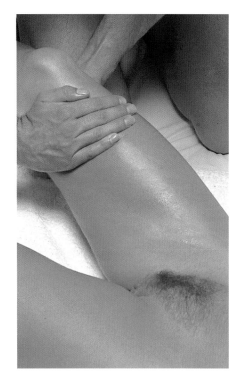

frontiers. A loving touch which brings reassurance and joy to the skin will ultimately infuse the whole body with a feeling of well-being.

Touch is an essential form of nourishment for the psychosomatic processes of body, mind and spirit throughout our lives. Adequate loving touch, in the form of affectionate caressing, hugging, stroking, cuddling and kissing, is vital in the early stages of infancy for the healthy development of a growing child. Through these pleasurable skin sensations, the infant can begin to define its sense of self-worth, and to develop an understanding and an appreciation of its own body.

Touch deprivation in early childhood can retard physical and emotional growth, potentially leading to health, behavioural and sexual problems in later years. Lack of adequate touch, even in adulthood, can rob someone of the feelings of vitality and ease within the body. This will often manifest itself as an

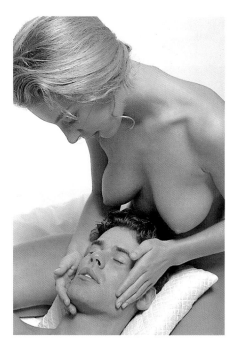

Healing Touch

▲ *By letting massage become a regular feature of a relationship, partners can learn to develop whole body sensuality, increase skin sensitivity to both external stimuli and internal feelings, and to develop a growing confidence and trust in the nurturing and healing qualities of touch.*

inability to express or receive affection adequately.

Loving touch, through the medium of massage, will help to heal old emotional wounds whose memories remain locked within the body, establishing a new and positive sense of body image, confidence and responsiveness to physical sensuality.

When couples experiment with touch techniques they discover, often to their surprise, that to give a massage is as satisfying as receiving one. This is because by touching and using your feeling senses, you open up the depths of your own emotions, and have a means to express them. Within a massage sequence, you can be playful, tender, strong, creative and loving. By coming to know and understand another's body, you begin to become more aware of your own physical needs.

It is important, however, to give massage only when willing to do so, for it is a caring act and the message imparted from your hands always

Tender Outpouring

▲ *By opening your heart and pouring tenderness into your hands as you stroke each part of his body, you can impart to him a deeply nurturing sense of love and care which will increase his feelings of physical well-being and of self-worth. Massage expresses and heightens emotional bonding in a unique way.*

Fluid Movements

▲ *In an intimate and sensual massage, use your hands, forearms, and other parts of your body to stroke the skin, letting the touches flow like water over the body. At some moments it will seem as if the two bodies have melted and merged into one another, dissolving the physical boundaries between you.*

Overture to Lovemaking

▼ *If both of you are clear that a sensual massage is a luxurious prelude to lovemaking, then once you have warmed and relaxed the whole body, you can stroke over the erogenous areas to increase excitement.*

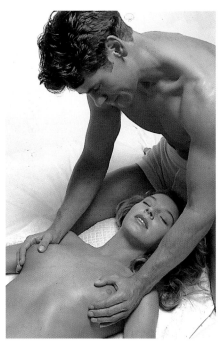

conveys your innermost feelings. Equally, it is important to know whether the massage you plan is purely for sensual pampering, relaxing or revitalizing, or whether it is an erotic encounter as a prelude to making love.

Naturally, if there is mutual consent, a massage may transform from one experience into the other, but it is wrong to use the situation as a means of seduction if your partner has not given you clear signals of consent. If the massage is intended purely to soothe, comfort and relax, or your partner is unwilling to engage in sexual activity, then it is better to avoid direct contact with the genitalia or other erogenous areas which could provoke an unwanted sexual response in either of you.

Selecting the Oils

Choose a light, preferably unrefined vegetable oil for lubrication, such as grapeseed, safflower or sunflower oil, to which you can add a much richer oil, such as almond, avocado or jojoba.

Learn about the soothing, romantic and erotic qualities of essential oils, so that you can create aromatic blends to enhance the sensuous mood of your massage. Place your oil in a ceramic bowl or a bottle that will allow you to pour the right amount into your hands. Warm the oil before applying it. Keep tissues or towels nearby for oil spillage or to wipe your hands.

If your partner does not like oil on his skin, then use a body lotion with nourishing skin properties. Talcum powder can also be used, though its dryness will prevent you from performing the flowing, soporific motions of a truly sensual massage.

Learning to receive massage is also a helpful process for those people who predominantly identify with the role of the main giver in a relationship, often unconsciously taking control of events and denying the other partner the chance to reciprocate love and concern. To receive massage is one of the few occasions in life where all you need to do is become totally receptive. Even in lovemaking, there is usually a constant interaction of activity.

To allow yourself to become passive, and simply receive touch, means you must open yourself up to a certain degree of trust and vulnerability and this, in itself, is a gift which you can offer to your partner. Make sure you take it in turns to give and receive massage so that you can both learn from all aspects of the experience.

The Strokes of Massage

Confidence, quality of touch in your hands and sensitivity to your partner's body are essential if the massage is to be mutually satisfying and pleasurable. But do give each other scope to experiment with different strokes, pressures and touches. Treat the whole experience as a game, make it fun, and tell each other what feels good. Give one another a chance to explore the techniques without being too directive, but make your feelings clear to your partner if you do not feel comfortable with what is happening to your body.

There are some basic rules to follow and certain strokes to learn that will improve the experience and enhance your mutual repertoire of techniques. By learning how to apply different movements and pressures you will be able to give the right massage for the occasion. You can also expand on your techniques by reading suitable massage manuals, or participating in a massage workshop with your partner.

The first step is to lubricate the area of the body you are about to massage. Pour a little oil into one palm and then rub both hands together to warm it before spreading the lubricant with soft, free-flowing motions, using the flat surface of your palms.

Apply sufficient oil to ensure your hands slide sensuously over the skin. These soporific strokes will help your

Liquid Warmth
◀ *Your liquid movements as you spread the oil will warm the muscles, boost the circulation, and prepare the body's tissues for other strokes. There is no need to hurry this part of the massage as it will give you both time to relax, focus your attention, and tune in to one another.*

Following the Contours
▼ *Allow all the tension to leave your hands so that they are able to glide, melt and sculpt the underlying contours and curves of your partner's body and bring to both him and yourself a much clearer definition of its shape and structure.*

Close Contact
◀ *By straddling your partner, you can comfortably enfold the circumference of his back in one long flowing sweep, stroking your hands up along his spine, over his shoulders and back down the sides of his body. Your physical closeness will add to the sensuality of the massage, but take care to support your own weight.*

Rounded Movements
▶ *Sensual massage movements should be smooth and rounded and never finish abruptly mid-way on the body. Always glide your hands around the body's contours, such as the shoulders or hips, or sweep them out along the limbs.*

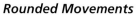

Circle Strokes

1 To circle stroke, place both hands flat and parallel on the body, with fingers pointing away from you. Your hands should be about 10cm/4in apart. With a steady pressure, begin to slide both hands in a circular clockwise motion with your right hand leading the movement.

Lift and Pass

2 Lift your right hand slightly away from the body, crossing it over the top of your left hand which continues to circle underneath.

Completing the Circle

3 As your left hand completes its circle, your right hand drops down to perform a half-circle, then lifts off again to let your left hand pass. Now repeat this sequence.

partner forget any stressful thoughts he might have and become more receptive to your touch.

You can create a truly relaxing and sensual massage using only soft gliding strokes in a variety of unbroken and flowing motions that embrace the whole body. By letting your hands slide from the back to the legs in simple easy stretches, or, when stroking the front of the body, from the thighs to the belly, you will bring a sense of unity and integration to your partner's body.

Circle and Fan Strokes

Circle and fan strokes stretch and ease the tension out of the body's soft tissues, bringing a lovely fluid and hypnotic movement to a session of sensual massage.

Circle strokes are applied to any broad surface area of the body, such as the back and sides of the body, the thighs, belly and chest. The art of this stroke is to keep it constantly spiralling over the skin until you are ready to move with an unbroken motion into the next sequence of strokes. The circle stroke is shown (*left*) in three stages.

Fanning Strokes

◄ *Fanning motions can be applied upwards or downwards. Once your hands have reached the base of the back on a downwards sequence, return to the top of the spine by gliding them up along the sides of the ribcage.*

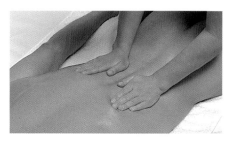

Fan Strokes

1 To fan upwards, place both hands flat, pointing to the head, on each side of the lower end of the spine.

Fanning Out

2 Glide both your hands upwards for a distance of about 15cm/6in before fanning them out towards the sides of the body.

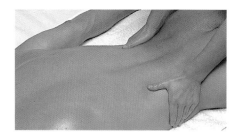

Gliding Downwards

3 Mould both hands firmly to the sides of the body and pull downwards. Then, with a turn of the wrists, glide your hands towards the centre of the back before stroking upwards again.

Essential Oils

All that is necessary for sensual massage is a basic carrier oil, such as sunflower or almond oil. But by blending in a few drops of one or more essential oils you can make the massage a truly memorable experience. Essential oils have their own unique therapeutic qualities – some are highly beneficial in relieving stress, for example. You and your partner should both decide on the blend of essential oils, otherwise if one of you finds an aroma unpleasant the massage will not be so pleasurable. Some oils such as rose, jasmine, sandalwood, rosewood, and the exotic ylang ylang enjoy a widespread appeal.

Warning: Essential oils are highly concentrated and should never be spread directly onto the skin. Always blend them with a suitable carrier oil first. For a whole body massage, add 10-15 drops of one, two or three essential oils to five teaspoons of base carrier oil.

Fan strokes are applied to most areas of the body with an upward, flowing and steady pressure using the surface of both palms. One fan stroke should merge into the next in a constant upward movement, which boosts the circulation towards the heart. When your hands reach to the top of a body part, fan them out to the sides and slide them back down to repeat the sequence. The fan stroke over the lower back is shown opposite in three stages.

Invigorating Strokes

Invigorating strokes add variety and spice to your sensual massage. They have a revitalizing effect on the system, boosting the blood circulation, loosening stiff muscles and ridding the tissues of trapped toxins. Your partner will enjoy the stimulat-

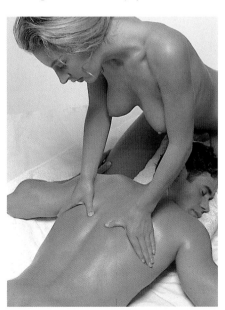

Soothing Strokes
◀ *Large circle strokes on the abdomen are very soothing, helping your partner breathe more deeply, so that she is more in touch with her sexual and emotional feelings. Always approach the abdomen sensitively as it is a vulnerable area.*

ing effect and the sensation of different pressures. Introduce friction, kneading and percussion strokes to the massage, once the muscles are warm and relaxed.

Always precede and follow invigorating movements with sensual strokes to soothe the skin and to integrate the part of the body under focus with the surrounding area. Friction grinds the tissue towards the bone and is excellent for relieving specific areas of tension. Pressure is applied slowly and sensitively from the heels of the hand, the thumbs, fingertips, or knuckles. The movement can be a steady slide, a short stretch, or small circular motions in which the pressure is greater on the outward half of the circle. Use friction whenever you are working close to the bone, such as alongside the

Spinal Relaxation
◀ *The spine is often one of the most tense areas of the body. The deeper stretching movement of a friction stroke over the muscles and ligaments running alongside the vertebrae will help to relieve stiffness from your partner's back, enabling him to relax more fully and enjoy the massage. In this movement, the thumb pads are pressed slowly at the top of the back into the grooves either side of the spine, while the hands rest on the body. Lean your weight steadily into the stroke as you slide your thumbs down towards the base of the back. Then glide your hands around his hips, up the sides of the ribcage and over the shoulders to repeat the whole sequence with a deeper level of pressure. To vary the stroke, make small circular movements with your thumbs moving down each side of the spine.*

Fleshy Zones

◀ *Kneading strokes are perfect for the fleshy erogenous zones of the buttocks and thighs, as the invigorating action helps to release tension from their large muscles and stimulate the sensory nerves that affect sexual response. When massaging the buttocks, begin with smooth, gliding motions that shape their ample contours, and then proceed with the kneading.*

Brisk Strokes

▼ *The brisk staccato movements of hacking can be a fun addition to sensual massage, particularly over the buttocks and thighs, as they will enliven the skin and may even stimulate your partner erotically. However, if he is feeling particularly vulnerable, or the mood of the massage is very relaxed, save these strokes for times when invigorating stimulation is the desired result.*

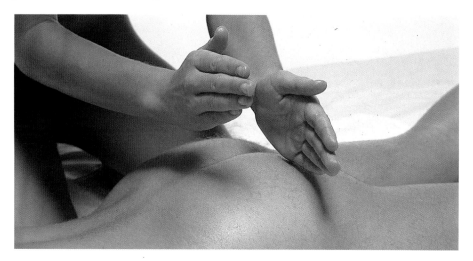

spine, around the shoulder blades, under or over the scalp, or on the hands, feet and face.

Kneading is applied to the fleshy parts of the body such as the shoulders, sides of the body, buttocks and thighs. Kneading, as the name suggests, replicates the action of a baker kneading dough, and is performed by scooping up and squeezing a portion of flesh between the fingers, heel and thumb of one hand before pushing it towards the other hand. The waiting hand then repeats the action, and in this way the flesh is rolled back and forth between both hands. Work thoroughly over an area, ensuring that your wrists and shoulders remain relaxed so that the kneading has a fluid and wave-like motion.

Percussion strokes are rapid, vibratory movements used to revitalize the system and tone up the skin by enriching the blood supply to its nerve endings. There are a variety of percussion strokes, all made with one hand following the other in quick succession to strike the flesh briskly before flicking immediately back off the skin. They feel best when applied to fleshy areas and should never be used directly over the bones.

Pummelling is done by rhythmically striking the sides of loosely made fists against the body, while hacking is performed with a series of gentle chopping movements made from the sides of open, straight hands. Relax your wrists so the percussion strokes remain bouncy but not heavy-handed.

Maintain Good Posture

Whether you are kneeling, sitting or standing while massaging your partner, it is always important to take care of your own posture, pausing to relax and breathe deeply whenever you feel tense. By remaining at ease in your body and breathing, your own vitality is sustained throughout the massage. This boosts your enjoyment of giving the massage and brings a comforting warmth and vitality to your hands. As a consequence, good posture improves the quality of your massage strokes.

Preparation for Massage

When you set the scene for a luxurious and sensual massage, take time to create a romantic ambience so that your partner will know this is a special occasion. Place flowers around the room for their delicate aroma and colourful effects, and light candles to create a mellow mood, putting them at a safe distance from the place you are giving the massage.

You should cover the mattress or surface you are working on with fresh, clean sheets, and also keep extra sheets and towels close by in case your partner gets cold. Have your favourite romantic style of music playing softly in the background but take care not to let the sounds invade the natural rhythm of your massage strokes.

Choose the setting for massage carefully, so both of you can relax fully. The room must be warm and draught-free if clothes are to be removed. Try to ensure privacy so the person receiving the massage has a chance to put all concerns aside, and the one giving it can devote his or her attention to the session.

In a full-body massage, both partners need a firm base such as a futon, a layer of foam, or a strong mattress to support their body weight under the pressure of strokes and movements. Folded blankets, a covered sleeping bag or firm cushions laid on the floor will also suffice. Towels and oils should be kept close at hand.

Spontaneous Massage

Different locations and occasions can turn a massage into a spontaneous treat. For instance, when bathing together you have the perfect opportunity for an impromptu massage, especially as your skin-to-skin

The Gossamer Touch

Feather touches are a sensual, skin-teasing way to carry out a series of strokes over any area. Using only the minimum of pressure from your fingertips, stroke very lightly over the skin, one hand following the other, and moving in one direction at a time. This will activate the skin's peripheral nerve endings, exquisitely heightening its sensitivity. Some people may find the touch just too light and ticklish, while others love its euphoric effects and would quite happily surrender to a whole body massage of these strokes alone.

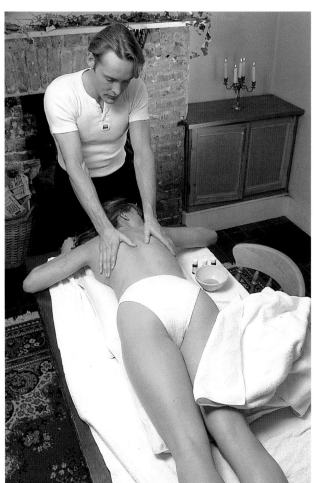

Massage Table

◄ *You can use a table for a massage base if it is sufficiently long and strong to take the size and weight of your partner, and narrow enough for you to reach her body. Pad it with blankets or cushions for comfort. A table of the right height and dimensions has the advantage of allowing you more freedom of movement, although it will inhibit close physical contact.*

contact will feel deliciously natural and uninhibited. In the bath, take turns to give each other a shoulder and neck massage. Your soothing strokes will assist the therapeutic qualities of warm water as it draws the tension out of the muscles.

If you have a fireplace, take the opportunity to massage your partner in front of a lighted hearth at the end of the evening or after a bath. The heat of a fire adds a primal earthiness to your nakedness and physical contact, and you can give a full body sensual massage to your partner as he or she lies on folded blankets or a thin mattress in front of the flickering flames. Or simply take it in turns to give a head, neck and shoulder massage to relax your partner before going to sleep.

Lather as Lubricant
In the bath, the rich soapy lather on her skin acts as a lubricant for you to glide your hands soothingly over the top of her back and shoulders. Then relax her spine with friction strokes. Hook your fingers over her shoulders and work your thumbs in small circular motions up alongside the bones.

Friction Rub
Use a loofah or soap glove to massage the skin. The gentle friction leaves it soft and glowing. Rub over the chest and arms, and then the back and shoulders.

Relaxing Aromas
You can add a few drops of essential oils into your basic oil to increase the relaxing effect of this fireside massage. Use soft, sensual strokes to sculpt the upper back and ease the tension from the shoulders and neck.

Targeting Tensions
Focus on tight areas between the shoulder blades, and at the base of the neck. Hook your fingers over his shoulders, and sink your thumb pads into the muscles, then use small circular motions over each tense spot in turn.

Tingling Vibrations
Hack briskly and firmly over the top of the shoulders and down along the sides of the shoulder blades, but avoid striking the spine. The rapid vibrations will loosen stiff shoulders and leave the skin flushed and tingling.

Soothing the Mind
A head massage can calm the mind when your partner is feeling under stress. Firmly circle the fingertips of both hands over his entire scalp, then comb your fingers through his hair to complete your fireside massage.

Tender Loving Care

Some people find it difficult to express their love verbally. Often, a tender touch conveys these feelings more directly than words. It is an instinctive human response to embrace a person as a gesture of affection, to take hold of the hand to comfort, or to soothe away pain with a gentle rub. When you make love, the way you touch the whole body is as important as the sexual act itself, because it communicates your loving feelings.

A sensual massage is a wonderful opportunity to give and receive tender, loving care but even if you do not have time for a full-body session, you can still pamper your partner with shorter programmes of massage which will leave him or her feeling cherished and relaxed. At the end of a tiring day, a twenty-minute massage is still an excellent treat.

A foot massage will dissolve stress and soothe body and mind. The soft strokes over the feet have a calming effect, while the stronger pressures will boost low energy levels. Massage one foot at a time, and spread a little lotion over the top and sole with gliding, sensual strokes. When the foot is

warm and supple, stroke your fingertips or thumb pads around the sides, front and back of the ankle to release any tension. Press or slide your thumbs firmly all over the sole to stimulate its countless nerve endings.

Pay attention to the toes as touch here is surprisingly sensual. Palpate each toe gently between thumb and finger, then slide your little finger between each toe and rub the soft webs of skin with little corkscrew motions. Add the strokes shown here to your massage and then repeat them all on the other foot.

Cradling the Foot
▶ *When you have completed the strokes on one foot, cradle it between your hands for a while, focusing all your attention towards your touch. The soft, enfolding embrace of the foot will deeply relax your partner.*

Position for Foot Massage
◀ *Foot massage gives you a chance to relax together, to chat and catch up on the news of the day while enjoying physical contact at the same time. Make sure your partner is sitting comfortably while she receives the massage, and her leg is supported by cushions. Position yourself so you can easily apply strokes to both sides of her foot.*

Tension-free Toes
▲ *The toes tend to retain tension, which adds stress to the posture. Stretching them brings relief to the whole body. After pressing gently over the toe, hold it between your thumb and index finger, and pull steadily along its length from the base to its tip. You will need to swap the position of your hands to stretch the big toe.*

Feather Touches
◀ *Feather-stroke down the leg and over the foot several times towards the end of the massage if your partner enjoys these exhilarating, skin-tingling touches.*

Many of the strokes used on the feet can be adapted to a hand massage. If your partner's work is manual, or involves gripping a pen or using a keyboard all day, a hand massage can alleviate the strain of repetitive movements which accumulates in the tendons and muscles. Make sure he is sitting or lying comfortably, so that his shoulders and arms are relaxed while you massage his hands.

A face massage is one of the most intimate and loving ways to give pleasure through touch. Use soft caresses to calm and reassure, and steady, firm pressures to relieve

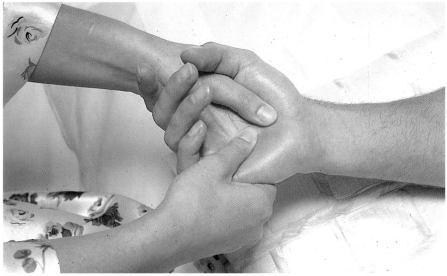

Loving Lotion
▲ Hand-to-hand contact conveys a silent message of love, friendship and support. Spread lotion over the hand with gliding strokes and then hold it between the warmth of your palms.

Slide and Stretch
◀ Make short, firm, sliding strokes with one thumb following the other, over the palm and up to the wrist to stretch away tension. Rest the back of the hand against your fingers. Rest his arm on a cushion during the massage.

tension spots in this most revealed and revealing part of the body.

Every thought and emotion expresses itself in the face and, often, its muscles tighten to present an acceptable mask to the world. When your lover comes home, help him to become more vulnerable and allow his true feelings to rise to the surface by stroking away the stress.

To give a face massage, kneel or sit behind your partner's head so that it rests between your legs. Place a cushion under his head to take the

strain off the back of his neck. Begin by cupping your hands very lightly over each side of his jaw and letting them rest there in a calm and still hold for up to a count of ten. Then stroke with the palms of both hands continuously, one after the other, along the jawbone from the chin to the ear until you feel the whole area relaxing under these loving caresses.

Take the lobes of the ears between thumbs and fingertips and gently press them, then make tiny circle

strokes all along the rims of the ears. Sweep your fingers in outward-flowing circles over both cheeks to move and loosen tense muscles. Follow this by tracing the fingertips of one hand lightly round and round the sensuous curves of the lips.

Using the tips of the first two fingers of each hand, stroke deftly around the eye socket up to ten times from the outer bridge of the nose to the edge of the temples, continuing lightly over the top of the cheekbones back towards the sides of the nose.

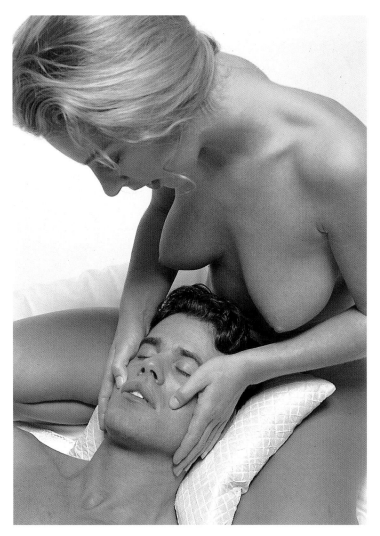

Steady Pressure

◀ *When massaging the face, your strokes should be smooth, steady and consistent. Apply a gentle but firm pressure as you move over tension areas, such as directly under the cheekbones. In this movement, your hands softly clasp the sides of his face while your thumbs slide down the edges of the nose and continue stretching outwards under the bone. Lighten the pressure as you get closer to the ears. Draw your hands lightly over the head before repeating the stroke twice more.*

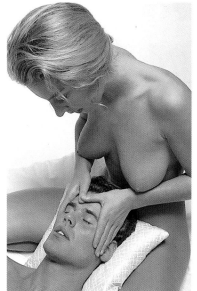

Glide your fingertips smoothly in clockwise motions around the temples, increasing the pressure slightly on the outward sweep. Now soothe the brow by softly drawing each hand consecutively across the forehead from the opposite-side temple, repeating these hypnotic movements for up to two minutes. Then work the fingertips of both hands simultaneously in small circles over the scalp as if shampooing the hair.

Help for Headaches

◀ *To relieve a tension headache, place your thumbs over the centre of the forehead just above the eyebrows while resting your hands on the sides of the face. Steadily draw your thumbs outwards over the brow, completing the stroke with a sweep of the temples. Continue repeating this stroke to cover the whole forehead, moving up a little at a time until you reach the hair line.*

Complete the face massage with a still and tender hold by placing your thumbs over the centre of his crown, so that his head nestles between your hands and your fingers lay symmetrically over his temples. Close your eyes and focus your attention on your hands to pour your loving feelings into them. After a minute or two, slowly withdraw your hands from the head but sit quietly with your partner so you can both enjoy these precious and peaceful moments together.

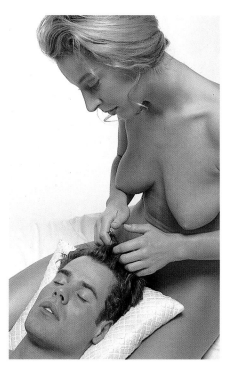

Soothing Strokes

◀ *Your partner will love the feeling as your fingers comb through his hair, as if they are drawing the last of the day's stresses out of his mind and body. It is a very soothing motion to add to the last few strokes of a face and head massage.*

Games & Exercises

Games and exercises offer a great opportunity for you and your partner to relax and have fun together, while renewing your physical vitality as you breathe more deeply, tone up your muscles and stretch your joints. It is a chance to enjoy your own and your lover's body outside of sexual contact.

These exercises provide a non-threatening and playful opportunity in which to discover whether there are any subtle physical and psychological tensions within yourself and your relationship that may be inhibiting harmonious and spontaneous interaction. Tension often reflects an internal state of mind, such as a fear of letting go or of losing control, which shows itself outwardly as hesitation, resistance or even aggression.

The games will help you find a point of balance in yourself where you are at ease and relaxed within your body and mind. From this position you then co-operate with your partner, to find a mutual point of harmony and balance between you.

Before attempting the exercises, warm up with one or both of the two

Exercise One
1 Get the passive partner to stand in a balanced posture, feet a shoulder-width apart and knees flexed, taking a few moments to relax all joints. He then drops his head forwards and leans his upper body towards the ground. The head and neck hang relaxed between the shoulders, and his arms dangle loosely down. As the active partner, pummel briskly, one hand following the other, up along each side of his spine, and between the shoulder blades. Take care not to strike the spine itself.

Soothe the Spine
2 After the invigorating pummelling, soothe your partner's spine and back with overlapping strokes from the fingers of each hand. Start the motion from the lower back, drawing one hand after the other up along the spine and over the neck. Repeat this action several times.

Stimulating Strokes

3 Move to your partner's side and hack briskly over the large muscles of the buttocks to invigorate and stimulate this area and to loosen its tension. Aim for the fleshy areas, taking care not to strike the lower spine or pelvic bones. You can continue this hacking motion down to the thighs.

Friction Rub

4 Position yourself behind his posterior, and apply a friction rub over the kidney area to warm and revitalize the whole body. Using the flat surface of each hand alternately, briskly rub them back and forth for about thirty seconds to generate a tingling heat. Then, soothe the back with some sensual strokes. Now ask your passive partner to extend his upper body, uncoiling the spine slowly from its base, vertebra by vertebra. The last area to lift is the neck and head which then rests, relaxed and balanced, over the spine. Give him a few moments to experience this sensation of easy graceful length through the upper body.

Clear the Chest

5 Now ask your partner to expand his chest, by pushing his fists into his lower back, while letting his shoulders and head drop backwards. Encourage him to clear tension from his throat by emitting sounds while you pummel thoroughly over the chest. The pummelling dispels carbon dioxide from the lungs, helping him to breathe more deeply and to release sensations of tightness in the ribcage. When you have completed these strokes, your partner should stand straight and shake his arms and hands, and then legs and feet, to loosen up their joints.

Exercise Two

1 In the second warm-up exercise, the partner who is lying down first relaxes her whole body, and then focuses her breath and attention softly towards her abdomen. Lay your hands gently but with total presence on her belly to develop warmth and contact. Encourage her to become aware of her belly's expansion towards your hands with each inhalation, and its contraction with each exhalation.

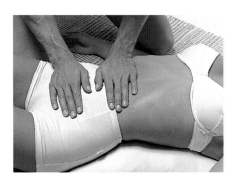

Take the Weight

2 Cradle your partner's pelvis and lower abdomen between the reassuring contact of your hands, by slipping one hand beneath the lower back, and the other just above the pubic bone. Wait patiently for her to drop the weight of her back and pelvis into the support of your lower hand, while she directs her breathing and mental concentration to her pelvic girdle and genitals, allowing those areas to relax more with each cycle of breath.

Breathing Away Tension

3 Stress causes the diaphragm, the sheath of muscle separating the chest and the abdominal cavity, to tighten, constricting breathing, increasing feelings of anxiety and cutting you off from basic emotions. Scoop the hand which is closest to your partner's head under her body to rest beneath the middle of her back. Encourage her to consciously release the tension in her back towards this hand. Place the other hand softly over the diaphragm area, above the solar plexus, and just below the ribcage. Ask your partner to breathe gently into the area between your hands and allow her tension to melt with each exhalation.

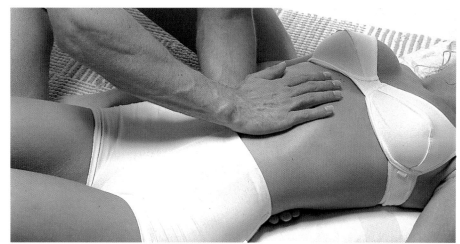

ten-minute tactile contact programmes shown here. The first exercise uses some of the percussion strokes explained in Sensual Massage to enliven the body and help ease strain from the back, shoulders and chest. The second exercise encourages greater relaxation and more fullness of breath, while helping you to make a deeper connection with the abdominal and pelvic area, the centre of gravity and balance in your body.

Physical relaxation and emotional trust come from a sense of being at ease with your body and feelings, so you can trust your basic instincts. Those feelings are deeply rooted in the body, and in particular, within the abdominal region.

After each exercise, take some time to assimilate its effects, and discuss with each other what feelings or sensations occurred. Then you can reverse roles.

Developing Trust and Synchronicity

Fundamentally, the following exercises centre on developing trust and attaining synchronicity. Both factors represent a huge dynamic in any relationship. Our basis of trust develops within us as children through the experiences of our primary relationships, and is generally replayed unconsciously in other relationships throughout our adult lives. Learning to trust more does not mean that we must throw caution to the wind; our inner self-protection mechanisms have developed for good reason and need to be respected.

Through physical game-playing we can become aware of our fears about developing real trust – and the body is the most manifest place for this observation – and can sometimes gain insights into our earlier childhood experiences. We can then begin

Game One: Synchronizing

1 Both of you should squat, facing each other and maintaining eye contact, but with sufficient distance to let your arms stretch out to make contact. Keep your backs straight, and your neck and head loose and relaxed. Focus your breath and attention on your pelvic region to allow this point of gravity to give you balance. Let the genital area, and especially the anus, relax, and drop the weight of your buttocks towards the floor. Weight should be distributed evenly throughout the feet. Once you feel comfortable in your own squatting position, reach out and clasp each other's hands or wrists.

to undo some of our fears and inhibitions, while regaining more natural spontaneity. Awareness occurs the moment we draw something from the unconscious into our conscious minds, and is always the first point of any change.

By playing these games, you also learn how to become attentive and aware of whatever is happening, both within yourself and your partner. You cannot expect your lover to relax deeply and trust in the situation if you are self-absorbed, or your attention is wandering, or if you are neither sensitive nor receptive to the mental and bodily signals he or she is giving out.

Try not to overpower your partner, or demand results, and be patient whenever you meet a moment of physical or emotional resistance. Explore those experiences together, trying to gain insight into their

messages and learn from them. These games are intended to be fun and should not become a serious encounter, even if they evoke some profound feelings. They are an experiment, allowing you both to interchange constantly between passive and active roles, and to become confident and attuned to your bodies, so that you can develop a more harmonious relationship.

A successful relationship between two people also results when synchronicity is attained on energetic, physical and mental levels. Many couples are drawn to each other in the first place because of a certain rapport, although initially this may be an unconscious factor in their mutual attraction. There is a kind of ebb and flow in a happy relationship, where a balance exists between knowing when to take the lead and when to yield.

Push and Pull

2 When you are ready, begin to lever yourselves upwards from the squatting position. The thrust of the upwards movement should come from your leg muscles and hips, so always keep your spine lengthened and your shoulders relaxed. The art of this exercise is to find a mutual point of balance between you as you gently push and pull on each other to rise upwards. Too much or too little assertion from either partner will tip this delicate balance, causing one or both of you to topple over.

Lift and Descend

3 Raise up your bodies until you are both standing, then begin the process again as you lower yourselves back down to a squatting position. Repeat the exercise several times until you have found a fluid balance of movement between you.

Synchronicity is the moment when these two facets of the one phenomenon come together and form a unity of thought and action. Perhaps this can best be witnessed when two people dance together and their bodies flow as one motion, because they are able to respond equally to one another's subliminal signals indicating when to take the initiative and when to surrender to the movement.

This fine tuning manifests itself in bed too, when lovemaking can become a congruent interplay of

Game Two: Letting Go
1 In this exercise, your partner lies on the floor with her back relaxed and her legs raised in the air. Gently, but firmly, push both legs to one side of her body and then remove your hands.

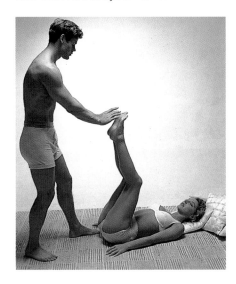

Back Swing
2 When you have released contact, she then swings her legs back to a central position. At this point, decide on the direction of the next push so that one movement flows into another.

mind, heart and body, or adversely, a battleground of subtle domination, control, resistance or submission.

Synchronicity, which tends to exist naturally in the first stages of a relationship, should not be taken for granted. It can be lost as the individual personalities and egos emerge, or when either one or both partners becomes enmeshed in the normal stresses and strains of daily life.

The four exercises in this section will help you become more attuned to each other, as they require both trust and synchronicity while finding a harmonious balance between taking passive and active roles.

The first exercise involves squatting, the importance of which, as a pelvic floor exercise, has been fully explained in the section on

Change Directions
3 Try to use a whole range of directions, this time pushing the legs to the left side of the body. The side-to-side and back-and-forth movements of the legs will exercise and strengthen the abdominal muscles. Gently make her aware of whether she is resisting or aiding you as she should be yielding to these passive movements.

Exercises for Sexual Fitness. Turn it into a game with your partner, so that both of you can benefit from its muscle-strengthening and balancing effects, while making it a playful exercise of mutual movement co-ordination.

The next two games use a push-and-let-go technique, which requires the active person to take charge of moving the other's body, while the passive partner yields to the movement. The motions must be confident but gentle so your partner can trust you and relax. You must become sensitive to his or her body and its range of movement. If you are jerky, too fast, or too aggressive, your partner will resist you and tighten up. In the first exercise you work just with the legs, and in the second exercise you move the whole body.

The last exercise is a trust game in which you stand as a support for your partner as he or she falls backwards into your arms.

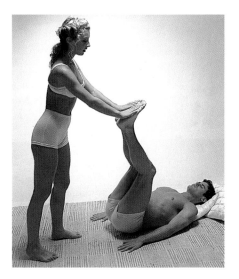

Reverse Roles
4 When you have completed a whole range of movements, swap roles. By pushing the legs towards the body you are giving a stretch to the lower back and hip joints.

Game Three: Taking Charge

1 This exercise is performed in a standing position. Ask your partner to stand in a relaxed posture so that she feels secure and balanced. She should close her eyes and focus on her breath and the sensations of movement. Position yourself behind her body and, with the lightest of touches, begin to direct her, pushing her gently to the side with one hand, and catching her with the other. Stay relaxed as you confidently take charge of her movements, keeping perfectly in tune with her sense of balance.

Gentle Rolling

2 Gracefully and quietly move around her body so that she is unable to guess the angle of the next movement. Roll her gently from side to side and back and forth, so that her body falls easily from one hand into the other.

Loosening Circles

3 Help her to loosen the hips and pelvis by circling this area between your hands. As she relaxes, and yields and allows her whole body to surrender to your hand directions, the movements can be gradually enlarged.

Learning to Surrender

▲ Initially, your man may find it difficult to surrender his body to these movements, fearing he is too big or heavy to let you take charge. If he is able to relax and release body rigidity, you will be able to move him with ease.

Game Four: Trust

1 This game is definitely about trust, and also requires the total attention of the active partner; only play it if you are confident about catching and supporting the weight of your partner's body. Ask her to stand in front of you, fully relaxed and with eyes closed. Position yourself behind, allowing enough space for her to fall back into your arms.

Falling for You

2 When she is ready, she allows herself to fall slowly backwards, trusting that you are there for her. The more physically relaxed she is able to remain, the easier it is for her to fall.

Safe Catch

3 As she tilts back, catch her securely in your arms, so that her upper back is supported and her head and neck rest against your chest or shoulder. Hold her against you for some moments, so she becomes aware of what she is feeling, then gently ease her back to a standing position. Repeat the exercise twice more.

Enhancing Sex

Back To Back

Most of the time we relate to others face to face. We spend inordinate amounts of time taking care of the front, ensuring we present a good image to our partners or to the world at large. Normally, we have very little sense of ourselves as viewed from the backs of our bodies. It is to correct such a gap in our self-knowledge that this book has emphasized the great importance of touching, stroking and making sensual contact with the back of the body during foreplay and love-making, as well as dealing with the more obvious intimate and directly sexual areas located at the front.

The back acts as a protective shell, often harbouring tensions which shield a deeper level of vulnerability. If you have practised your sensual massage strokes on each other, you may have noticed how, once the muscles of the back are relaxed, the whole body seems to become more alive and sensitive. Often, touch, massage and contact to the back can help someone let go of their inner emotional tensions.

Here are some exercises you can enjoy with your partner to develop more familiarity with your own and each other's back. Through them, you develop a clearer feeling of its shape and structure and, there-fore, a stronger sense of your body image.

In addition, these back-to-back exercises can help you dissolve the tensions which tend to keep you rigid, and allow you both to melt more with each other, both physi-cally and emotionally.

Again, you need to be sensitive to each other and find a mutual point of balance, where your weight and movement are evenly and gently distributed. (It is not advisable to do these exercises if you are suffering from back problems of an acute or chronic nature.)

Begin by sitting with your backs to each other on a firm and supportive base, so that the surface of your backs and your spines are in comfort-able contact. How much contact depends, of course, on the differences in your size and structure. It is important not to slump, but to keep your spines relaxed yet extended upwards.

Link your arms loosely together, and spend about three minutes directing your awareness and breath to areas of the back which feel tight and withholding, gradu-ally allowing the tensions to melt.

Lean gently into each other, taking care not to burden your partner with your weight, espe-cially if he or she is smaller or lighter than you. Close your eyes and begin to focus on the skin-to-skin contact of your backs, the shape and structure, how and where they fit together perfectly, and where there is tension. Imagine those tensions are beginning to dissolve so that both backs are merging together.

Start to sway gently together, finding a natural rhythm to your motion, and becoming more aware of the moments when the movements jar. Change the rhythm every so often, but always aim to remain harmoniously in tune with your partner's body.

Try to stay aware of any feelings which arise in you or you may be

Fitting Together

◄ Bend your knees to lower your body so that she can fit her buttocks comfortably into the small of your back. Before moving, ensure that she is ready and relaxed for the lift.

picking up from your partner as you let go of muscular tensions.

Now, sit silently together, eyes closed, but staying as deeply in tune with each other as possible for at least a minute. Once you are ready to separate, it is a good idea to discuss with each other what you experi-enced during this exercise, both in relation to your own body and your partner's body.

This back-to-back attunement game will prepare you for the spinal stretch exercise shown here, in which one partner lifts the other onto his or her back and balances the weight.

If you are lifting your partner, stabi-lize your own body by placing your feet a shoulder-width apart, and focus your breath towards your abdomen. This movement requires the recipient to trust the active partner enough to relax the weight of the whole back while being lifted upwards.

Spinal Stretch

1 As you tilt from your hips to lower your upper body, the passive partner sinks her back down onto yours, allowing her head and neck to relax backwards. Check that she is feeling safe before you lift her upwards.

Lower Your Torso

2 Begin to lower your torso to lift your partner's feet away from the ground so the full weight of her back is released towards your body. It is important for her shoulders and neck to remain relaxed. Move very slowly and in tune with her. Stay balanced and secure on your own feet and legs, and breathe easily, taking care to remain relaxed in your own body.

Lifting Off

3 As you lift her higher off the ground, her spine receives a good slow stretch. She should breathe fully into her chest and abdomen. Remain in this position for some moments, and then slowly put her back down, by extending gently upwards from your hips. Her feet need firm contact with the floor before you straighten up.

Contrasting Physiques

▶ It is possible for two people of different sizes to do this exercise provided you maintain stability and relaxation. However, common sense will guide you as to whether the weight or height differences are too great to attempt it. The first priority is to ensure that there is no danger of you straining your back or spine in any exercise.

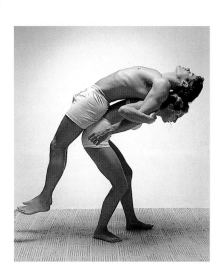

Tantric Concepts of Sex

In many mystical practices throughout the world, sexuality has been regarded as a gateway, helping adepts to experience profound spiritual realization. There is a great deal of evidence, some going back thousands of years, of teachings, rites and rituals which uphold the sacredness of sexual union between a man and woman. Some of the principles behind mystical sex practices can help the loving union between a man and woman become physically, emotionally and spiritually ecstatic.

Mystical teachings on sexuality perceive the sex act, in which the total energies of a man and woman merge, to be a microcosm of the divine laws which govern the macrocosm of universal creation. It is the perfect union of the polar opposites, of the male (active) principle with the female (passive) principle, that creates universal harmony and equilibrium.

Nowadays, there is a renewal of interest in mystical sexuality, and as sexual issues are discussed more openly than ever, many people have sought to understand the ancient teachings on sexual practices to enrich their own relationships.

One of the most widely acknowledged systems of spiritual sexuality is Tantra, which flourished in India,

and can be traced back to 3000 BC. Tantra is a path which is designed to teach its disciples and adepts the way to achieve a state of enlightenment or cosmic consciousness.

Under the spiritual guidance of a realized teacher or guru, the disciples were initiated into a series of practices which included yoga, meditation, breath awareness, chanting mantras, gazing on scientifically formulated designs called mandalas, and sexo-yogic positions.

Tantra, which means expansion, sought to take the ordinary man and woman through initiation and training into a higher state of consciousness and self-realization where the individual sense of ego could dissolve

into an ecstatic oneness with the cosmic consciousness. To follow the true path of Tantra it would be necessary to find a Tantric teacher. Yet some of the principles of Tantra can be adopted into a bonded relationship, to enrich it and to bring greater sexual joy and satisfaction.

Tantric or sacred sex practices honour the whole body and the whole being of the lovers involved. It celebrates both physical sensuality

Mystical Sex

▼ *Sex is sacred when a meditative quality is flowing spontaneously within it. You can't actually "do" it, but you can allow it to happen. You are then able to dissolve yourselves fully into the sensations which arise.*

Forming a Bond
◀ *A strong commitment is needed when entering into the practices of mystical sex. It will enhance your lovemaking and bond you into a deeper level of honesty, sharing and intimacy on all levels of your relationship.*

Celebrate Your Divine Essence
▲ *The concept of mystical sex has flourished in cultures where men and women have been regarded as true equals, and where the divine essence of both sexes is acknowledged. In Tantric practices the woman is seen as the embodiment of creative consciousness. Dance for your lover to celebrate the goddess within you.*

If you and your partner wish to try out the Tantric concepts of sexual union, you may need to change some of the most fundamental patterns of your sexual habits. Try to talk to each other honestly about your sexual relationship, and discover if there is mutual agreement between you to explore another sexual path.

There is no need to reject all the other enjoyable ways you make love. Variety adds spice to your love life. You will need, however, to commit time and practice to these ideas. Perhaps you will discover that you are both looking for something different to happen in your sex lives without knowing exactly what that is.

Even the most successful and orgasmic sexual relationships can begin to feel repetitive and empty after a period of time. This is not necessarily a reflection on your attraction or love for each other. It may simply be a deep longing for

and the powerful psychic forces which reside within the human body. Tantra, for instance, upholds that when two people enter into an intimate relationship with the right intentions, their sexuality is not separate from their spirituality.

your intimate relationship to become spiritually uplifting as well as physically and emotionally bonded.

Tantric sex puts emphasis on meditative lovemaking and the avoidance of orgasm. It regards ejaculation and climax as a waste of vital life energy which can be used, instead, to transform the spiritual consciousness of the lovers. A meditative state of mind is essential to the science of mystical sex. By approaching lovemaking meditatively, we are able to control the mental processes of thought, fantasy and desire which are seen to interfere with the process of physical, emotional, energetic and spiritual merging.

Meditation in Relationship

It will be helpful for you and your partner to practise meditation both alone and together. Meditation helps focus your full attention into the present moment, away from the endless distractions of thoughts which course through your mind. The purpose of meditation is not to suppress these thoughts and feelings, but to harness all this potential energy and bring it to one focal point. Then, whatever you are doing in a meditative way has a different quality about it.

You are able to function more spontaneously and creatively, trusting yourself more and responding intuitively, letting one moment give birth to the next, without the constant interference of your mind. When this quality of totality enters into your lovemaking it can become more spontaneous and a true vehicle for mystical experience.

Awareness of breath is one of the basic tools of meditation. By focusing total awareness onto the breathing cycle, it becomes easier to detach from all mental images. Breathing is a natural, involuntary process, our most fundamental link to life and the

Synchronize Your Breathing
▶ *Meditation can take your relationship deeper and beyond its everyday parameters. Gradually extend your meditation time to between forty minutes and one hour as you learn to escape the hustle and bustle of your lives and enjoy a new tranquillity. Initially, your focus will be on your own breathing, but after some time, as you continue to meditate together, your breathing patterns may begin to synchronize without effort.*

doorway between the internal self and the external environment.

However, our breathing is affected by our thoughts, physical tensions and emotional states. When we are under stress, breathing may become too rapid or shallow. By focusing awareness on the breath during meditation, we begin to breathe in a more relaxed way, creating greater equilibrium between inhalation and exhalation. Meditative breathing brings balance to the body, mind and spirit.

Do not try to change or force your breathing in any way. First, close your eyes and focus attention on the sensation of breath as it is drawn into your nostrils, and then exhaled out of your nostrils or mouth. After about five minutes, start to focus on the subtle movement of your abdomen as it rises with each inhalation, and falls back with each exhalation.

When thoughts and feelings distract you, bring your attention back to your breathing. It is actually quite difficult

to remain focused on your breathing. Do not worry about this. Each time your attention begins to meander, lead it gently back. Gradually, your mind will become calmer and allow a transcendental quality of consciousness to arise within you.

Make a commitment to meditate together at least once to three times a week, setting aside a regular time when you can sit together, undisturbed and in total privacy. Try to meditate even if you feel preoccupied. Sitting with your partner will calm and refresh you both. However, do not try to force each other to sit and meditate. If your partner is unable to meditate with you, then be happy to meditate alone.

If you have never meditated before, start off with fifteen-minute sessions. The ideal position for meditation is to sit cross-legged on the floor, with your hands relaxed, palms facing upwards, on your thighs. Avoid slumping by placing a cushion

Form a Circuit of Energy

▶ *Sit together with your right palm turned downwards to represent the active male principle, and the left palm facing upwards to represent the passive female principle. Rest your hands lightly on your partner's. Imagine that as you inhale, you are drawing your partner's breath and vital energy into yourself through your left hand. As you exhale, you are pouring out your breath and vital energy through your right hand into your partner. Visualize yourselves joining together to form a balanced circuit of energy through the mutual breathing and contact. When you feel ready, slowly draw your hands away from each other to rest them on your lap for several minutes.*

beneath your buttocks, tilting your pelvis to support your upper body. Keep your spine straight but relaxed, and let your neck and head extend gracefully above your spine. If sitting on the floor is too uncomfortable, then sit on a straight-backed chair.

Connecting and Merging

The three meditation exercises which follow all involve a degree of physical interaction to deepen your mutual bond and intimacy. They will heighten your sensitivity and encourage you to open your hearts to one another so that your sense of merging energetically becomes stronger. This fusion of body and spirit is what Tantric, or sacred, sex is all about.

Tantra teaches that when the male and female energies merge harmoniously, their union creates a powerful, moving, loving and transforming force. Use these exercises on a regular basis to connect with one another on

subtle levels, especially at times when the pressures of everyday life have caused an emotional or physical distance between you.

In the first meditation for merging, both of you contemplate this union of opposite polarities, while connecting palm to palm, for up to 15 minutes, allowing your breathing to synchronize naturally. To complete this meditation, open your eyes, and slowly perform the namaste ritual which is designed to honour one another's intrinsic divinity.

The second exercise is an eye-gazing technique which gives truth to the saying, "the eyes are the mirrors of the soul". By looking softly into each other's eyes for periods of between ten and twenty minutes, you can both see and be seen. It will

Signal Your Respect

◀ *In the East, people place their hands together in the position of prayer, and incline towards each other as a gesture of respect. This is the beautiful traditional greeting of namaste, also used to signify gratitude, and recognition of the divine self within each person. At the end of each meditation, acknowledge each other sincerely with this symbolic ritual.*

create trust and deep intimacy as you look within each other, and let go of your normal defences to reveal your inner vulnerability.

Make palm-to-palm contact so that you feel connected on the physical level. Focus attention on your breathing, your body and the tactile contact of your hands. If your face becomes tense, relax the muscles, particularly around the jaw and mouth. Do not out-stare or try to dominate your partner with your gaze; keep your eyes softly focused.

At first, you may feel exposed, almost naked, as different emotions emerge, such as embarrassment, fear,

Creating a Meditative Ambience

Set aside a room for meditation, or if this is not possible, create a specific area in your bedroom or living room which is dedicated to your Tantric rituals. Treat this space as a temple to your love. Place flowers, light candles and burn incense, or carry out any ritual which is appropriate and meaningful to you both, to make yourselves feel as if you are on consecrated ground.

Try to ensure complete privacy, and plan a time when you know you will be left undisturbed.

Place a clock with a soft-sounding alarm some distance away from you, or have it muffled beneath a pillow, to alert you when your allotted time for meditation is over. Be prepared to give yourselves at least five to fifteen minutes for re-orientation back to a normal functioning state of consciousness. You may want to lie down on the floor next to each other, bringing your full attention to your body as it rests on the ground.

Gaze Into Your Partner's Eyes

◀ *During the eye-gazing meditation, breathe gently into whatever feelings arise, letting them come and go without analysis. Remain relaxed, and allow yourself to be seen by your loved one. At the same time, look deep within your partner's being as you continue to gaze steadily and softly into his eyes.*

Tune Into Your Heart

◀ *Place your right hand very lightly over your heart. Take some moments to bring full awareness to the physical sensations of your heart pumping beneath your hand. Now tune in more deeply to the feelings of the heart. Imagine your heart centre becoming more open and vulnerable as you breathe out any tensions.*

Feel Yourselves Merge

◀ *Now stretch out to place your right hand gently over your lover's heart. Take some moments to feel the warmth of the skin, the beat of the heart and the rhythm of the breath. Connect to the feelings within your partner's heart and pour yourselves into this contact, so you both merge on a heart-to-heart level.*

happiness, sadness, love and joy. Do not suppress these feelings or try to change them, but stay with the eye contact and breath. When you are ready to complete the eye-gazing meditation, close your eyes and release your palm-to-palm contact slowly so your hands rest against your lap. Focus on your breathing and body sensations. After some minutes, open your eyes and thank your partner with the namaste bow.

The third exercise has four five-minute stages and connects you directly, heart to heart, with one another. When we are "in our hearts" we long to share and merge with each other. The first step is to sit facing your partner in a meditative posture, close your eyes and begin to focus on your breathing. During the second stage, you bring your attention to the feelings within your heart and allow yourself to become more

open, vulnerable and receptive. In the third stage, you make contact with each other to allow a fusion of heart-to-heart loving energy. The fourth step is to draw your hands slowly away from one another's heart centre and to bring that sense of merging back within yourself by placing your hand back onto your own heart. When you are ready, open your eyes and namaste to each other to conclude this meditation.

Opening the Body's Energy Channels

Tantra teaches that within the human body resides a vast and dynamic psychic energy known as the Kundalini. Tantrikas, or exponents of Tantra, believe that in normal circumstances, when human beings are concerned only with the basic matters of survival, the Kundalini power is a dormant energy, symbolically portrayed as a coiled serpent sleeping at the base of the spine.

The potential of its powerful and transforming effects on the psycho-physiological processes may never be realized. When the Kundalini energy is awakened, through yoga, meditation and sexual practices, it arises to travel upwards along a central pathway in the body where it interacts with, and transforms, the subtle energy centres, releasing new levels of consciousness at each stage. At its ultimate pinnacle, the Kundalini energy opens the crown chakra, which is slightly above the head, to bring the disciple into communion with cosmic consciousness.

Tantra teaches that all seven energy centres of the body must be fully open and engaged for spiritual transformation. This is why it regards sexuality as a potential path to higher consciousness.

The following programme guides you towards becoming more sensitive to the subtle energy vibrations within the body. The simple hands-on techniques will show you how to bring balance and harmony between the energy chakras.

First, return to the section on Sensual Massage. When using massage as part of your Tantric ritual, ensure that you touch each other without sexual desire. Let massage become a meditation in itself, functioning from a place of asexual and infinite love. Trust your hands, allowing them to move and stroke over your lover's body in response to the messages you are intuitively picking up. The more you trust yourself as you touch the body, the more sensitive your hands become, not only to the physical body but also to its energetic essence.

When you massage meditatively, the physical boundaries between you seem to dissolve, and you experience a meeting and merging of energies. If you are receiving the session, try to relax deeply and focus your breath and attention towards the healing quality of the touch that you are getting from your lover.

The more attuned you become to one another through massage, the

The Seven Energy Centres of The Body

Tantra originated the science of the seven chakras, or subtle energy centres, within the human body, all of which are associated with different psycho-physiological aspects of human nature. Each chakra is located in a different area of the body, and is associated with one of the rainbow colours in the spectrum of light. In everyday life, we experience the chakras on subtle psychological and physical levels, and while we may be unaware of their source or full potency, we are aware of their effects. We talk about our "gut" level feelings when we experience strong, instinctive emotions, we feel the bitter-sweet pain of love in the heart centre, and we trust the "sixth sense" of our intuitive faculties.

The base chakra: Located at the base of the sex organs. Associated with sex drive, survival, pain, pleasure, elimination. Colour: Red.

The belly chakra: Located just below the navel. Centre of gravity and balance in the body and source of vital life energy. Associated with emotion, reproduction, vitality. Colour: Orange.

The solar plexus chakra: Located at the centre point at the base of the front of the ribcage. Associated with intellect, self-confidence, power and action. Colour: Yellow.

The heart chakra: Located between the breasts or nipples. Associated with love, empathy, vulnerability, joy and external merging. This chakra is the point where the earthly instincts unite with the higher spiritual conscious. Colour: Green.

The throat chakra: Located in the throat. Associated with communication, self-understanding and self-expression. Colour: Blue.

The brow chakra: Located at the point between the eyebrows, and sometimes called the "third eye". Associated with intuition, insight, cognitive faculties, compassion for all things. Colour: Indigo.

The crown chakra: Located above the crown of the head. Associated with the higher mind, self-realization, harmony of body, mind and spirit, and merging with cosmic consciousness. Colour: Violet-white.

Massage as Meditation

▶ *Use massage as a part of your programme of honouring each other's bodies. Let the massage become an act of meditation as if your hands are worshipping her body. As you receive the massage, surrender your body to your lover. Breathe towards his hands as they stroke your skin.*

more you experience the pulsation of energy within the body. You may feel this as a flowing stream, a current, or vibrations of energy. At other times, if your partner is tired, or under stress, the chakra centres may feel undercharged or overcharged with energy. Use the following hands-on techniques to restore equilibrium to body, mind and spirit, and balance within the chakras.

Lay your hands very lightly and meditatively over the chakra centres, or slightly above them. Trust your intuition and let you hands rest, softly and meditatively, over the areas to which they are drawn. You can also ask your partner to guide you. Or you can do a complete energy-balancing session, working slowly over all the chakras. If you sense your partner needs to come "down to earth", follow a sequence moving down the body.

Alternatively, if your partner's spirit needs to be more uplifted, then work up the body towards the head. Spend up to three minutes with each hold, letting your intuition direct you as to when and where to sensitively approach the body and when to withdraw from it.

When you both feel that, through meditation, massage and energy balancing practice, you are more in

Balance the Pathway

▲ *To balance the Kundalini Pathway, ask your partner to curl up on her side into a comforting foetal position which exposes her back and spine. Hold one hand above the crown of her head, while the other hovers over the base of her spine. Pour breath and love into your hands.*

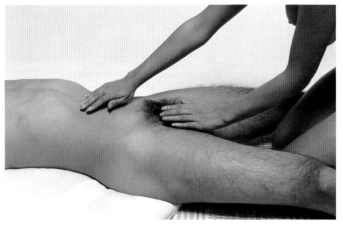

Direct His Breathing

▲ *To help your partner connect to his vitality, cup one hand gently over the sexual organs and perineum and lay the other on the lower abdomen for three minutes. Encourage him to direct his breath towards your hands and feel the vital forces radiating from him.*

Integrate Mind and Body
◀ *Lay your hands tenderly over the heart and brow to integrate mind and body and to encourage more connection between the centre of love and the centre of intuition.*

Dispel Negative Feelings
▼ *Work at balancing the energy centres while in the sitting position. Place one hand over the heart and rest the other hand over the solar plexus. Gentle contact here dispels feelings of insecurity, fear and jealousy.*

Comfort and Support
▼ *Your partner can lean her weight into the support of your body as you put one hand over her belly and the other on her chest. This contact with her belly will reassure and comfort her, especially in times of stress.*

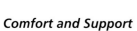

Aligning the Energy Centres
▲ *This chakra meditation helps bring you both into close proximity so that your energy centres become aligned.*

harmony with each other physically, mentally and energetically, begin to experiment with the following chakra alignment exercise.

In this practice, the female sits astride the man's lap. Use a chair if necessary. Relax and lengthen your spines so the Kundalini Pathway is without tension. If there is some sexual arousal, the man can enter his penis into the woman's vagina, and both partners can move slightly to sustain the erection, taking care not to become sexually over-stimulated. Otherwise, the penis can remain flaccid close to the entrance of the vagina. Gradually, naturally and easily let your breathing synchronize.

When you feel in harmony, direct your breathing towards the base chakra around the centre of your perineum, the area between your genitals and anus, for 60 seconds. Visualize this chakra opening up and becoming charged with warmth and light with your in-breath, and relaxing deeply with your out-breath. (Don't force your breathing, just imagine it flowing gently towards the chakra.) Breathe together through each chakra for about one minute, then visualize your breath and energy pouring into the crown centre above your head. As your bodies become charged with energy, let them vibrate and move together.

When you have completed the cycle of breathing, remain in the sitting position in a close embrace for up to five minutes, allowing yourselves to feel the pulsating sensations within. Then, lie down next to each other for up to 15 minutes to rest and complete the meditation. You may need a quiet time after these exercises if you have to resume your normal activities.

Focus on the Vibrations

▼ *Release all tension so your bodies relax and mould together. Bring your attention to the sensations of skin-to-skin contact, the sound and rhythm of inhalation and exhalation, the beating of the hearts, the throb of the pulses. Become totally immersed in the bodily vibrations.*

Give Into the Emotion

▲ *As energy begins to stream up through your bodies, let them sway or vibrate as powerful emotions such as love, sadness and joy emerge. Abandon yourselves to the movement but remain bonded and secure in each other's arms.*

Honouring the Sacred Body

All mystical sex practices regard the sexual act between men and women as something beyond the purpose of pure physical gratification or procreation. For instance, great honour is given to the symbolism of the sexual organs, both male and female. In more ancient cultures, images of sexual organs were sculpted in wood and stone and became shrines of worship.

These have been commonly regarded by modern societies as ancient fertility symbols erected to incite Nature to bestow her blessings in the form of a good harvest or a healthy brood of children. In fact, these symbols often represented something more profound, and acknowledged that sexual union of the opposites could lead towards cosmic consciousness.

Throughout India there are many thousands of shrines, some simple and some elaborate, which have stone images of the linga and yoni, which symbolise a divine male phallus set within a divine female vagina. These symbols are objects of great devotion and worship.

To regard the most intimate sexual organs of the body with this degree of honour and respect drastically transforms an intimate relationship. You can create some beautiful rituals together in which you honour completely your own and your partner's body.

Make up your own rituals, or use some of the ideas in the photographs shown here, to add this new element to the previous meditation exercises.

In the shrines in India devotees often spread petals and flowers around the sacred phallic sites. To

Honour Her with Rose Petals
▶ In this ritual, you honour her whole body as a manifestation of her inner and outer beauty. As she lies with her legs wrapped around your waist so your genital organs are in close proximity, scatter scented rose petals over her entire body.

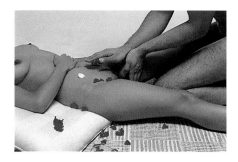

Symbol of Creativity
▲ The woman's sexual organs embody the divine principle of cosmic creativity. Kneel before her and scatter petals onto her sexual area as a way of honouring her intrinsic feminine power.

Repecting the Male Principle
▶ The male organ is the symbol of cosmic consciousness. The woman can show her respect for the male principle by kneeling before her man to drop the rose petals onto his lap.

Experiencing the Cosmic Union
◀ The entry of the penis into the vagina symbolises the union of the male and female cosmic polarities through which joy and ecstasy can be attained. Immerse yourselves into this union to feel fully the depth of your physical, emotional and psychic connection.

make your ritual more special, use scented petals such as the delicate rose whose perfume is known to be spiritually, emotionally and sexually uplifting. Take turns to perform the ritual, scattering the petals over the body, and to acknowledge through touch and words that you honour each part of the other's body. Make the phrases simple, such as "I honour your beauty/skin/breasts", and so on. Or, "I have the deepest respect for your inner feminine/masculine power". Kneel before your partner's penis or vagina, and say something like "I worship your most intimate part as a manifestation of the god/goddess within".

When the ritual of honouring each other's body is over, lie together in a deep embrace. If it feels right, stimulate the penis so it is erect enough to enter and remain in the vagina. Try to stay together in this meditative position for as long as you both want, focusing only on the present moment of your union, without becoming too sexually excited. The idea is not to go full steam ahead into lovemaking or orgasm but simply to be united as one.

Sex Without Orgasm

This last Tantric ritual can be practised regularly in your relationship and can keep you intimately connected, even when you do not have the time or will for a full love-making session. For instance, when you awake in the morning and you must soon go separate ways, you can lie together for five to fifteen minutes just holding each other in this intimate conjugal embrace.

All mystical sex practices have upheld the importance of containing

Timeless Lovemaking
▲ *Real joy and ecstasy can be attained by letting your lovemaking enter into a totally new dimension of precious timelessness. Eye-to-eye contact will enable you to stay deeply attuned to each other.*

ejaculation and orgasm during love-making. The concept of non-orgasm while making love is considerably different from most edicts of modern sexology with their emphasis on achieving great orgasms. In fact, orgasm is usually seen as the ultimate goal of sex. This can make the man afraid of ejaculating prematurely before his partner has reached her climax, and leave the woman concerned about not having an orgasm before the lovemaking session is over. Some women fake orgasms in order to protect their lover's ego.

The pressure in modern sexual relationships is for bigger, better orgasms, simultaneous orgasms, and even multiple orgasms. There is no doubt that an orgasmic capacity enormously increases the pleasure and satisfaction of lovemaking. Yet the whole physical and psychological pressure on achieving orgasm can rob sexual intercourse of its natural spontaneity, its deep sensuality and tenderness, and the exploration of its intrinsic spiritual dimension.

When orgasm becomes the main goal of sex it is almost impossible to remain with the pure sensual feeling of the present moment. Orgasm-orientated sex has a finite purpose and is in danger of becoming a performance-related programme aimed mostly at achieving a satisfactory conclusion.

The essence of meditation in sex is when two people pour body, heart and soul into that which is actually happening spontaneously and intuitively between them, without purpose or goal. When this happens,

all the bodily senses become heightened and movement, breath and mutual interaction start to flow effortlessly, without interference from thoughts, fantasies and pre-conceived expectations.

Slowing the Pace

◀ *The woman-on-top position helps the man slow his pace of lovemaking. In this position, he is also more able to touch, and remain sensitive to, her whole body.*

Achieving True Harmony

▼ *Tantric lovemaking does not preclude any sexual position or behaviour but it does add a more intuitive and spontaneous quality of effortless movement because the lovers are in harmony with each other's bodily responses.*

Merging into One

▼ *The orgasmic energy which arises during Tantric lovemaking continues to pulsate throughout your body for as long as you want. You may feel that your individual egos are disappearing and that you and your lover are merging into one being.*

The Tantric idea of containing orgasm during sex applies to both men and women as it is seen as a way to prolong lovemaking and to create a force of transforming energy within the body, without dissipating it through ejaculation and climax. By avoiding over-excitement – which leads to hasty orgasm – during Tantric lovemaking, both lovers remain in a milieu of potent sexual and sensual forces for as long as they wish.

The following are some of the benefits:

❖ A couple can make love for as long as they want as they do not

become exhausted by effort or orgasm.

❖ Lovemaking becomes a continuous, unbroken theme to the relationship, so that the couple can interrupt sex when necessary and begin again when convenient, without feeling frustrated, because they remain deeply sexually connected.

❖ Mental thoughts, judgements, goals and expectations which interfere with the intimacy of sexual bonding can be dropped so that the truly natural and spontaneous body and feeling responses take over.

❖ The uncomfortable sense of using each other's bodies for sexual gratification disappears. Mutual honour and deep respect develops for the body and its inherent sexuality as they are both perceived as divine sources of transformation.

When practising Tantric lovemaking, the following suggestions are important for both partners to remember:

❖ Ensure that this sexual exploration is a mutual decision, otherwise it may become a subtle means of controlling one another. If you or your partner have reached the point where one or both of you want passionate sex and orgasm then you should go ahead and enjoy yourselves. Always try to respect each other's needs, as this is just as important as any ideal.

❖ Do not turn the containment of orgasm into another mental programme of sexual achievement. Remember, that "being together" rather than "doing together" is what it is all about.

❖ Tantric sex means making love meditatively. It is "cool" sex rather than "hot" sex. Slow down long before you reach the orgasmic point of no return. Stop moving, if necessary, or change positions if you are getting too excited. Lie together in a still embrace, breathe together, or look into each other's eyes.

Blissful Sex

Mystical union requires slow lovemaking. Every time you feel yourselves getting too excited, make a conscious effort to cool down and bring awareness back to each other and the immediate sensations of your tactile contact, your breath, your senses and your love for each other. When you practise making love like this over a period of time, your bodies will begin to moderate their orgasmic responses. At first you may feel as if you are controlling your sexuality, but gradually the whole pattern of your lovemaking will change. You will become so attuned to your own and your partner's sexual responses that it will seem as if you are riding of a wave of pure energy together. Making love in this way can become blissful and ecstatic.

Peaceful Union
▼ *The sense of closeness during the union of lovemaking can continue as you rest peacefully together.*

Contraception

Contraception is an important consideration for most sexually active people, as a way of avoiding unwanted pregnancy or as an aid to family planning. It is important to keep in mind, however, that no method is 100 per cent reliable, and some forms of contraception do not protect against HIV or other sexually transmitted diseases. Condoms have been shown to be effective against these risks and to play an invaluable role in safer sex, as well as guarding against conception.

There is now a much wider choice of contraceptive methods than ever before, and most are readily available. The various forms are discussed below, and their suitability for you can best be determined by consulting a health practitioner. Changing lifestyles or needs, or relevant health issues, may require that you re-evaluate the type of contraceptive you are currently using. This is easily done in consultation with your doctor or local family planning clinic.

It is important, as a sexually active person, to take a responsible attitude to contraception and to avoid spreading sexually transmitted diseases. Some forms of contraception carry health risks, which you should take into account when choosing the most suitable method for you, bearing in mind factors such as your medical condition, weight, age and lifestyle.

However, it is worth bearing in mind that pregnancy and childbirth also involve slight risks, to say nothing of the distress of an unwanted pregnancy. The various methods now available should make the decision on these matters easier and ensure your choice is best suited to the specific needs of you and your partner.

The failure rates quoted in this section are based on the theoretical number of pregnancies that can be expected within one year among 100 couples having regular sex and using the particular form of contraception mentioned. The risk of failure is obviously increased if a contraceptive method is used incorrectly.

HORMONAL METHODS

Oral Contraceptive Pill

The oral contraceptive pill has been used by millions of women since its introduction in the early 1960s. There are currently over 60 million women world-wide using this method. If used correctly, the pill is a highly reliable form of contraception – up to 99 per cent effective. The advantage of the pill is that couples do not have to think about contraception (so long as it is taken on the days and at the times specified) and so it does not interfere with their spontaneity.

The pill works by suppressing normal control of a woman's sex hormone system, thereby artificially regulating her menstrual cycle. Most forms of the pill contain a combination of progestogen and synthetic oestrogen, which mimic the female hormones progesterone and oestrogen. The effect is to prevent ovulation, make the cervical mucus impenetrable to sperm, and alter the lining of the uterus so that a fertilized egg cannot implant in it.

The combined pill is taken on 21 days out of 28 – with seven pill-free days. It is available in three forms: monophasic, biphasic and triphasic. Monophasic pills release constant doses of hormones. Biphasic and triphasic pills release staged doses – in two phases and three phases respectively – to mimic the normal pattern of female hormone production more closely.

The combined pill may be less effective if it is taken more than 12 hours late, or if there is any vomiting or diarrhoea. Other medications, such as antibiotics, sedatives and some painkillers, may also alter the efficacy of the combined pill. In any of these cases, an additional form of contraception should be used until the end of the cycle.

Studies have linked the combined pill with an increased risk of cardiovascular disease, and liver and cervical cancer, but it seems to offer protection against ovarian cancer, cancer of the endometrium (the lining of the uterus), ovarian cysts, non-cancerous breast tumours, fibroids, and ectopic pregnancy. Medical opinion is divided on the link between hormonal pills and breast cancer.

All women who use hormonal contraceptive methods should have regular breast examinations, cervical smears, and six-monthly check-ups of blood pressure and weight.

The combined pill does have some serious side-effects such as increased risk of blood clots in the arteries and veins. This risk is much greater in women over the age of 35, smokers, and those who are very overweight. It is not usually prescribed for women in these high-risk categories. Some of the other side-effects of the pill reported include breast tenderness, mood swings, weight gain, water retention, and loss of libido. Vaginal infections, such as thrush, are also more common among contraceptive pill users.

Mini-Pill

Another form of hormonal contraception is the progestogen-only pill, or mini-pill, which is taken every day, without a break. It uses only very low doses of progestogen, so it must be taken at the same time each day to prevent fertilization, and never more than three hours late. It has fewer side-effects than the combined pill but there is a higher failure rate (up to four per cent).

Because it does not contain oestrogen, which is the hormone that has been linked to thrombosis, or blood clots forming in the veins and arteries, it may be a better alternative in certain cases. It is associated with a higher risk of breast cancer than the combined pill, particularly among women who have taken the drug for over five years. Some women who use it may have irregular periods, or light spotting between periods.

Implants

Implants are another hormonal method of birth control. Six tiny, flexible capsules are inserted under the skin of the upper arm. This requires minor surgery, which is carried out under a local anaesthetic. Once in place, the capsules release low levels of progestogen directly into the bloodstream. Implants rarely cause discomfort, and they provide contraceptive protection for up to five years. They may cause changes in menstruation, producing either heavier periods or irregular periods, and weight gain. They also require minor surgery to be taken out.

Fertility is restored soon after removal of the implants. As this method does not contain oestrogen, it may be suitable for women who cannot use the combined pill.

Injectable Contraceptives

In this method, an injection of progestogen is given in a muscle during the first five days of menstruation. It provides contraceptive protection for eight to twelve weeks. Though its effectiveness rivals that of the pill, it is mostly prescribed in exceptional circumstances. These include women who have just been immunized against rubella, when pregnancy could result in birth defects in the foetus; women whose partners have recently had a vasectomy, until tests can show there are no longer sperm present; and women who are unable to use other forms of birth control. Once injected the contraceptive action cannot be reversed and there may also be a delay before fertility returns. Menstrual disturbances, weight gain and a delay in fertility are the most common side-effects.

BARRIER METHODS

IUD

The IUD (intra-uterine device, or "coil") is a T-shaped appliance that is inserted through the cervix into the uterus. It is not known exactly how the IUD works. It was previously thought that it prevents a fertilized ovum implanting in the lining of the uterus, but research now suggests its main action is to make conditions in the uterus hostile to sperm.

Many IUDs are made of plastic, or copper wire on a plastic frame. Some have a silver core and there are versions that also release progestogen. IUDs have two nylon threads that hang down into the vagina, enabling the woman to check each month whether the device is still in place. Some forms must be replaced every two to three years, others can be left in the womb for up to five years, and some last over ten years. Regular check-ups will be necessary.

An IUD should only be inserted by a doctor. This is usually done during menstruation because the cervix is slightly dilated at this time, and there is little likelihood that the woman is pregnant. An IUD can, however, be expelled from the uterus soon after insertion or in the first three months. Sometimes, though rarely, the IUD can dislodge and perforate the wall of the uterus. Usually, this is signalled by sharp pains in the lower abdomen and vaginal bleeding. Many users experience heavier, more painful periods, especially in the first few months. It also makes a woman's reproductive system more vulnerable to infections such as PID (pelvic inflammatory disease) which, when untreated, can lead to infertility. It is therefore not advised for younger women, or those who have had no children, or women with a history of sexually transmitted diseases.

The IUD is a very effective form of birth control with a protection rate similar to the combined pill. However, if pregnancy does occur with an IUD in place there is a higher risk of miscarriage, either if it is left in place or at the time of removal. It does not protect against STDs and is better suited to women in monogamous relationships.

Spermicides

Spermicides are available in many different forms, most often as vaginal creams, gels, foams, pessaries and tablets. A contraceptive film is also available, which is packed between squares of silver foil for easy handling. Spermicides are available from the chemist without a prescription and most contain the active ingredient Nonoxynol-9. They usually offer protection for only one episode of intercourse, and must be re-applied before sex is repeated. On their own, they are not highly effective as a contraceptive, with failure rates as high as 25 per cent.

Spermicides are most effective when used in conjunction with another barrier method, such as the condom, diaphragm, cap or sponge (see below). They may cause minor irritations or allergies in either partner. Some spermicides may damage condoms and diaphragms, so only recommended types should be used. Recent tests show that Nonoxynol-9 can kill the HIV virus, the disease responsible for AIDS.

The Diaphragm

The diaphragm is a soft rubber dome, reinforced with a flexible metal spring in the rim, that is placed inside the vagina so that it covers the cervix. It is easily fitted by the user herself, simply by pressing two sides together so it can be inserted. When used consistently with spermicide, placed on the surfaces of the diaphragm before insertion, it can provide a very safe form of birth control – up to 98 per cent effective – and does not interfere with a woman's hormonal balance. However, when used without spermicide, the failure rate can be as high as 15 per cent. The diaphragm must be left in place for at least six hours after sexual intercourse, but no longer than 24 hours. Additional spermicide must be applied before intercourse is repeated.

As the diaphragm is made of a relatively thin form of rubber, it must be checked for signs of deterioration, such as small cuts or tears, before each use. It should also be checked for size every six months as childbirth, miscarriage, or weight gain or loss of more than 3kg/7lb in the user can make it less effective. In such a case a more appropriate size should be fitted. Some women find it difficult to insert, though with practice it usually becomes easier. It can also impair spontaneity for it needs to be inserted before lovemaking. Some women cope with this by inserting it earlier in the evening, but they should keep in mind that spermicide loses a great deal of its potency after three hours and more should be added prior to intercourse.

The diaphragm puts pressure on the bladder and so is not recommended for women who suffer from recurrent cystitis or other urinary infections. A few women are allergic to the rubber of the diaphragm and will not be able to tolerate it. There is a risk of toxic shock syndrome if the diaphragm is worn continuously, especially during a period.

The Cap

The cap functions very much like the diaphragm but is smaller, fitting snugly over the cervix where it is held in place by suction. It has the same success rate as the diaphragm and must be used in conjunction with spermicide to be most effective. It must also be left in place for six hours after sexual intercourse. Additional spermicide should be inserted if sexual intercourse is repeated. Like the diaphragm, its main drawback is that it may detract from spontaneity as it needs to be fitted prior to intercourse.

The Condom

The condom is one of the oldest forms of contraception. Condoms are enjoying renewed popularity for their ability to provide protection against HIV and other sexually transmitted diseases. They are made of fine latex rubber with a teat at the end to collect sperm. To provide maximum protection, the condom should be fitted prior to any genital contact. The condom should be rolled down evenly over the erect penis, taking care to expel all the air from the tip. After ejaculation, the man should withdraw his penis, holding the base of the condom so that no sperm escapes into the vagina.

Only water-based lubricants should be used; oil-based products can cause the rubber to deteriorate. Most condoms contain spermicide and this usually provides sufficient lubrication. Condoms should always be handled with care and checked for signs of damage or ageing. They should not be carried in pockets or wallets where they can get damaged.

Some men complain of a loss of sensation when using condoms, but this is less of a problem nowadays as modern condoms are made of a very thin form of latex. Indeed, any reduced sensitivity may be an advantage for men who suffer premature ejaculation, or who wish to extend lovemaking. Fitting a condom can become part of foreplay so it does not detract from the spontaneity.

Apart from a very small number who are allergic to rubber, there is nothing to prevent most people from using them. Condoms play an invaluable role in safer sex. Their use is particularly recommended with new or casual partners. Used consistently, they are up to 98 per cent effective.

The Female Condom

The female condom, which was developed by a Danish physician in the 1980s, is an innovation in birth control. Like the male condom, it has the added benefit of protecting the user against sexually transmitted diseases, including HIV.

The female condom is a long, loose tube, about 17.5 cm/7in in length, which is closed at one end. It has a smaller fixed ring which is inserted into the vagina and pushed in as far as possible to cover the cervix. A larger ring remains outside and is pushed back against the labia during intercourse. The female condom is pre-lubricated, and made of flexible polyurethane, which is thinner than latex, so there is not so much loss of sensitivity. It is also very loose so it does not have the same constricting feeling as its male counterpart, but is likely to affect sensation nevertheless.

Some women find it rather uncomfortable, but it has the advantage of not requiring the man to withdraw immediately, as is the case with the male condom. Polyurethane is also stronger and more durable than latex, so is less likely to break during intercourse. As it is heavily lubricated, the female condom may be of benefit to women following childbirth or suffering vaginal dryness, around the time of the menopause, for example. Some trials claim a success rate similar to the male condom, though other studies suggest it may be less effective, with failure rates of up to 25 per cent.

The Sponge

The sponge is made of soft polythene foam, impregnated with Nonoxynol-9 spermicide. In order to activate the spermicide, the sponge should be moistened with water before insertion. It is placed as far into the vagina as it will go, and should cover the cervix. It can be inserted any time before sex and must be removed no longer than 30 hours afterwards (but must be left in for at least six hours).

The spermicide component kills sperm for up to 48 hours, regardless of the number of times intercourse takes place. Its major disadvantage is that it has a high failure rate, up to 25 per cent, and should be used with a condom to protect against the risk of pregnancy. A small number of women, between three and five per cent, are allergic to the spermicide.

POST-COITAL CONTRACEPTION

The "Morning-After" Pill

If a woman has had unprotected sexual intercourse, or suspects her method of contraception has failed and is concerned about pregnancy, she can obtain the morning-after pill from her doctor. This emergency contraception is a form of hormonal pill which is taken in double doses – that is, two pills at a time. The first dose is taken within 72 hours of intercourse, and the second dose 12 hours later. Many users experience nausea and breast tenderness.

If vomiting occurs, another dose will be necessary as the pills may not have been absorbed by the body. It does not seem to have any other adverse effects, though it may be unsuitable for women who have been advised not to use other forms of hormonal contraception. Should the morning-after pill fail, it is not yet known what effects there may be on the developing foetus.

Post-Coital IUD

The IUD can also be used as a method of emergency contraception, and has the advantage that it can be used up to five days after unprotected sex, or within five days after the release of an egg. It is not recommended for women who have not had children, or where there is a risk of sexually transmitted disease, for example in cases of rape. As a method of post-coital contraception the IUD is credited with a 100 per cent success rate, to date.

STERILIZATION

Sterilization is a permanent form of birth control, and though it may be reversed, there is no guarantee that fertility will be restored. It is an option that is favoured by people who already have children. It is usually inadvisable in young people, or those who have not had children, for if they have a change of heart later, reversal may not be successful. Counselling is advisable prior to deciding on sterilization.

Vasectomy

A vasectomy is a relatively minor surgical procedure that is usually carried out under local anaesthetic, taking around ten to 15 minutes. It involves cutting and tying back the vasa deferentia, the tubes which carry sperm from the testicles. Most men will need one or two days to recover fully from the operation.

The man's semen may still contain active sperm between six to eight weeks after a vasectomy, so it is important that an alternative means of birth control is used during this time until two separate semen samples have been examined and shown to be free of sperm.

Quick Guide to Contraception

METHOD: **The Combined Pill**

Risks:

✘ Side-effects: mood swings, nausea, weight gain, loss of libido, headaches

✘ Increased risk of blood clots, especially in the overweight and smokers aged over 35

✘ Possible increased risk of cardiovascular disease, and liver, breast and cervical cancer

Benefits:

✔ Highly effective as a contraceptive

✔ Protection against cancer of the ovaries and endometrium

✔ Lighter periods

✔ Reduced risk of ovarian cysts

METHOD: **The Mini-Pill**

Risks:

✘ Small increased risk of ovarian cysts

✘ Less effective than the combined pill

✘ Possible increased risk of breast cancer

Benefits:

✔ Possible protection against ovarian cancer

✔ Side-effects are less severe than the combined pill

METHOD: **Hormonal Implants**

Risks:

✘ Complications have been reported in some women during insertion or removal of implants

✘ Heavy, irregular or absent periods

✘ Weight gain

Benefits:

✔ Does not interrupt spontaneity of sexual intercourse

✔ Provides effective contraception for up to five years or until removed

METHOD: **Hormonal Injection**

Risks:

✘ Heavy, irregular or absent periods

✘ Weight gain

✘ Delay in return of fertility

Benefits:

✔ Reduced risk of ovarian and endometrial cancer

✔ Reduced risk of ovarian cysts

✔ Does not interrupt spontaneity of sexual intercourse

METHOD: **IUD**

Risks:

✘ Increased risk of PID and other pelvic infections

✘ Increased risk of ectopic pregnancy

✘ Heavier periods in many users

Benefits:

✔ Very effective form of birth control

✔ Can be removed without delay in return of fertility

METHOD: **Diaphragm/Cap**

Risks:

✘ Slight risk of toxic shock syndrome

✘ Can interrupt spontaneity of sexual intercourse

✘ Not as effective without the use of a spermicide

Benefits:

✔ Does not interfere with a woman's hormonal balance

✔ Some protection against genital warts

✔ Some protection against cervical cancer

✔ Some protection against HIV and other sexually transmitted diseases, particularly when used with spermicide

METHOD: **Condom**

Risks:

✘ It may break or tear during intercourse

✘ Can interrupt spontaneity of sexual intercourse

Benefits:

✔ Protects against HIV and other sexually transmitted diseases

METHOD: **The Sponge**

Risks:

✘ Relatively high failure rate

Benefits:

✔ Once in place it can be left for 24 hours

METHOD: **Vasectomy**

Risks:

✘ Psychological regret about loss of fertility

✘ Must generally be considered irreversible

Benefits:

✔ Freedom from fear of impregnating partner

METHOD: **Female Sterilization**

Risks:

✘ Psychological regret about loss of fertility

✘ Must generally be considered irreversible

✘ Some women experience heavier periods

Benefits:

✔ Freedom from fear of pregnancy

METHOD: **Natural Family Planning**

Risks:

✘ Without adequate tuition, motivation and commitment, this is an unreliable form of birth control

Benefits:

✔ Morally acceptable for couples that don't want to use artificial means of contraception

✔ Gives better insight of how a woman's body functions

METHOD: **Coitus Interruptus**

Risks:

✘ Too unreliable

On rare occasions, the ends of a vas deferens may rejoin spontaneously, but usually a vasectomy is a highly effective form of birth control. Reversal techniques using microsurgery are becoming increasingly successful, but there is always the risk that anti-sperm antibodies will have been produced that will render the man infertile. Vasectomy should therefore be considered irreversible and only contemplated if the man is sure he has completed his family.

Female Sterilization

Female sterilization is growing in popularity, particularly among those women who have had children. It is a more complicated operation than a vasectomy, and as it is usually carried out under general anaesthetic carries a greater risk. It involves blocking the Fallopian tubes, which carry eggs from the ovaries to the uterus, by cutting, cauterizing or attaching clips to them. This is normally done via a small incision made in the lower abdomen just above the pubic bone.

Sterilization does not usually require an overnight stay in the hospital and its effect is immediate. There may be some pain for a couple of days, while gas pumped into the abdomen during the operation gradually disperses. For many women who have had children, sterilization removes the fear of pregnancy. It is not recommended in younger women or those that have had no children. Some women do experience heavier periods after sterilization. Reversal is a costly and difficult process, and not always effective, though there is a 40 to 80 per cent chance of success. Like male sterilization, it should only be considered if a woman is sure she has completed her family.

NATURAL FAMILY PLANNING (THE RHYTHM METHOD)

Once an egg has been released at ovulation it can only survive for around 24 hours. Sperm have a longer life span, but conditions must be suitable for them. About six days before ovulation, the cervix starts producing a special kind of mucus that provides just the right kind of environment for the sperm. They cannot live long without it, but when it is present they can survive for up to five days, lying in wait ready to fertilize the egg as soon as it is released. Natural family planning is about learning to recognize the changes in a woman's body that indicate her fertile time. Then, unless the couple plan to have a baby, they can abstain from sex during those days or use a barrier method of contraception.

It may be the only option for couples who, for moral or religious reasons, choose not to use artificial means of birth control. It can also be used by women who want to feel they are in tune with their bodies, or who do not find other methods of birth control satisfactory, or who are actively trying to get pregnant.

There are various forms of natural family planning. The most widely practised is the sympto-thermal method, which uses a combination of factors to recognize the fertile stage. These include changes in basal body temperature (her temperature at rest, usually taken soon after waking in the morning), changes in cervical mucus, and changes in the softness, firmness and position of the cervix. Other signs include pain or discomfort in the back, lower abdomen, or breasts. Such changes need to be recorded on a chart, and a woman will usually have to monitor these symptoms and signs over several cycles before she begins to recognize a pattern.

For example, following ovulation a woman's basal body temperature rises by a very small amount and stays at this level until the onset of her next period. This slight change can only be detected by a special fertility thermometer, available from chemists and family planning clinics. Her mucus also alters, from scant, sticky, white or absent, often becoming more profuse, and usually changing to a slippery and stretchy texture that may be clear or slightly cloudy. Some women also experience pain or discomfort at the time of ovulation. Careful monitoring of these various signs should pinpoint the fertile days.

Natural family planning is a complicated procedure that requires motivation, commitment and careful observation of the rules. Women need to learn the correct method from a properly trained natural family planning teacher before they use it as their only form of birth control. When practised conscientiously it has a 97 per cent success rate, which compares with the IUD and hormonal contraception.

COITUS INTERRUPTUS/ WITHDRAWAL

Coitus interruptus, also known as the withdrawal method, is probably the most widely used form of birth control in the world and also the most unreliable. It involves withdrawing the penis from the vagina just prior to ejaculation. As a man's pre-ejaculatory fluid can contain millions of sperm, and accidents are unavoidable, this method has a very high failure rate.

STDs *(Sexually Transmitted Diseases)*

Sexually transmitted diseases (STDs) can have unpleasant and often serious consequences. The world-wide spread of AIDS, a potentially fatal condition arising from a sexually transmitted disease, has highlighted more than ever the need to avoid high-risk sexual practices. If you suspect that you have caught a sexually transmitted disease, it is vital that you seek medical attention at the first opportunity. With all STDs, the infected person should inform all known sexual partners so that they too can be examined and receive the appropriate treatment.

Never ignore the symptoms of a sexually transmitted disease. Most STDs respond well to prompt treatment but delay can allow the disease to spread and risks infertility, crippling side-effects and even death. Medical aid is available from your doctor or, if you prefer, at an STD or GUM (genito-urinary medicine) clinic, where medical staff have specialist knowledge. At such clinics, treatment is confidential and visitors can remain anonymous, if they wish. They will, however, be asked for the names of sexual partners who may be at risk, as the clinic will need to get in touch with them to arrange treatment. They will be contacted in strict confidence. Below, in alphabetical order, are listed the most common sexually transmitted diseases.

Candidiasis (Thrush)

Candidiasis, or thrush, is a common complaint. It is caused by a yeast-like fungus called *Candida albicans* that lives, usually quite harmlessly, in the mouth, intestinal tract and vagina. It is normally kept under control by bacteria that also live in these locations. A warm, moist environment is needed for the fungus to thrive, so the vagina makes an ideal home.

Anything that alters conditions in the vagina can tip the balance in favour of the fungus and enable it to multiply. Tight and confining clothing, illness, or antibiotics, which can destroy the beneficial bacteria, may trigger an outbreak. It is more common in pregnant women, diabetics, and those using hormonal contraceptives. Thrush can also be contracted through sex, and every year thousands of people with the condition visit STD clinics.

Symptoms vary. In women, there may be intense itching of the vulva, with soreness, redness and swelling around the vagina, vulva or anus. They may experience a burning sensation during sex, and when urinating, and some may notice a thick, white, yeast-smelling discharge, which has the consistency of cottage cheese. Not all women show this symptom, however.

In men, a rash may appear on the penis and can occasionally spread to the scrotum. Some may notice a slight burning sensation on the penis during or after sexual intercourse. Thrush can cause considerable discomfort, particularly in those who are prone to recurrences.

The condition is usually treated with antifungal drugs, often as creams or pessaries. The partner should be treated at the same time to prevent re-infection. Other measures may be needed such as wearing loose, natural clothing, and sterilizing underwear and towels. Women who use hormonal contraceptives may be advised to use an alternative form of birth control.

Chancroid

Chancroid is a sexually transmitted disease caused by the bacterium *Haemophylus ducreyi*. It is most often found in tropical countries, mainly through contact with prostitutes, but is becoming more common in the West because of increased international travel. There is an incubation period of up to one week before a painful ulcer forms on the penis or near the entrance to the vagina. There may also be a painful swelling in the groin. If the disease is not treated, abscesses can form in the groin which leave deep scars. Chancroid is usually treated with an antibiotic such as erythromycin.

Chlamydia

Chlamydia trachomatis, a microorganism similar to a bacterium, is the most prevalent STD in the West. It is one of the main causes of a disorder called non-specific urethritis, or NSU (see below) which can lead to infertility. Chlamydia can be transmitted by vaginal, anal, or oral sex, or it can be passed on to a baby during childbirth.

Men may experience a burning sensation when urinating, a whitish discharge from the urethra, and pain and swelling of the testicles, but often there are no symptoms. In women, symptoms are even less common but some may notice pain or a burning sensation when urinating, or a cloudy, white discharge.

If chlamydia remains undetected it can spread through the reproductive tract resulting in a potentially life-threatening condition called pelvic inflammatory disease (PID), itself a major cause of infertility. Chlamydia is treated with antibiotics such as tetracycline and erythromycin. Partners should be treated at the same time, to avoid re-infection.

Genital Herpes

Genital herpes is caused by the *Herpes simplex* virus, which produces painful blisters on or near the genitals. *Herpes simplex* occurs in two main forms. The first, type I, causes cold sores. It is type II that causes genital herpes. The latter form is usually transmitted by sexual contact, including oral sex, and can enter the body through the mucous membranes, or through tiny tears in the skin. It is very infectious and the risk of catching the disease greatly increases if an individual has multiple sexual partners.

There is an incubation period of three to six days, followed by the appearance of a group of small, painful blisters on or near the genitals. These blisters break open and then heal, over a period of 10 to 20 days. The initial attack of genital herpes is usually accompanied by symptoms such as fever, headaches, muscular pain and itching. Further outbreaks will usually cause a recurrence of the blisters.

Once a person has become infected the virus is with them for life, although up to 20 per cent only have one attack. For the rest, the flare-ups usually grow steadily less intense over time. Various factors can cause outbreaks, including stress, anxiety, depression, or illness. Some people are able to anticipate an attack, two or three days beforehand, when they notice symptoms such as tingling, itching, or burning sensa-

tions in the genitals. Sexual contact should be avoided during and just before an outbreak, as the condition is highly infectious at this time. There is no cure for genital herpes, but anti-viral drugs such as acyclovir can reduce the pain and speed up healing. Genital herpes may play a part in cervical cancer, so infected women should be sure to have annual cervical smear tests.

Genital Warts

Genital warts are caused by the human *papillomavirus*, which is sexually transmitted. The warts are soft and dry, and greyish-pink in colour. Usually painless, they are found on or near the genitals and anus. There is an incubation period of six to eight weeks after exposure. The virus is transmitted by direct contact with the warts, although the virus has also been found in semen. Like genital herpes, genital warts have been linked with cervical cancer, so yearly cervical smears are advisable for affected women.

Genital warts may be destroyed by caustic chemicals, such as podophyllin, or by laser surgery, or liquid nitrogen. As the virus remains in the tissues, however, genital warts tend to recur. Even when warts are not present, affected people should use condoms to avoid transmitting the virus to partners.

Gonorrhoea ("The Clap")

Gonorrhoea is an infection caused by the bacterium *Neisseria gonorrhoea*. It is one of the most common sexually transmitted diseases and is found principally among teenagers and young adults who have several sexual partners. It can be passed on during vaginal, anal, or oral sex, and an

infected woman can transmit the disease to her baby during childbirth. Men are more likely than women to show symptoms. They may experience soreness or swelling at the tip of the penis, and a burning sensation when passing urine, often accompanied by a milky discharge from the urethra, two to ten days after infection. The discharge may become thicker, and yellowish in colour, and sometimes contains traces of blood.

Up to 60 per cent of infected women have mild symptoms, or none at all. They may urinate more often, and urination may be painful. There may be a watery, yellow or greenish discharge from the urethra. If the cervix has been infected, there may be vaginal discharge and abnormal menstrual bleeding.

Gonorrhoea is a common cause of infertility and can lead to pelvic inflammatory disease (PID). In a few cases, the infection can spread through the bloodstream, causing conditions as diverse as arthritis, skin rashes, and septicaemia, and even leading to brain damage and death, in severe cases. The disease is easily treated with penicillin antibiotics (or suitable alternatives, for those allergic to such drugs) and, as with all STDs, sexual partners must be contacted so they can receive treatment as well.

Hepatitis

Hepatitis is a serious and potentially fatal disease in which the liver becomes badly inflamed, leading to serious tissue damage. It can be caused by alcohol abuse, drugs, poisons, chemicals, and certain viruses. Of the different forms of viral hepatitis, the two most common are hepatitis A and B. Type A is usually caught from contaminated food or water. Hepatitis B is mainly passed on during sex, or via contaminated needles, particularly among drug users.

It has an incubation period of a few weeks to several months. Sufferers may have a flu-like illness, with nausea and vomiting, followed by jaundice. Some carriers, however, show no symptoms and yet are still be able to infect others. Up to ten per cent of sufferers go on to develop the chronic, or long-term, form of the disease resulting in steadily increasing liver damage.

There is no specific treatment, other than bed rest, a good diet, and anti-inflammatory drugs. However, there is a vaccine against hepatitis B which is recommended for anyone at particular risk, including those with multiple sexual partners (homosexual or heterosexual), intravenous drug users, health care workers, and relatives of carriers.

HIV/AIDS

HIV (human immunodeficiency virus) is a disease that is most often transmitted through unprotected sexual intercourse and by sharing needles and syringes among intravenous drug users. HIV can attack the brain directly, but most often it targets white blood cells called T-4 cells, which are vital to the body's immune system.

Over a period of time, the immune system is so badly impaired that the body becomes vulnerable to a range of opportunistic infections and cancers. This latter, potentially fatal, stage is called AIDS (acquired immune deficiency syndrome). Some of these illnesses, such as Karposi's sarcoma or Pneumocystis carinii, are rare or relatively harmless among non-AIDS sufferers, but life-threatening in those with impaired immune systems.

The rate at which HIV progresses to AIDS is highly variable. Some people develop AIDS within months, while others have milder symptoms for years, a condition known as ARC (AIDS-related complex). They may have periods of good health, interspersed with periods of illness. Some infected people show no symptoms and yet are capable of infecting others. It can take up to ten years or more for the symptoms of full-blown AIDS to develop.

HIV is easily killed outside the body and there is no known risk through ordinary social contact, such as hugging, sharing a meal, or using another person's cups, cutlery, or crockery. The main risk is through the exchange of body fluids. This is why HIV can be passed on through all forms of penetrative sex, especially if there are cuts, tears, or sores in the vagina or anus, or on the penis or cervix.

There is a greater risk if a person has already contracted genital herpes or warts. While HIV is present in all body fluids of an infected person, particularly in semen, vaginal fluids and blood, the risk of transmission in saliva is considered to be minimal. Mothers can transmit HIV to their babies, at birth or through breast-feeding. In the past, HIV has been contracted through contaminated blood and blood products, but this risk is now negligible in the West, with the introduction of screening and heat treatment of donor blood. Health workers can be at risk through accidental injury with a contaminated needle.

Those who suspect they may have HIV, especially people in high-risk categories, can have a blood test to determine whether they have been infected. This test detects whether the body has developed antibodies to try to fight the disease. Those found to have developed antibodies are said to be HIV-positive. A negative result means either that individuals do not have the virus, or that their body has not yet made antibodies, which take two to three months to develop. If you're considering having an HIV test it is vital that you first get specialist counselling to help you understand the implications if the result is positive.

At present there is no vaccine against HIV and no cure for HIV or AIDS, though symptoms and complications can often be treated with antibiotics, anti-cancer drugs and radiotherapy. Anti-viral drugs such as AZT (zidovudine) and acyclovir may reduce the speed at which AIDS develops.

To reduce the risk of HIV infection, individuals should practise safer sex if they are unsure of a partner's sexual history. This means finding safer alternatives to penetrative sex, such as mutual masturbation, or using condoms or other forms of latex barrier. This applies both to casual sex, and sex with long-term partners who might previously have been at risk of acquiring HIV. Intravenous drug users should never share needles and syringes.

NSU

NSU (or non-specific urethritis) is inflammation of the urethra, the tube through which urine passes out of the body, due to causes other than gonorrhoea. It is a fairly common complaint. The main symptom is pain when urinating, which is sometimes, but not always, accompanied by a discharge. There can be over 70 causes of NSU, the most common being chlamydia (see previous page) and trichomonas (see below) infection. It is usually sexually transmitted.

Treatment can be difficult unless the disease responsible is identified. This is usually done by taking samples from the opening of the urethra, or by examining a urine sample (usually taken in the morning when there is the highest buildup of organisms). The choice of medication depends on the underlying cause, although it is most likely to be cured by antibiotics. Partners of those with NSU should also be treated to avoid re-infection.

Pubic Lice ("Crabs")

Pubic lice, *Phthiris pubis*, are a parasitic form of insect. They are more commonly known as crabs because of the crab-like claws by which they attach themselves to hairs. They are most likely to infest the pubic region, but they can be found on all body hairs – even the eyebrows. They do not usually infest the scalp.

Crabs are mainly spread by sexual contact, though they can also be caught from infested bedding or clothing, or from lavatory seats. The eggs are laid at the base of the pubic hairs and hatch about a week later. Pubic lice puncture the skin to feed on blood, which causes the intense itching and irritation. Treatment is with insecticide lotion, available on prescription or from the pharmacist, applied to infected areas. Partners should also be treated to avoid re-infection, and clothes and bedding should be washed in very hot water.

Syphilis

Syphilis, a sexually transmitted disease caused by the bacterium *Treponema pallidum*, was introduced into Europe from North America during the late 15th century. It soon reached epidemic proportions, causing many deaths. Syphilis continued to spread in the following centuries, although its virulence abated. The discovery of penicillin in the 1940s brought it under control.

The bacterium enters the body via broken skin or the mucous membranes, in and around the mouth, genitals and anus. It is highly contagious and can be passed on by any intimate contact, including penetrative sex, oral sex, and even kissing. Unlike with most other STDs, condoms do not give total protection against syphilis.

The disease has four stages: primary, secondary, latent and tertiary. During the primary stage, the first symptoms of syphilis appear after an incubation period of just under a month. A small, painless ulcer will appear at the site of transmission, usually around the genitals or anus, but sometimes the lips, throat or fingers. This ulcer usually disappears after six weeks.

The secondary stage usually occurs up to three months after initial infection. It is marked by a variety of symptoms, the most common being a skin rash, but there may be fever, headaches, sore throat, swollen lymph nodes, aches and pains, loss of hair, and pink patches may appear on the skin. In some cases, there may be meningitis (inflammation of the membranes surrounding the brain), eye infection, or kidney problems.

If untreated, the sufferer enters the latent period, when symptoms may lie dormant for twenty years or more. Symptoms may recur in some sufferers. The tertiary phase is very serious and usually involves destruction of tissues and internal organs, such as damage to the heart, blood vessels, nervous system, and brain, resulting in heart disease, mental disorders, paralysis, and death.

Syphilis is usually identified with a blood test. The disease can be tackled effectively with penicillin or other antibiotics, although 50 per cent of infected people suffer a severe reaction to treatment as the body responds to the death of large numbers of bacteria.

Trichomoniasis

Trichomoniasis (TV) is an infection caused by a single-celled parasite, or protozoon, called *Trichomonas vaginalis*. This highly infectious microorganism is a common cause of vaginitis, or inflammation of the vagina, and is almost exclusively transmitted sexually.

Symptoms, if any, start between four days and three weeks after sexual contact and can show as a thin vaginal discharge that is yellow or green, and frothy, and usually has an offensive smell. In addition, some women may experience vaginal pain and itching, especially during sexual intercourse. These symptoms usually worsen during or after menstruation. Many women, however, suffer no symptoms at all.

Men don't usually show symptoms, although a few may notice a slight discharge and find urinating painful. The condition usually responds to treatment with the antiprotozoal drug metronidazole. The sexual partner should also be treated to avoid re-infection.

Index